THE
UNDERACHIEVING
SOCIETY

▲▲▲

THE
UNDERACHIEVING
SOCIETY

▲▲▲

Development Strategy and Policy in Trinidad and Tobago 1958–2008

Terrence W. Farrell

University of the West Indies Press
Jamaica • Barbados • Trinidad and Tobago
www.uwipress.com

University of the West Indies Press

7A Gibraltar Hall Road, Mona

Kingston 7, Jamaica

www.uwipress.com

ISBN 978-976-640-319-5

A catalogue record of this book is available from the
National Library of Jamaica.

Cover design by Gabby Woodham.

Dedicated to Lloyd Best, Eric St Cyr, Euric Bobb and
Wendell Mottley, and, with love and affection, to
Sandra Welch-Farrell, Krista Farrell and Marc-Kwesi Farrell

Contents

Preface and Acknowledgements

This work chronicles the evolution of development strategy and policy in the small but resource-rich island state of Trinidad and Tobago, the southernmost islands in the Caribbean archipelago. Part 2 of the book is based on my master's thesis done over thirty years ago at the University of the West Indies, St Augustine, under the supervision of Eric St Cyr. In 2003, I was a member of the Multisectoral Core Group of the Vision 2020 exercise and chairman of the macroeconomics subcommittee. During what is described here as the lost decade (1983 to 1992) I was a senior official of the Central Bank of Trinidad and Tobago and closely involved in macroeconomic management in those difficult years, which involved dual exchange rates, import restrictions, debt restructurings and an International Monetary Fund (IMF) programme, followed in 1993 by the floating of the TT dollar.

I had therefore studied the early "planning years" closely and was integrally involved in policymaking in subsequent periods. I came to know several of the key figures who were involved in the "planning years" and in the period of the "lost decade". Euric Bobb had encouraged me to leave academic life and join the central bank as a senior economist, and I was subsequently director of research, senior manager of research and information and, lastly, deputy governor. Patricia Robinson, who had worked as a very young economist on the second plan, was also a former director of research at the Central Bank of Trinidad and Tobago, and I later worked with her in setting up the Institute of Banking when she was at the National Institute for Higher Education Research Science and Technology (NIHERST). William ("Willie") Demas, the architect of the second and third five-year plans, joined the Central Bank in 1988 and I worked under him until he left in 1992. From my perch in the Central Bank, I met Frank Rampersad and Frank Barsotti who were then powerful and influential technocrats in the Ministry of Finance during the 1980s, and I was privileged to be able to work with those legendary economists on various committees. They had both played key roles during the planning years working out of the "stables" at Whitehall with Willie Demas. Ewart Williams, who had also worked with Eric St Cyr for his master's at University of the West Indies a couple of years before me, took time off from his job at the IMF to work with Demas at the Central Bank on the debt restructuring and IMF negotiations during the latter years of the lost decade. He would return some time later as governor of the Central Bank.

Later on, while in the private sector at Guardian Holdings Limited the insurance group, I was asked to work on the Vision 2020 exercise by Arthur Lok Jack, then chairman of Guardian Holdings Limited and one of the region's leading businessmen and entrepreneurs. The Vision 2020 project not only put me back in contact with economic research and analysis, it also allowed me to work with excellent economists like Shelton Nicholls, Patrick Watson and Philip Colthrust. Later, I also worked with Arthur Lok Jack as a member of the BWIA Task Force.

My motivations in writing this book have been several. First, I wanted to tidy up my master's thesis with which I was never completely satisfied. Revisiting it revealed the naïveté, even silliness, of a youthful academic. But the fact that most of what I wrote then has survived into this book indicates that I have either not changed my mind about a lot of things or that not all of it was that bad. Second, having started the work of revision, I realized that I also needed to document the Vision 2020 experience and then try to bridge the early planning years and Vision 2020 exercise. The process of attempting to do that brought home the central theme of this work, which is the underperformance of Trinidad and Tobago in terms of its economic development and exploration of the reasons for that underperformance. Third, I do think it is important to document our history and the people who made that history. Those who come after us must appreciate that they stand on the shoulders of those who went before them and that it is important to see what challenges their predecessors faced, standing as it were in their shoes and looking at the world through their eyes at the time. Doing so only makes all of us humble, realizing that change does not come easily or quickly. It is heartening to see that recently several leading figures in the formative years of the country's independence have "put pen to paper" to document their experiences or to provide their perspective on various aspects of the country's economic social and political development.[1]

Writing the book presented certain difficulties in structuring and organizing the material. I strongly believe that economics is a technical discipline grounded in evidence interpreted by sensibly constructed theoretical frameworks. Mathematical and econometric techniques are useful in assisting in this process. However, in order to make the work accessible to more general readers, interested primarily in the economic history of Trinidad and Tobago, I have tried to make the exposition clear and readable without, I hope, losing much if any of the analytical rigour I hoped to achieve. I also believe that economic processes play out as "*local* processes", that is, how economic processes evolve or can be influenced depends on the specific sociopolitical matrix and cultural behaviours in the economy under study. This is why in demarcating and introducing the periodization of the evolution of policy, I have devoted sections to the international and domestic sociopolitical contexts that seemed to me to have shaped or influenced the thinking and approach to policymaking at those times.

I have no one to blame for the many shortcomings of this work. I am very grateful for the detailed and incisive comments of Norman Girvan, which resulted in many amendments and considerable restructuring of the material. There remain some issues on which we disagree, notably whether the strategy pursued in the 1950s and 1960s is attributable to the influence of Arthur Lewis. I am grateful to Mark Figueroa, expert on Arthur Lewis, for joining and clarifying the issue, happily in agreement with my own position. Alvin Hilaire, chief economist and director of research at the Central Bank of Trinidad and Tobago, also made detailed comments on the first draft of the manuscript, and these have improved the exposition significantly. I also received useful comments and encouragement from Selwyn Ryan, Sunity Maharaj and Euric Bobb.

I would like to thank Republic Bank for assisting with the publication of this work through their sponsorship and thereby making this effort a reality.

Finally, I would like to acknowledge the enormous contribution the following persons have made, not necessarily or directly to the work itself, but to my own growth and development as a professional in the discipline of economics. Eric St Cyr was my first-year mathematics and statistics lecturer at the University of the West Indies, supervisor of my master's thesis, who became an academic colleague and a friend. It was Eric who taught me that when you set out to critique someone else's work, you need to understand it as well as or better than they do. Lloyd Best was my most influential teacher, even though I never became an acolyte. It was Best who picked me, still a graduate student, to teach his iconic course "Caribbean Economic Problems" when he went on leave in 1974. While the language and categories of "Plantation Economy" are not evident in this work, Best is always there lurking beneath the surface, as every proposition and position is implicitly tested by asking, "What would Lloyd Best think about this?"

Euric Bobb extracted me from academe and launched me on a career trajectory for which I have absolutely no regrets. Despite his awesome intellect, Euric did not dictate, but gave me "room to run", charged me with ever greater responsibility and reposed trust in a very young economist to lead his research department. We coauthored several pieces, and I think we did much to give the central bank a strong voice amid the angst of the national discourse during the difficult 1980s. He too has become a firm friend. Finally, Wendell Mottley, as minister of finance, was brave enough to support my elevation to the position of deputy governor in 1992. We sallied forth to do Trinidad and Tobago's first Eurobond issue and other debt-raising road shows, articulate and confident in the face of investment bankers sceptical about the prospects of this small island economy with a dubious record in the 1980s and having just emerged from an attempted coup in 1990. Under his watch as minister, I was deeply engaged in the dismantling of exchange controls and the engineering of the flotation of the TT dollar. Wendell too remains a firm friend.

I thank these mentors – Eric St Cyr, Lloyd Best, Euric Bobb and Wendell Mottley – for their trust, support, encouragement and friendship, and I dedicate this work to them.

I also dedicate the work to my wife, Sandra, a constant source of support and encouragement, and to my children, Krista and Marc-Kwesi, both high achievers.

"Because of their long history of economic dependence on the metropolitan countries, the people of the Caribbean have never been forced to utilize their own resources. We have preferred to view our material progress in terms of handouts from the metropolis – handouts of aid, of capital investment, of sheltered and preferential markets, of opportunities for emigration and the brain drain. We have never fully looked inwards. And when we do, we look to the government as a source of handouts. . . . The whole country is operating way below maximum capacity."

— Eric Williams, "The Chaguaramas Declaration", November 1970

Part 1

Setting the Stage

1

The Roots of Ambivalence

This work documents and analyses the effectiveness of the sets of policies employed by the Government of Trinidad and Tobago over a fifty-year period, from 1958 to 2008, in the effort to foster the growth and development of the nation's economy. Our focus is on the country's *economic* development. The meaning of "development" is discussed extensively in chapter 2. Issues related to social and cultural development policies are not treated, except insofar as they bear on resource allocation or on economic development more broadly. Nor have we sought to address issues relating to physical planning or environmental policy, although both these aspects of policy are important in a country of small size pursuing the development of heavy and environmentally impactful industries such as oil extraction and refining, iron and steel, and various petrochemicals.

The southernmost islands of the Caribbean archipelago, Trinidad and Tobago are together only about 1,980 square miles (5,128 square kilometres) in area, with a population of about 0.5 million in 1938, 789,000 in 1958 and only 1.3 million in 2008. Small size is certainly a defining characteristic of the Trinidad and Tobago economy, and there has been debate as to the extent to which small size constrains policy options and affects development.[1] The issue of size is discussed later in this chapter. The other critical defining characteristics of the country are its ethnic composition and diversity, and the relative abundance of oil and natural gas.

The Ethnicity Factor

The history of Trinidad, and to a lesser extent, Tobago, is one of immigration and, in later years, emigration. Founded by the Spanish, settled by the French, and colonized by the British, Trinidad was never really a plantation economy within a "hinterland of settlement" like Jamaica or Barbados, and indeed at the close of the slave trade in 1808, there were only 21,895 slaves in Trinidad out of a population of 31,478.[2] Indeed many of these slaves had come to Trinidad from other southern Caribbean territories, and several slave-owners in Trinidad were themselves black or "free coloured".

It is estimated that the population of Trinidad in 1844 was 73,023, compared with 122,198 in Barbados and 377,433 in Jamaica. After emancipation in 1838, labourers for the sugar estates were imported from India. East Indians began to arrive in considerable numbers from 1845 until indentureship was halted in 1917. A total of 143,900 East Indians come to Trinidad under indenture. East Indians settled on or around the sugar estates in rural Trinidad while the African ex-slaves moved into or close to the towns, making for geographical and occupational distribution based on ethnicity. In the latter half of the nineteenth century and the early part of the twentieth century, there were immigrants who were Chinese, Syrian-Lebanese, Portuguese mainly from Madeira and even a few Jews.

The population of the colony swelled to 365,913 in 1921 and reached 732,300 on the eve of self-government in 1955, the fastest rate of growth of population in the Western Hemisphere.[3] The society is therefore characterized by diversity or heterogeneity, with peoples of East Indian, African, European, Chinese and Syrian-Lebanese, and mixtures of most if not all of these. These groups were also divided by religion (Hindu, Muslim, Christian and various Christian sects). Elements of caste remained within the East Indian community for some time but eventually began to attenuate under the impact of education and the exigencies of life in a new society. The society was also stratified along class lines with the European (English or French creole) classes ruling the government as well as business, and social status ascribed based in part on gradations of colour or "complexion".

Ceded to England in 1763, captured by the French in 1781, Tobago was fought over by several colonial powers until the English finally established full control in 1803. However, its constant interchange between colonial powers had inhibited its development as a plantation colony. It was better known in the eighteenth century for its production of tobacco, indigo and cotton, but these products all eventually yielded to sugar. Tobago's economy declined throughout much of the nineteenth century, exacerbated by a hurricane in 1847 that destroyed much of the capital stock.

In 1808, Tobago had 439 whites and 17,009 enslaved African, almost as many as in the much larger island of Trinidad. When emancipation came in 1838, Tobago was unable to finance an immigration scheme along the lines of Trinidad or Guyana and as a result the population of Tobago remained almost entirely of African descent. In order to slow the decline of the sugar industry, a *métayage* system was introduced as in St Lucia and Antigua. Tobago was annexed to Trinidad in 1889 and made a ward within the colony of Trinidad and Tobago in 1899.[4]

The table below shows the evolution of the ethnic distribution of the population of Trinidad and Tobago in the postwar period. The decline in the shares of the African-descended and the European-descended population is noteworthy, as is the increase in the shares of the East Indian and the "mixed" populations. While the share of the East Indian population has stabilized at around 40 per cent, the share of the "mixed" population has continued to increase. Notably the share of Chinese in the population fell from 1 per cent in 1946 to just 0.3 per cent in 2000. No one ethnic group commands a majority of the population.

Ethnicity is not readily correlated with religion in Trinidad and Tobago society. While most East Indians are Hindu, not insignificant percentages are Christian or Muslim. African-descended persons may adhere to a range of Christian beliefs ranging from Catholicism to Spiritual Baptists, with some practising syncretistic forms of Christian and African religions. Since 1970, there has been a growing, though still numerically small, number of Africans who have embraced Islam.

This polyglot assemblage of races and ethnicities makes for a rich cultural mosaic of religious practices, superstitions, cuisine, dress, speech patterns and behaviours, perhaps unlike any other place in the world. Trinidad's Carnival has become world famous, evolving from its post-emancipation celebrations rooted

Table 1.1 Ethnic Distribution of Population, 1946, 1970, 1980, 1990, 2000 (%)

	1946	1970	1980	1990	2000
European (White)	2.5	1.2	0.9	0.6	0.6
East Indian	35.0	40.1	40.8	40.3	40.0
African (Black)	46.8	42.8	41.0	39.6	37.5
Mixed	14.0	14.2	16.4	18.4	20.5
Chinese	1.0				0.3
Other			0.9		
Not stated				5.5	0.8

Source: M.G. Smith, *Pluralism, Politics and Ideology in the Creole Caribbean* (New York: Research Institute for the Study of Man, 1991), from 1946 Census; Central Statistical Office, Population Census, various years.

in African traditions as well as the French, Catholic pre-Lenten fêtes to massive street parades of masqueraders. In the postwar period, Carnival incorporated the steel pan invented in Trinidad in the twentieth century. But there are also to be found Hindu (Divali, Ramleela and so on), Muslim (Eid ul Fitr), Baptist and Christian (Corpus Christi, Pentecost and so on) festivals, several of which are now commemorated by national public holidays.[5] Trinidad and Tobago gave calypso music first to the Caribbean region and then to the world, and has given birth in recent years to unique combinations of Indian chutney and calypso music. The steel pan, the only new musical instrument of the twentieth century, was invented in Trinidad, and the sound it produces has become associated with all the Caribbean islands. In recent decades, there has been an increasing cross-fertilization and fusion of music and dance forms between the cultural expressions of the two major ethnic groups. Trinidad and Tobago is perhaps the quintessential "plural society".[6]

The dominant Euro-creole culture was largely displaced by the dynamic and creative Afro-creole culture that had been evolved by the ex-slaves after emancipation and that became dominant after self-government and independence. Indian, or more precisely Hindu, cultural expressions were for a long time suppressed and kept out of the mainstream, until the growing economic and political power of Indo-Trinidadians, together with a commensurate assertiveness and the opening up of the media, brought East Indian cultural expressions increasingly into the mainstream.[7] With this came demands for a more equitable sharing of state funding for cultural activities and festivals. There was a major debate on the country's highest national award – the "Trinity Cross" – which was resolved by the high court on a constitutional motion from a representative East Indian group that argued that the use of the symbolism of the Christian cross was offensive and discriminatory.[8] There was also a debate on the designation of the steel pan invented in Port of Spain by Afro-Trinidadians, as the national musical instrument.

The Syrian-Lebanese community, which had started immigrating to Trinidad in the early twentieth century and established itself in small retail and commercial enterprises, began to challenge the hegemony of the French creole elite in large-scale business activity in the second half of the century.[9] Indeed, by the last quarter of the twentieth century, East Indian–owned businesses were also gaining prominence in several areas of commerce and industry, as well as in the professions. In contrast, black-owned private businesses were comparatively fewer and generally small or microenterprises.[10]

This is not to suggest that this "rainbow country" has not been without ethnic competition and conflict. However, it would be true to say that such competition and conflict as has occurred has not degenerated into violence, as has happened in other ethnically divided societies, including neighbouring Guyana, though Trinidad apparently came close to open ethnic violence in the general election of 1961.[11]

The greater significance of Trinidad and Tobago's ethnic or "tribal" segments is that the political parties have tended to draw the majority of their membership and support from one or other of the main ethnic groups. The support for the People's National Movement (PNM) has come mainly from the urban Afro-creole population distributed along the East-West Corridor and San Fernando, the second largest city, whereas the support for the main opposition party has been drawn from the East Indian population located in Central Trinidad. Tobago has shifted allegiances depending on which party more resources and more autonomy for Tobago are likely to come from. This has meant therefore that the policymakers have come predominantly from one ethnic group or the other, depending on which party has emerged successful in the general elections.[12] M.G. Smith has written: "In such segmental pluralities as Trinidad, Guyana and Suriname, the political competition of large racial and cultural blocs had tended to produce a virtual monopoly of power and state resources by representatives of one social segment *to the exclusion of others*."[13] This immediately raises the questions as to whether (1) policymaking is influenced by the ethnic provenance of the policymakers; (2) there are systematic differences in governance between the two main ethnic groups; (3) policymaking is influenced by the fact that the government of the day knows that it has a bloc of support irrespective of how it performs in office, and (4) the *outcomes* of policy decisions have unintended consequences for ethnic equilibrium and/or perceptions of equity.[14]

The Oil Factor

In addition to the challenge of growing and transforming a small island state with a complex social structure, there is also the challenge of managing the boom and bust of an economy blessed (or cursed) with petroleum and natural gas resources and hence subject to the volatility characteristic of oil and gas economies, as well as to some of its other deleterious effects such as "Dutch Disease". Revenues from oil and natural gas account for a significant proportion of government revenues and dominate foreign exchange earnings.

If Trinidad and Tobago is sufficiently different from other Caribbean countries in terms of its ethnic composition and cultural dynamics, it is also different in its atypical Caribbean geology. Only seven miles from Venezuela at its closest point, Trinidad is geologically an extension of the South American continent and more particularly the oil- and gas-bearing rock strata that extend eastward from

Venezuela.[15] Commercial oil production began in the early twentieth century, and Trinidad was to become the most important source of oil for the British Navy. Oil attracted multinational corporations and significant foreign investment, technology and skills, placing Trinidad and Tobago in a unique position compared to its agriculture- and tourism-dependent Caribbean neighbours. Resource-rich countries have a different menu of development choices and different management challenges compared to those not so endowed. Yet, the experience has been that resource-rich developing countries have not outperformed less well-endowed countries over time, and indeed resource riches may have inhibited growth and development through a variety of effects.[16]

Some authors have argued that "petro-states" are characterized by a particular structural and institutional legacy that "reduces the range of decision making, rewards some decisions and forms of behavior more than others and shapes the preferences of officials in a manner that is not conducive to successful development".[17]

The argument has been articulated by Karl thus:

> Commodity-led growth induces changes in prevailing notions of property rights, the relative power of interest groups and organizations, and the role and character of the state vis-à-vis the market. These institutional changes subsequently define the revenue basis of the state, especially the tax structure. How these states collect and distribute taxes, in turn, creates incentives that pervasively influence the organization of political and economic life and shapes government preferences with respect to public policies.[18]

This perspective invites into our consideration the role of multinational corporations and even the role of external governments for whom production and export of the commodity may be strategic. This structural-institutional approach to development policy in the context of the petroleum economy is discussed further in the next chapter, and the Dutch Disease phenomenon in the context of Trinidad and Tobago is discussed in part 3, "Resource-Based Industrialization".

The Size Factor

Demas's seminal contribution to the Caribbean economics literature and thought was his work on the influence of size on economic development.[19] The constraints imposed by small size had been recognized by other writers, but Demas was writing specifically about the microstates of the Caribbean. Small states have small internal markets that make it difficult or impossible for economies of scale to be attained. They also have limited and insufficiently varied domestic resources. Size in the context of this analysis refers to population rather than geographical extent, so that Guyana, whereas larger than say the United Kingdom, has only a small population living along the coast.

Demas argued that the route to development lies through the export of manufactures, and as a result of the disadvantage of small size, the development path is more difficult. In addition to the disadvantage of small markets, small countries are more likely to be affected by export of savings and the "sacrifice of domestic employment to balance of payments equilibrium". Demas contended that small size does confer some advantages such as being "unimportant", more unified national markets, greater flexibility and "perhaps greater social cohesion". The last mentioned may not prove to be the case in ethnically diverse societies. He also advocated regional economic integration to help overcome the constraints of small size.

The other aspect of size is vulnerability to natural disasters such as earthquakes and hurricanes that have a considerably greater impact on smaller territories. While Trinidad and Tobago is located in a seismically active zone and does experience earthquakes, there have been few that have caused massive damage and loss of life. Similarly, although located in the hurricane belt, its location at about ten degrees north means that most storms and hurricanes tend to track north of Trinidad, but occasionally do hit the island of Tobago.

The Challenge of Development in a Small, Ethnically Diverse Petro-State

Trinidad and Tobago makes an interesting case study in economic development and in development policy. How does size influence policy choices? How and to what extent does the history and social psychology of a people influence the policy choices they make? How do policymakers deal with the volatility inherent in a commodity like petroleum? How does resource abundance influence the choice of policies? How does the government manage the perception of inequitable distribution of state resources among ethnic groups that are concentrated in particular geographical areas or associated with particular occupations? How can powerful multinational corporations be made to operate in the national interest? How can the local private sector be harnessed in support of development? How can a small state build implementation capacity quickly and effectively? How are social and economic crises managed?

Over the fifty-year period of the analysis, there were major policy shifts, from the articulation of import substitution industrialization in the 1950s, to the pursuit of development planning in the period 1958 to 1973, resource-based industrialization in the period 1974 to 1982, followed by structural adjustment in the 1980s and then the embrace of a modified version of free markets, where development is led by the investments of a revenue-rich state in directly productive activities and in infrastructure.

These development policies are based on the premise that it is possible to engineer an economy to achieve faster economic growth and/or to engineer "structural transformation" of the economy so as to place incomes and the overall standard of living on a sustainable basis. In the next chapters, as the stage is set for examination of development policies pursued over the years, theories of economic growth and development are reviewed in chapter 2 and the theory of economic policy is elaborated and discussed in chapter 3. Chapter 4 on colonial economic policy is included in part 1 as it also sets the stage for the consideration of development policy under self-government and independence.

2

The Determinants of Growth and Development

I n this chapter, various theoretical approaches to growth and development are summarized and discussed briefly. The objective of this review is to iden- tify the factors and relationships that various development theorists have thought to be important in promoting or achieving growth and development and that have therefore influenced particular development strategies. Although "de- velopment strategy" and "development policy" are sometimes used interchange- ably, even in this work, one should understand "strategy" to mean a coherent approach to the achievement of a defined goal. "Import substitution industrial- ization", "infrastructure development", "export promotion industrialization", and "resource-based industrialization" are proper examples of development strate- gies. Strategies are comprised of a set of policies that may cover, for example, tax- ation and tax incentives, foreign direct investment, monetary policy (low interest rates or selective credit controls), and exchange rate policy (undervaluation or overvaluation), which is formulated and implemented in the pursuit of a given strategy.[1] A particular policy may be consistent with more than one development strategy, and this can make distinguishing strategies and periodization of strate- gies difficult.

The first section of the chapter discusses the meaning of "development", a topic that surfaces quite often when particular outcomes are being evaluated or comparisons are made between and among countries. The other sections of this chapter are not intended to be comprehensive reviews of the literature of development economics, but rather to assist in the elucidation of the theoretical underpinnings of thinking on the formulation of economic policy in Trinidad and Tobago.

Methodologically, this is important. First, policymakers do operate within some sort of theoretical framework or paradigm, even if they may not be entirely aware of it. Explicitly or implicitly they have in mind some "model" of how variables hang together and the impact of one on the others. Second, one has to analyse and make sense of policy by using some theoretical framework. Without such a framework, policy actions can perhaps only be assessed as capricious or whimsical. The underlying assumption here therefore is that the advisors and policymakers in Trinidad and Tobago were influenced in some way, perhaps through schooling, membership and participation in international organizations, and attendance at conferences and seminars to embrace one or another theoretical framework or paradigm. Readers who have no interest in the nuances of the theories of economic development might be content to read the first section on the meaning of "development" and the concluding section of this chapter where the key lessons are distilled.

The Meaning of "Development"

It would perhaps be inappropriate to press on to the documentation and consideration of development policy in Trinidad and Tobago or to outline theories of growth and development and economic policy without first addressing the definition or meaning of "development". Used in conjunction and in contradistinction to "growth", most people would understand and appreciate that while "growth" refers to quantitative increase in output and income, the word "development" implies more than this.[2] As "growth" in the biological sense means that the animal or plant gets physically bigger, "development" means that there are qualitative changes – faster, smarter, psychologically more mature, more capable of dealing with or adapting to the environment, more robust or resilient. Arguably, growth is a necessary but not a sufficient condition for development. Increase in quantitative capacity facilitates increase in qualities or attributes needed to sustain further growth, coping and adaptability. But equally, certain attributes or qualities may facilitate increases in investment and output.[3] Output growth and qualitative attributes or factors are mutually reinforcing in the process of growth and development.

Between these positions, development over the decades has been related to or identified with structural and sectoral change – hence "industrialization", forward and backward linkages, development of the financial sector, infrastructure or "social overhead capital";[4] and institutional change – land reform, democratic and political reforms, access to credit, agricultural extension, access to health care, gender equality and female participation in the workforce. Economists and other social scientists have placed emphasis on one or another of these factors as being the key to development, or in fact constituting development. At different times, emphasis has been placed on the presence or absence of natural resources, climate, population growth, capital accumulation, entrepreneurship and investment in human resources. Underdevelopment or "backwardness" was caused by the absence of some key to growth and development, whatever that key was perceived to be.[5]

Some economists sought to shift the focus from growth in per capita income as "development" by a change of terminology. Hence Demas viewed development as "structural transformation", which was reflected in elimination of surplus labour and subsistence production, a higher share of manufacturing and services in gross domestic product (GDP), greater interindustry linkages, lower import propensity over the long run, and a more flexible, diversified and adaptable economy.[6] Indeed, following Demas's lead, "transformation" became the preferred word for many Caribbean economists.

Nobel Prize–winning economist Amartya Sen has argued that "development can be seen . . . as a process of expanding the real freedoms that people enjoy".[7] These freedoms concern not only growth in GDP or industrialization or technological advance, they also depend on social and economic arrangements – for example, education and health care, and political and civil rights. Sen argues that these freedoms are both means (instruments) and ends of development.

> The instrumental roles of freedom include several distinct but inter-related components, such as economic facilities, political freedoms, social opportunities, transparency guarantees and protective security. These instrumental rights, opportunities and entitlements have strong inter-linkages, which can go in different directions. The process of development is crucially influenced by these interconnections. Corresponding to multiple inter-connected freedoms, there is a need to develop and support a plurality of institutions, including democratic systems, legal mechanisms, market structures, educational and health provisions, media and other communication facilities and so on. The institutions can incorporate private initiatives as well as public arrangements and also more mixed structures, such as nongovernmental organizations and cooperative entities.[8]

Walter Rodney, approaching the problem from a Marxist perspective provides a definition of development that is quite similar to that of Sen, who is decidedly not a Marxist:

Development in human society is a many-sided process. At the level of the individual, it implies increased skill and capacity, greater freedom, creativity, self-discipline, responsibility and material well-being. Some of these are virtually moral categories and are difficult to evaluate – depending as they do on the age in which one lives, one's class origins, and one's personal code of what is right and what is wrong. However, what is indisputable is that the achievement of any of those aspects of personal development is very much tied in with the state of the society as a whole.[9]

Rodney's perspective that development has a *moral* dimension resonates with the social doctrine of the Catholic Church, in which the question of development has been addressed by successive papal encyclicals. Notably, the social doctrine of the Catholic Church describes the "model society" as one founded on a few central values: the person and its spiritual dignity, freedom and responsibility; the family, as the basic cell of society; the sense of solidarity among citizens that inspires care for the common good of society and a special attention for the poor; the right to private ownership, to be reconciled with the common destination of all material things created for the benefit of all; the principles of justice, equity and responsibility, applied to all partners of economic activity; the value of work considered in its individual and social aspects, the worker being more valued than the product of his work; the moral accountability of civic leaders; and the search for universal brotherhood and peace through a just international order.[10] The Catholic Church has encapsulated these values in what John Paul II called "authentic development", which avers that "progress" is to be seen not only in quantitative economic terms but also in moral and cultural growth.

Kari Levitt who has worked extensively in the Caribbean over almost five decades and was a significant collaborator with Lloyd Best, describes "meaningful economic development" in the following terms: "Development cannot be imposed from without. It is a creative social process and its central nervous system, the matrix which nourishes it, is located in the cultural sphere. Development is ultimately not a matter of money or physical capital, or foreign exchange, but of the capacity of a society to tap the root of popular creativity, to free up and empower people to exercise their intelligence and collective wisdom."[11]

The recognition in recent decades that economic growth consumes resources and may do so without due regard for the likely impact on future generations, either by overproduction or by the environmental impact of resource extraction and use, led to the emergence of the concept of "sustainable development", that is, development that meets the needs of current generations without compromising the ability of future generations to meet their own needs.[12]

A holistic approach would embrace all of these factors as constitutive of "development". Moreover, these factors are mutually reinforcing, creating either vicious or virtuous circles. GDP growth and improvements in personal incomes influence values and attitudes, and induce changes in product and labour markets. The assertion of rights and freedoms and the shift from sovereign rule to democratic governments that are responsible and accountable induces the creation of new institutions and reform of existing institutions or relationships. The empowerment encouraged by institutional reform and the growth of individual freedom facilitates structural changes in markets, liberating and unleashing increases in productivity. At the same time, recognition of the impact on poverty within and across countries together with the impact on the environment, condition and influence resource use and production, as well as the institutions for income distribution and poverty alleviation. This holistic, mutually reinforcing perspective on development is illustrated schematically in figure 2.1.

What we can conclude from this is that development is a complex, multifaceted, interactive process. The word "process" is important. "Development" is not an "end state". Viewed as an ongoing process, no country can be said to be "developed", nor indeed another "underdeveloped".[13] Development policy needs to address at various times all of the constitutive elements or factors in development, but at certain times, one or another of these constitutive elements is likely to be seen as the most important.

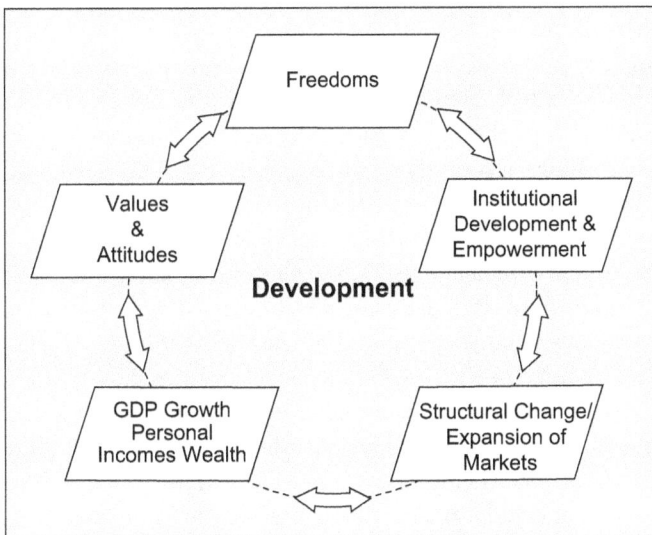

Figure 2.1 The nature of development

Theories of Growth and Development

If "growth" (quantitative increases in output and income) is seen to be a necessary but not sufficient condition for "development", then an examination of theories of growth is a good place to start.[14]

Classical and Neoclassical Growth Theory

Classical and neoclassical theories of economic growth focused on the race between population growth and investment or capital accumulation. Land was assumed to be fixed and hence largely ignored. Labour force growth was a function of population growth and labour force participation. But the real driver of growth in the classical and neoclassical models was the accumulation of capital.

The early models as developed by Harrod, Domar and others, assumed closed, one-sector economies, paid no attention to the role of money, ignored prices, and took no account of technical progress. It is important to appreciate that these theories were not focused on the problem of growth in developing countries *per se*, but the problem of growth generally and at a high level of abstraction.[15] These theorists were of course keenly aware that neither labour nor capital was homogeneous, and capital in particular was a very difficult variable to conceptualize, to model and to measure. The defining characteristic of these early models was the exogeneity of the determinants of growth. Later models sought to endogenize many of these factors.

The simplest models assumed that the capital-output ratio and the capital-labour ratio were fixed. Output is either consumed or invested to increase the stock of capital. Thus the rate of growth of output (income) depends on the savings rate and inversely on the capital-output ratio or the capital intensity of output.[16] The other condition to be satisfied is the full employment condition. Since by assumption the capital-labour ratio is fixed, the growth rate of output (income) must also be equal to the growth rate of the labour force.

Growth theory after Harrod-Domar can be assessed as analysts seeking to relax these restrictive assumptions to ascertain how well the basic conclusions stand up and also exploring the dynamics of the models to assess how the growth paths of economies are likely to behave. The determination of the growth path was important especially as the Harrod-Domar conditions imply a "knife-edge"; that is, since all the determinants of the growth rate are exogenous, the fulfillment of all the Harrod-Domar equilibrium conditions are likely to be met only by accident.[17]

The neoclassical growth models, of which Solow's is emblematic, posit a production function exhibiting constant returns to scale in which capital and labour are substitutable so that the capital-output ratio can be varied as growth proceeds. Solow's model incorporates exogenous labour-augmenting technical progress. Given the rate of increase of the labour force, an increase in the savings rate moves the economy to a higher capital-labour ratio and to a higher output per capita. It can also be demonstrated that the shares of wages and profits in total output are constant in equilibrium.

In extending the Harrod-Domar model to an open economy it can be shown that the rate of growth of output increases with the savings rate and with the import propensity, but output growth varies inversely with the capital-output ratio and with the ratio of exports to output. This counterintuitive result in respect of the role of exports comes about because in the Harrod-Domar model, output growth is investment driven and the capital-output ratio is fixed. A trade deficit results in an inflow of investment on capital account and increases the growth rate, while a trade surplus results in an outflow of investment and reduces the growth of output.[18]

In the neoclassical model extended to the open economy, an increase in the export-labour ratio lowers per capita output. The difference in the neoclassical formulation is that the capital-labour ratio can vary during the adjustment to a new equilibrium position, but the basic outcome is the same.

The Harrod-Domar and neoclassical models for both the closed and open economy are cast in terms of real variables; that is, they abstract from changes in money and prices (terms of trade). The exchange rate is fixed and trade imbalances can persist apparently without adjustment. Neoclassical models were subsequently developed to include money to assess under what conditions money balances were non-neutral, that is, the conditions under which monetary policy could influence the equilibrium growth path.[19]

W. Arthur Lewis and Unlimited Supplies of Labour

St Lucia–born Nobel laureate W. Arthur Lewis articulated an approach to economic growth and development over a distinguished career spanning three decades. He was one of a group of "high development" theorists that included Rosenstein-Rodan, Albert Hirschman, Ragnar Nurkse and Gunnar Myrdal. Rosenstein-Rodan was the author of the "big push" theory of development. Albert Hirschman developed the idea of "forward and backward linkages", whereas Myrdal spoke to the idea of "circular and cumulative causation".[20]

Lewis's own work ranged from extensive and detailed studies in international economic history seeking to explain growth and development, policy studies, and prescriptions for countries in the West Indies and Africa, and theoretical explorations of the problem of growth. It was his *Economic Development with Unlimited Supplies of Labour* that was perhaps his definitive contribution.[21]

The classical and basic neoclassical models of growth view the economy as one sector producing one good that could either be consumed or invested. Lewis articulated a one-good, two-sector model. One sector is the capitalist sector that uses reproducible capital, and the other sector is the subsistence sector that does not. The economy as a whole is characterized by overpopulation and in the subsistence sector, the marginal product of labour is zero but workers are paid the average product of labour as the subsistence wage. The wage paid to workers in the capitalist sector is determined by what workers can earn outside that sector, the subsistence wage. The capitalist sector employs workers up to the point where their marginal product is equal to the subsistence wage plus a margin or premium. At that wage rate, the capitalist sector has available to it an "unlimited" supply of labour comprising the subsistence workers, females who are not in the labour force and the openly unemployed.

Growth is produced by the reinvestment of the capitalist surplus, which increases output, draws more labour out of the subsistence sector at a fixed wage, further increases the capitalist surplus and so on until the labour surplus is completely absorbed. Lewis argued that the rate of profit on capital does not fall as capital accumulation proceeds because the capital-labour ratio holds constant because of the labour surplus. In addition, the average product of labour in the subsistence sector must be lower than in the modern or capitalist sector (and remain lower until the entire labour surplus is absorbed) or else the capitalist sector would not be able to generate a surplus and capital-using technology would not be used.

Lewis considered the role that money and credit could play in the process of economic growth and development. That role was essentially to permit the expansion of capital without causing a diminution in consumption as assumed in the classical model. The drawback was that if labour was put to work to create new capital and paid using new money, there was the possibility of inflation if the output of consumer goods remains constant. Inflation is obviated or stopped if savings rise to equal the increase in investment.

Lewis also brought government into the picture. He concluded that government could accelerate growth and development depending on whether its expenditure served to raise output or merely increased consumption. Government expenditure could also impact inflation depending on what proportion of incremental income was taken back in taxation. Lewis stated that "no government should consider deficit financing without assuring itself that a large part of the increases in money income will automatically come back to itself".[22]

For Lewis,

> The central problem in the theory of economic development is to understand the process by which a community which was previously saving and investing 4 or 5 per cent of its national income or less, converts itself to an economy where voluntary saving is running at about 12 to 15 per cent of national income or more. This is the central problem because the central fact of economic development is rapid capital accumulation (including knowledge and skills with capital).[23]

As in the traditional growth theories, fostering economic growth and development in the Lewisian world reduces ultimately to increasing savings and investment. But for Lewis, the accumulation of savings and hence investment in the hands of the capitalists in the modern sector is critical to growth and the transition to a modern economy. Lewis's capitalists are assumed to have a higher savings propensity than the workers in the subsistence sector, and the surpluses generated are invested to accelerate growth. However, it was critically important that wage rates in the capitalist sector do not rise above the level needed for steady state growth or else capital accumulation and growth would stall. In terms of income distribution, the profit share in total output increases during the transition to a modern economy.

Increasing Returns

Increasing returns has a distinguished pedigree in the history of economic thought going back to Adam Smith's notion of the division of labour and Alfred Marshall's elucidation of internal and external economies. Allyn Young's contribution was significant in pointing to the importance of increasing returns for "economic progress".[24] Young stated: "Every important advance in the organisation of production, whether it is based on anything which, in a narrow or technical sense would be called an new 'invention', or involves a fresh application of the fruits of scientific progress to industry, alters the conditions of industrial activity and initiates responses elsewhere in the industrial structure which in turn have a further unsettling effect. Thus change becomes progressive and propagates itself in a cumulative way."[25] As with the Smithian division of labour within the single firm, the realization of increasing returns through division of labour among firms and industries was also dependent on the size of the market.

However, the Harrod-Domar formulations of growth theory with their emphasis on diminishing returns to capital and steady-state equilibrium conditions came to dominate thinking on growth and capital accumulation and Young's contribution was ignored by mainstream economic theorists, although it does seem to have influenced the development theorists. Rosenstein-Rodan's "big push", Myrdal's "circular and cumulative causation" and Hirschman's "forward and backward linkages" can be seen as pointing to increasing returns as key to economic development, even if the analytical frameworks employed did not elucidate this clearly.[26] These "high development theorists" were not concerned like Lewis to keep their analysis within the restrictive bounds of the classical assumptions of diminishing returns and perfect competition, but rather saw the development process as a disequilibrium process involving increasing returns to scale not necessarily across the entire economy, but certainly in respect of manufacturing industry, and some markets that were characterized by imperfect competition.

Moreover, Hirschman's critical insight into the importance of social overhead capital – economic and social infrastructure such as roads, electricity generation, water and irrigation systems, health care, education – as promoting increasing returns to private industry must be noted here. As Hirschman pointed out, activities producing social overhead capital are characterized by the following: (1) they facilitate production across a range of economic activities; (2) they are typically provided by public agencies either free or at controlled prices; (3) they cannot be imported and (4) they are typically capital intensive.[27]

Romer's 1986 model marked an attempt to formalize increasing returns emphasizing the impact of "knowledge" (an "intangible capital good") as a factor in the production process that can grow "without bound". Murphy and colleagues presented a model of the "big push", which outlines the conditions for a successful big push. What turns out to be critical is again the relative wage rates between the traditional and modern sectors.[28]

The increasing returns model therefore also highlights the significance of relative wages between the traditional and modern sectors and hence, in our view, the significance of wages or incomes policy for the development process. Specifically, the modern sector will scale up for mass production where the wage rate is less than the marginal product of labour in the modern sector.[29] The increasing returns paradigm also introduces the role of government into the growth process in a direct way through the provision of social overhead capital. This also means that considerations of tax policy and the impact of taxation on profit rates and capital accumulation need to be factored into the process of growth and development.

Natural Resources and Dutch Disease

In the classical and neoclassical models of growth, natural resources play no part. Land as a factor of production is fixed and then ignored. However, consideration of the growth and development effects of natural resources, in particular oil and minerals, emerged from differing schools in the early twentieth century. The Canadian "staples thesis" and Myint's "vent for surplus" suggested that exports of resource-intensive products could have positive growth and development effects, whereas the Prebisch-Singer analysis of the terms of trade of primary producing countries suggested that these countries would experience negative growth and development effects as a result of secular adverse terms of trade. Parenthetically, Ros had pointed out that the observation that countries or regions with scarce natural resources might become more prosperous than resource-rich countries or regions goes back to the work of Graham on protection in 1923.[30]

The impact of natural resources can be demonstrated in an economy with traditional (agricultural) production with a given steady state capital-labour ratio and wage level. If this economy now discovers and begins to produce a natural resource that also uses labour, the equilibrium- and market-clearing wage will rise. This lowers the profit rate and hence the rate of capital accumulation in the natural resource–based economy that ends up with a lower real wage than the traditional economy and a lower equilibrium capital-labour ratio.

The Dutch Disease model gives a similar result except that the mechanism works through expenditure on nontradables. Higher rents in the resource-intensive sector are spent on nontradables, driving up the price of nontradables relative to tradables as well as the wage rate in that sector as labour is reallocated from the traditional sector to the nontradables sector. The market-clearing and equilibrium wage rises with the same results as before. Profits are lower in the tradables sector and hence the rate of capital accumulation declines.

Over time the resource-poor country will outperform the resource-rich country as it will invest incrementally in increasing returns industries and social overhead capital while the resource-rich country invests more in natural resources and comparatively less in increasing returns industries and social overhead capital. Empirical work over the last twenty years appears to bear out the hypothesis that countries that are resource-poorer outperform those that are resource-rich.[31] Auty has argued, however, that "economic theory provides no convincing explanation as to why resource abundance should be inherently disadvantageous. Indeed, the additional rents and foreign exchange obtained from commodity exports should permit higher levels of investment and greater capacity to import capital goods with which to accelerate economic growth."[32] And further, he argues that "variations in economic performance are caused by differences in the quality of governance that are linked through the type of political state and the pattern of structural change to the natural resource endowment".[33]

Some states are "developmental" while others are "predatory" in their use of the rents accruing from the exploitation of the natural resource. Auty's argument resonates as well with the work of Karl on petro-states.[34] The availability of these rents would delay diversification and investment in industries generating increasing returns. We note as well that whereas the classical and neoclassical theorists assumed that savings were fully invested in the local economy to produce additional output, the propensity to save out of the rents from natural resources might actually be much lower. The structural and institutional features of the economy were therefore relevant to its ability to grow and develop – factors that were central to the perspective of the dependency theorists to whom we now turn.

Dependency Theory, Structuralism and Plantation Economy

Even as Lewis and others were establishing their theories of growth and development and beginning to influence actual plans and policies in developing countries, another generation of economists, trained in the metropolitan schools but finding their intellectual feet in the post-Bandung, post-colonial era began to articulate alternative approaches to the problem of growth and development. They were influenced in part by Marxist economic theory applied to developing countries as articulated by political economists like Paul Baran, Paul Sweezy, and institutional economists like Joseph Schumpeter, Gunnar Myrdal and Karl Polanyi who provided sweeping reinterpretations of European economic history and Europe's relations with the "Third World" as well as reinterpretations of the economic history of developing countries. The Latin American structuralist school saw the emergence of writers like Raul Prebisch, Andre Gunder Frank, Osvaldo Sunkel and Celso Furtado. The Caribbean school saw the emergence of George Beckford, C.Y. Thomas, Lloyd Best, Kari Levitt, Alister McIntyre and Norman Girvan.[35]

The Latin American and Caribbean structuralists took as the starting point for their analysis of the problem of development the nature of the relationship between developed and developing countries. This gave rise to the "centre-periphery" description in Latin America and the "metropolis-hinterland" description in the Caribbean literature. Essentially, these writers saw that the developing countries were passively incorporated into the international economy as price-taking, primary producers, heavily dependent on the metropole/centre for imported consumption and capital goods, and afflicted by terms of trade that seemed to move relentlessly against them. The emphasis placed by structuralists on the nature of the trading and investment relationships between developing and industrialized countries was anticipated in the work of economists such as Hans Singer, Hla Myint and, of course, Prebisch.[36]

Moreover the organization of production in the periphery/hinterland by multinational corporations – the dominant unit of production – was such that surpluses generated in the hinterland were systematically siphoned off to the metropole to foster growth and development there, at the expense of the hinterland. The multinational corporation was just the modern-day form of the merchant class who organized economic activity in the past. The critical question was "To whom did the surplus accrue, and what did they do with it?"

Another factor that loomed, especially for the Caribbean writers, was the problem of size. Caribbean economies were physically small islands with limited or no natural resources and small populations. Small size would limit the extent of the market and hence the possibility for expansion of output and incomes driven by the growth of consumption, which in any event had very high import content.[37] This led to the advocacy of Caribbean economic integration as a means of expanding the market.

It is difficult to conclude, however, that the structuralist writers produced a theory of growth and development in the sense in which "theory" as testable hypothesis is normally understood in the scientific method.[38] In fact, most writers in the structuralist-institutionalist tradition eschewed conventional neoclassical economic analysis and considered its approaches and methods inappropriate to the analysis of the circumstances of underdeveloped countries.[39] The analysis of the mode of incorporation of these economies into the world economy prompted either an anti-imperialist stance, where capitalism itself was to be removed and replaced by a socialist construct, or else structural and institutional reforms, which promoted economic sectors and activities outside the pale of the "plantation economy". Economic policy was reduced to either social revolution or institutional reforms. As Girvan stated, "an analysis of underdevelopment which focuses on the effects of history, institutions, structure and foreign economic relations, implies that the solutions are long-term, and that they must be based on changes in institutions, the structure of production, and the nature of foreign economic relations".[40]

Girvan's remarks seem to imply that governments need to play a greater role than would be allowed in the classical or neoclassical frameworks, taking action to effect institutional reforms, using taxation and/or subsidies to influence the structure of production and actively addressing trade and external relations to improve trading conditions and influence the decision making of international corporations.

Alister McIntyre, long-time collaborator of Lloyd Best, has offered an excellent summary of the economic strategy proposed by the New World school of Caribbean structuralists. The elements of the strategy were as follows: (1) de-emphasizing "Industrialization by Invitation", Puerto Rican style; (2) import displacement by encouraging simple lifestyles, higher propensities to save, changing tastes and patterns of demand in favour of locally produced goods with higher value added; (3) developing local technology, encouraging the use of local raw materials; (4) integrating the regional market to achieve greater critical mass and economies of scale; (5) reducing dependence on external trade preferences and the commodity exports dependent on them; (6) pursuing an active monetary policy giving priority to economic growth over monetary and price stability; (7) pursuing an active exchange rate policy and (8) attacking poverty and income inequality through land reform, education and special employment programmes.[41]

Stabilization, Adjustment and the Washington Consensus

Stabilization and adjustment policies do not really derive from theories of growth and development. Rather they are concerned with restoring an economy to a stable growth path after it has deviated owing to either some adverse external shock, for example, collapse of commodity prices, or unsound macroeconomic policies, for example, excessive government spending leading to chronic deficits, inflation and devaluation. These policies dominated the discourse in developing countries including the Caribbean in the 1970s and 1980s.[42]

Inspired by the Keynesian macroeconomic theory, the notion developed that governments and central banks could "fine-tune" the performance of an economy through the careful calibration of fiscal and monetary policies. Central banks would control the demand for and supply of money through interest rate policies affected through open-market operations and adjustment in discount rates. Governments would influence the pace and growth of aggregate demand through the size and financing of deficits and surpluses.

In the context of developing countries where the manifestation of poor policy was usually massive balance of payments deficits and declining foreign exchange reserves, stabilization and adjustment, in the context of immature financial markets and governments anxious for accelerated growth even with inflation, tended to involve blunt instruments of policy wielded under the direction of the IMF, which was the only means of acquiring foreign exchange to avoid collapse and maintain access to international capital markets. The end result of all of this was volatile or weak growth, with deleterious consequences for income distribution and poverty alleviation.

The IMF itself had evolved what was characterized as the "monetary approach to the balance of payments", which according to Polak had its roots in Kahn-Keynesian macroeconomic theorizing.[43] The IMF approach, in the context of fixed-exchange-rate regimes, justified intervention by government to correct fundamental disequilibria in the balance of payments by manipulating domestic credit creation. This was in contrast to the other "monetary approach to the balance of payments", which evolved under the influence of Harry Johnson, Robert Mundell and the Chicago monetarists. Both approaches aver that excessive credit creation results in balance of payments deficits and loss of reserves.

The so-called Washington Consensus had its antecedents in the work of Milton Friedman and the Chicago School of Monetarists and the neo-neoclassical economists who published their work in the 1960s and 1970s.[44] This school was of the view that unfettered markets were quite capable of producing growth without the intervention of governments. The role of government was to provide public goods – essential infrastructure and the systems of law and order to protect property rights – reasonable and low taxation, and macroeconomic discipline, and leave the rest of the economy to market forces.

According the John Williamson, who coined the phrase "Washington Consensus", the approach has ten features or elements:

1. fiscal discipline
2. reordering public expenditure priorities in favour of basic health and education
3. tax reform – the construction of a tax system that combined a broad tax base with moderate marginal tax rates
4. liberalizing interest rates
5. a competitive exchange rate
6. trade liberalization
7. liberalization of inward foreign direct investment
8. privatization
9. deregulation, specifically easing barriers to entry and exit
10. property rights

Articulated in the context of the developed industrialized countries, this school of thought became influential in developing countries through the activities of the International Monetary Fund and the World Bank. Both these institutions insisted that developing countries should embrace free-market policies in order to receive funding. In practical terms this meant reducing or eliminating fiscal deficits, reducing the size and scope of the public sector, including the activities of state enterprises, lowering tax rates on companies and individuals, exchange rate adjustment and monetary policies that eschewed credit controls and favoured low reserve requirements.

Culture and Development

The earliest development theorists and economic historians sought to explain the differences in "levels" of development between industrialized and developing countries in terms of climate or in terms of cultural practices – attitudes and behaviours – in the latter that were inimical to savings, investment and growth. Among the cultural factors highlighted in the early literature were rapid population growth and low participation rates of women in the (formal) labour force. The unfortunate characterization of certain cultural practices as "primitive" led to a reaction to these theories by later writers.

In recent times economic and social historians have returned to the question of what explains why some countries became rich while others are poor. Social scientists in the Marxist-Leninist tradition explain the disparity as the result of the action of the industrialized countries on the developing countries through colonialism and other forms of exploitation. Other historians have rejected that explanation as being neither historically accurate nor sufficient to explain the observed disparities.

In his iconoclastic book, David Landes argues, "If we learn anything from the history of economic development, it is that culture makes all the difference."[45] He identifies what he perceives to be the values and attitudes of an "ideal growth-and-development society" which is one that is "fitter to produce goods and services". The ideal society would be one that "(1) Knew how to operate, manage and build the instruments of production and to create, adapt and master new technologies on the technological frontier; (2) Was able to impart this knowledge and know-how to the young, whether by formal education or apprenticeship training; (3) Chose people for jobs by competence and relative merit; promoted and demoted on the basis of performance; (4) Afforded opportunity to individual or collective enterprise; encouraged initiative, competition and emulation; (5) Allowed people to enjoy and employ the fruits of their labour and enterprise."[46] In addition, such a society would secure private property rights, secure rights to personal liberty, enforce contracts and provide stable, honest, responsive and efficient government.

The factors identified by Landes are not new. Bert Hoselitz, a founding editor of the journal *Economic Development and Cultural Change* and himself influenced by Max Weber and the German Historical School, argued the case for entrepreneurship as critical to economic development. Cultural factors were discussed extensively by Arthur Lewis, who approached development economics with a keen sense of the economic history of industrialized and developing countries and practical experience of working in such countries.[47] It is significant, however, that these cultural factors are being given new prominence following the tremendous strides made by East Asian countries, Japan and latterly China, employing development strategies that appear to be different from those pursued by the Western industrialized countries and achieving hitherto unprecedented rates of growth.

"Managerial" Theories of Development

Over the last fifteen to twenty years, several non-economists have stepped up to provide theories or explanations of growth and development deriving from non-traditional disciplines or perspectives. Significant among these efforts are management or business writers such as Harvard Business School's Michael Porter and McKinsey and Company partner, William Lewis.[48] Porter's insights are that (1) it is "competitiveness" that matters; (2) it is firms that compete, not nations; (3) productivity (the value of output produced by a unit of capital or labour) is the "prime determinant" of a nation's standard of living; (4) governments can facilitate and enable increases in productivity not by active "industrial policy" or "picking winners" but by fostering an environment that allows firms to become more productive and hence more competitive; and (5) the creation of "clusters" – groups of interconnected firms, suppliers, related industries and specialized institutions in particular fields in particular locations – is an important spur to increased competitiveness.

The traditional development economist would find little or nothing within Porter's framework with which to quarrel since the critical role of productivity, the importance of "agglomeration" of industries, and the external economies (increasing returns) these location advantages provide and the benefits of competition have long been incorporated into their discourses if not into their models. The "effective labour" concept of the neoclassical model sought to capture the impact of productivity.

Structuralists might argue that Porter's framework makes implicit assumptions about the concept of the nation-state, the provenance and objectives of the firms operating in the particular territory and the capacities and inclinations of the governments of these nations. What Porter's framework does do is to emphasize the *micro*economic over the macroeconomic, a perspective that was also emphasized by Lloyd Best.

The Question of Income Distribution

The neoclassical model with constant returns to scale has the result that in steady-state equilibrium the relative shares of profits and wages are constant. In the transition to the steady state however, as capital deepening occurs, the profit share rises relative to the wage share since the profit rate (marginal product of capital) rises faster than the rate of growth of the labour force and the wage rate. The model incorporating technical progress produces a similar result, although the wage rate is affected by the productivity factor.

Societies are not indifferent about the distribution of income and wherever trade unions are powerful, the distribution of income flowing from the required rate of capital accumulation may not be acceptable, leading to industrial relations conflict. This may have the result that wages increase faster than warranted and capital accumulation and growth slow down. A similar effect may result if government taxes profits at a high rate in order to effect transfers and subsidies to wage earners and the profit rate and capital accumulation decline.

Conclusions: The Determinants of Growth and Development

The simple Harrod-Domar model formulation, although built with a number of highly restrictive assumptions – constant returns to scale, fixed capital-labour ratio, closed economy – has yet been very influential in the thinking on the problem of growth by treating growth from a policy perspective as the encouragement of savings, the promotion of investment, and reducing the capital-output ratio through technical change and innovation. The neoclassical (Solow) model added technical progress to the mix and determined that in fact technical progress (increasing labour productivity) was ultimately of greater significance for growth than factor accumulation, that is, growth in the capital stock and growth in the labour force. In respect of income distribution, the neoclassical model suggests that the higher the marginal product of capital (profit rate), the higher will be the growth of output given the capital-labour ratio and the greater will be the share of profits in total income.

Lewis's two-sector model of a labour-surplus economy points out that we must pay attention to the reallocation of resources between the traditional and modern sectors and the role of the wage differential between the traditional or subsistence sector and the modern sector in that process. Increasing returns models are not only more realistic, but hint at a role for government that is completely absent from the classical and neoclassical models in devising initiatives that can effect a "big push", in providing social overhead capital, and also in devising wages or incomes policies that support the growth of the more productive modern sector.

The models of natural resources and Dutch Disease invite consideration of the characteristics of the industries to which incremental investment flows, the consumption and savings propensities of the rentier class, and the implications of those choices for the economy's long-run growth path. The structuralist-institutionalist discourse reminds us that we need to understand who the capitalists are, where they are domiciled, what their motivations are and what their savings propensities are. We also need an appreciation of the power of trades unions in terms of influencing the level of wages. Structuralists would also point out that identification of the "initial conditions" is critically important to understanding how the economy evolves.

The managerial "models" focus attention on microeconomic forces that determine competitive advantage at the level of the firm or industry. Broader cultural factors are also relevant to the analysis, including the rule of law and protection of property rights, achievement orientation, and values and attitudes that are conducive to work and the accumulation of capital. Account must also be taken of the evolution of the distribution of income between capital and labour and more broadly, inequality in the society as well as taxation and transfers and subsidies since these may have implications for the pace of capital accumulation and growth.

Our assessments of development strategy and policy in Trinidad and Tobago and its outcomes will therefore focus on savings and investment rates; sectoral wage rates and population growth; productivity; wage and profit shares, and inequality more broadly; taxation and transfers and subsidies; openness of the economy as an indicator of access to innovation via imports and extension of the market via exports; and the allocation of investment to increasing returns activities including social overhead capital. We will also take appropriate note of institutional changes and developments that may have impacted the processes of growth and development over the period of the analysis.

3

Theories of Economic Policy

In chapter 2, theories of growth and development were surveyed. Categories such as "savings", "investment", "natural resources", "wages" and "profits" were utilized in the construction of models of growth and development. However, the formulation and implementation of development policy is a purposive human activity concerned with the achievement of certain objectives for a given society. We need to ask who constitutes the "government" in a particular society, and what are the competencies and motivations of those persons who formulate and implement policy. We also need to address how, conceptually, governments define and set about achieving those objectives.

Tinbergen's Approach

While the theories of growth and development attempt to explain how growth as well as structural and institutional changes occur, the theory of economic policy is premised on the idea that certain variables that cause growth or structural change can be manipulated by governments to accelerate or slow down the growth process, or foster structural and institutional change. The theory of economic policy is outlined and discussed in this chapter.

There are two important sets of considerations here. First, should governments seek to influence the pace and direction of growth and development at all? Second, can certain variables reliably and consistently be characterized as instrument variables, others as target variables and yet others as exogenous variables?

In the heyday of "development economics" in the 1950s and 1960s, the first question would not have arisen at all. Keynesian macroeconomic theory had given governments a central role in economic stabilization, and tax and expenditure policies were acknowledged as potent tools in macroeconomic management. Postwar reconstruction efforts in Europe and Japan after World War II were driven by the initiatives of Western governments. Russia and the rest of the Soviet Union gained prominence after World War II as economies that embraced Marxist-Leninist politics and central economic planning. It was therefore only a small step for development economists emerging into a new branch of economics in the postwar period to embrace government-led initiatives to promote growth, structural transformation and "modernization".

It was in this postwar intellectual climate, dominated by Keynesian theory and central planning, that economists began thinking about a theory of economic policy. The other important strand that informed the initial theories was the growth of quantitative economic modelling using techniques such as input-output analysis and linear programming. The mathematical foundations of economics had been developing since the early twentieth century, but quantification came later in the second half of the century, along with the development of the discipline of econometrics and the application of computer power to econometric model-building and testing.

The second question springs directly from the model-thinking of the pioneers of the theory of economic policy, economists such as Jan Tinbergen and Bent Hansen.[1] These economists built models of the macroeconomy around consumption, investment, savings, exports and imports, wages and profits, and government taxation and expenditure. Within the models, variables were either endogenous, that is, the values of the variables were determined within the model itself, or exogenous, whose values were obtained from outside the model. The theory of economic policy naturally placed government (in its role of policymaker at least) as "outside" the model, and the variables manipulated by government – tax rate, expenditure, interest rates – were exogenous policy instruments. The settings of these instrument variables would determine the outturn of the target variables or variables of interest – consumption, investment, savings, and ultimately, income and employment.[2]

Tinbergen's approach to the theory of economic policy begins with the idea that economic policy employs a set of means to attain a specified set of objectives. Means and ends are established within a particular socioeconomic context, a context that is the product of historical forces at play in the particular society.

Thus the objectives of economic policy, which describe the desired course or events or future "state of the economy", and the means employed to achieve them will be circumscribed and defined by historically determined social, political and ideological structures. These structures provide the "data" the planner or policymaker has to deal with. The data are, in the words of Tinbergen, "natural, technical, psychological and international elements which the action of man has to take for granted . . . [such as] . . . climate, crops, technical processes, human preferences, habits, laws, political agreements, world market prices and world demand".[3]

Some data can be changed by policy, and these are classified as "means". Those which cannot be changed are classified as "other data". These latter would be the elements determined by nature (e.g., climate), and perhaps certain social structures and cultural attributes. The means of policy may be either quantitative or qualitative. "Qualitative means" refer to the fundamental elements of social and economic organization, such as spiritual values, constitutional rights, attitudes towards property, ownership and control of economic resources, and so on. There are also "less fundamental" elements such as the nature and role of the state, types of taxation, market structures and other such elements. Policy that addresses these qualitative means may be described as structural policy that brings about "structural change". "Quantitative means" refer to the instruments of "purely economic" policy such as tax rates, public investment, bank rate, exchange rates and so on, which are more frequently employed to direct or influence the economic process.

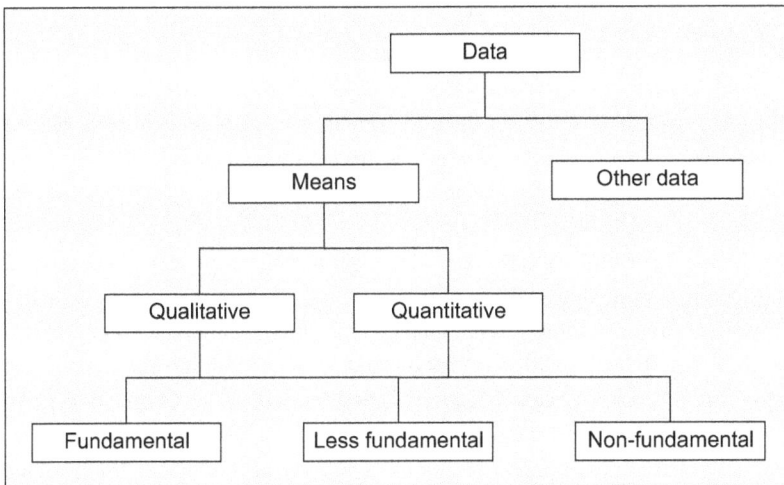

Figure 3.1 Tinbergen's classification

Dependence and Economic Policymaking

But the Classical theory of economic policy still leaves unaddressed the question of what determines the choices of policymakers and what induces policy change. At one extreme, implicit in the Classical approach, policymakers are assumed to be freely acting rational agents who weigh the options before them and make choices that optimize some objective (preference) function.

At the other extreme, social and political structures sweep the policymakers before them. Policy choices are constrained by historically and institutionally determined factors within which policymakers and decision makers in markets are embedded. In the context of petro-states, Karl has argued that the petro-state is characterized by an "unfortunate" gap between jurisdiction and its mechanisms of authority which works to the detriment of the state's ability to flexibly adjust to changing conditions. He states that

> The massive capital and organizational requirements associated with exploiting petroleum had the dual effect of further weakening the domestic bourgeoisie while simultaneously thrusting the state even further onto the centre stage. Because oil revenues poured into the state and not into private enterprise, each new discovery of reserves or price increase enhanced the role of the public sector. This rapid expansion of jurisdiction was accompanied by the intensive centralization of resources in the executive branch, where decisions about petroleum were made. As long as oil revenues continued to enter the national treasury and no conscious effort was made to reverse the process, intervention, centralization, and the concentration of power were virtually automatic.[4]

There is a similar notion in the Caribbean literature where a distinction was made between "structural dependence" and "functional dependence". McIntyre described "functional dependence" as "dependence which arises as a result of the particular policies chosen and can therefore be avoided if alternative policies are pursued". McIntyre made this distinction in the context of his consideration of West Indian trade policy choices as the system of Imperial Preference began to crumble in the postwar period, and his observation that policymakers were apparently unable or unwilling to frame a new set of policy options, but preferred to seek to maintain the status quo.[5]

Havelock Brewster attempted to formalize the vague concept of "economic dependence" which he defined as "a lack of capacity to manipulate the operative elements of an economic system".[6] This arises because of the lack of interdependence between the economic functions of a system such that the system had "no internal dynamic which could enable it to function as an independent, autonomous entity". Brewster sought to demonstrate that policy measures in such economies are of little or no effect because the economic relationships on which policy is predicated are nonexistent. In the face of the ineffectiveness of planning and policy, there is a retreat to the symbols of development, the creation of institutions which "flourish but do not function" and, finally, deceit, self-contempt and self-delusion, wherein compromise is elevated into a theory of achievement.[7]

Development Strategy and Policy

In developing countries, development policies and planning are based explicitly or implicitly on some overall development strategy. Such a strategy is necessarily constructed out of a conception, or theory or "way of seeing" the economy, and which conception determines what we choose to identify as the problems facing the economy that will require attention over some defined period; a statement of the society's fundamental goals, or what has been termed a "philosophy of the optimum social order" – such a statement comes out of the political process and may be ideologically based; and a statement of tactical objectives to be attained over the plan period or the fiscal year such as "an increase in manufactured exports" or "an increase in domestic savings" or "equilibrium in the balance of payments". More attention has been paid in the development economics literature to the latter two elements of "development strategy" than to the conception or theory of the economy, since such a conception is almost always that of the stereotyped "underdeveloped" or "developing" country.

The way in which those responsible for policymaking see the economy is conditioned by ideological, sociopsychological and political factors. Economic crises often change the policymakers' conception of how the economy works. For example, the Great Depression of the 1930s stimulated the Keynesian revolution, and governments embraced the idea that the economy was capable of manipulation by fiscal and monetary policy to maintain stability and/or stimulate growth in the short and medium run. This stood in contrast to the then prevailing Classical notions that disturbances to equilibrium were self-correcting and that government intervention was not required for macroeconomic stability.[8] The establishment of an avowedly socialist government in the Soviet Union, and the initially high rates of growth achieved under central planning, provided developing countries with an alternative model of development and apparently the means whereby the economy could not only be manipulated, but actually moulded as it were, in the national interest.

The earlier analysts of Caribbean economy adopted the conventional metropolitan thinking and approach to the analysis of the economies and their potential.

What struck the early analysts, many of whom were in fact from the United Kingdom, was the constraint on capital accumulation imposed by the small size of the individual Caribbean economies and the impact of rapid population growth on the prospects for development.[9]

The post-colonial analysts, who were born in the region but learned their profession in the metropolitan universities, were struck by what they perceived to be the central characteristic of these economies – their "dependence". There are, however, two problems with the use of the term "dependence". First, while the "economic dependence" of the Caribbean economies has been acknowledged, the attitudes towards it have differed. Some have tended to see it as natural and inevitable, either because of a set of sociopsychological attitudes, or because of what they perceive to be structural and perhaps unalterable facts of the Caribbean economic environment, its small size in particular.[10] Others saw dependence as having been institutionalized over the course of our history and observed that it was both possible and desirable to change the prevailing patterns. The structural characteristics of the economies are emphasized only to determine the ways and means through which the system of domination and subordination is created and reinforced over time.[11]

Second, and arising partly from the foregoing perspectives, the analytic framework used by the various analysts differ in content and emphasis, in some respects quite markedly. Some like Clive Thomas espoused an explicit socialist perspective on dependence and utilized Marxist categories in his analysis.[12] William Demas was rather more eclectic and mainstream in his views on dependence, and his policy prescriptions reflected this positioning. Lloyd Best and Kari Levitt eschewed the Marxist categories and method of analysis, as well as the mainstream development economics literature, and sought to define and stake out an independent position based on the theory of plantation economy.[13]

Class, Race, Ethnicity, Gender and Region in Development Policy

Classical and Neoclassical economics were concerned with categories such as "markets" "prices", "wages" and "profits". Political economy was concerned as well with categories such as "class", "corporations" and "trade unions", which had particular interests in the economic process and its outcomes. Political directorates emerge from particular class relations, and in certain societies, the ruling classes or the political elite might emerge from particular racial groups or tribes or ethnicities, or might be drawn from particular regions of the country. Members of the political elite may have access to information and plans that the rest of the population does not have and that they can take advantage of to their exclusive benefit. Given this reality, it is appropriate to ask whether or not, or to what extent, government policy tends to prefer the interests of one group or class or ethnicity over those of others. This may include for example the interests of migrants, guest workers or non-nationals residing and working in the territory.

It is also appropriate to ask whether a particular policy set *indirectly* favours one group over another or one region or community over another. For example, a policy of tax incentives that is intended to encourage higher profits and reinvestment on the part of the business class will prefer the racial or ethnic group that dominates business in the particular society. Or again, if the business class selectively employs persons from a particular ethnic group, government expenditure or incentives may disproportionately favour the employment prospects of persons from that group relative to other groups.[14] And again, certain policies may promote the creation of certain types of jobs that favour males versus females or vice versa, or create conditions that favour female participation in the labour force.

Development policy can therefore have political and social consequences beyond those intended by the formulators of the policy. It is difficult to know whether or not these effects or consequences are intended or unintended. The intentions are irrelevant if the effects lead to social unrest or social changes that ultimately disrupt the development process. Our working hypothesis in respect of Trinidad and Tobago, a society divided along class and ethnic lines with regional dimensions, is that the formulation of government policy (as distinct from its actual implementation) is not intended to favour one group or class or ethnicity over any other, but that such favouritism may indeed be an *unintended* consequence of the policy or initiative of the government of the day.

Efficiency and Effectiveness of Policy Implementation

In mixed economies, that is, economies where both private and public sectors are significant, the achievement of policy objectives will depend, *inter alia*, on the effectiveness of the policy instruments at the disposal of the government. Policy instruments may be classified as "market" or "non-market", depending on whether or not they operate through the market mechanism, and "direct" or "indirect" depending on whether the target is proximately or remotely related to the policy instrument. The following matrix in figure 3.2 represents a classification of policy instruments based on these categories. As countries become more developed and markets become broader and deeper, one can expect that there will be a shift from the use of nonmarket instruments to market-based instruments.

	Non-market	Market
Direct	• price controls • credit controls • exchange control • incomes policy • anti-trust or competition policy	• exchange rate • direct taxation
Indirect	• moral suasion	• interest rate policy • indirect taxation and subsidies

Figure 3.2 Classification of policy instruments

"Moral suasion" is an interesting policy instrument. More usually employed in the context of the central bank and monetary policy, it can be used at two levels. First, the government seeks the involvement of representatives of the private sector in the exercise of plan formulation – project identification, forecasting of production and demand, estimation of manpower requirements and generally the trading of information, expectations and plans. By this means the government seeks to get the "buy-in" or enrolment of the private sector and obtain co-ownership of the resulting plans and policies.[15] At the second level, the government exhorts and urges the private sector to meet this or that target, or refrain from a certain practice or behaviour so that the policy objectives may be achieved. This approach may be chosen as more effective because the use of market-based instruments may carry certain administrative or economic costs, may take too long to impact the objective, or may be seen to not work at all owing to certain market imperfections or market failure.

A given policy may be implemented or executed more or less competently, more or less corruptly, or more or less efficiently. Social overhead capital or infrastructure projects may impact more or fewer citizens, may be more or less socially useful, or may have a shorter or longer half-life. How policies and projects are executed will therefore have a bearing on the efficiency of the growth path. While it is obvious that these qualitative considerations will impact the growth rate achieved or the extent or pace of transformation, it is hard to know *a priori* the extent of that impact.

An important consideration in this regard is the question of corruption, a pervasive factor in all societies. It is particularly pernicious in developing countries, and more so again in rentier-type economies such as petro-states. As Rose-Ackerman has pointed out: "Corrupt high-level officials support too much unproductive public investment and under-maintain past investments. Corruption reduces total investment and limits FDI, but it encourages excessive public infrastructure investment."[16] And again: "Corrupt rulers favor capital-intensive projects over other types of public expenditures and favor public investment over private investment. They will frequently support 'white elephant' projects with little value in promoting economic development."[17]

Allegations of corruption in Trinidad and Tobago have bedeviled political life since colonial times, and have become stronger and more frequent in the period since the petrodollar boom in the 1970s. However, we do not pursue this question or the broader question of the efficiency of implementation of policy in any great detail, though its importance is unquestioned.

Policy Mapping: A Method for Describing and Assessing Development Policy

A development strategy is reflected or represented in a set of policies that are intended to achieve the goals of the strategy. Governments may employ taxation, subsidies, tariffs, exchange rate variations, interest rates, credit controls, and government expenditure on goods and services, among other policy measures to achieve the objectives specified.

The assessment of the stance or direction of policy is complex because of the several instruments or measures that might be employed, how these are deployed and the objectives or targets that policymakers are trying to achieve. Comparing strategies or the stance of policy from one period to the next is even more complicated. In figure 3.3 below, we outline a pictorial representation of the stance of policy at a particular period. There are eleven policy factors displayed in the policy map that are identified and described in table 3.1. The list of factors is not to be seen as exhaustive, nor does the listing suggest any hierarchy in the importance of the factors since the importance of one or another factor will vary depending on the circumstances of the economy. The configuration of the factors over a given period will reflect the strategy or policy stance of the government.

The stance of policy in respect of any specific factor or dimension of policy is described by a position on the ray from the centre. More conservative policy stances would be represented by a point closer to the centre, while more aggressive or expansive policy stances would be represented by points farther away from the centre.

In figure 3.2, two very different policy configurations are represented. The inner configuration might, for example, reflect a conservative neoclassical approach wherein property rights are strongly upheld, the role of the state is limited, foreign direct investment is encouraged, and fiscal and monetary policies are conservative – low interest rates, positive real interest rates and low inflation, with a fiscal deficit that respects inflation pressures and debt accumulation.

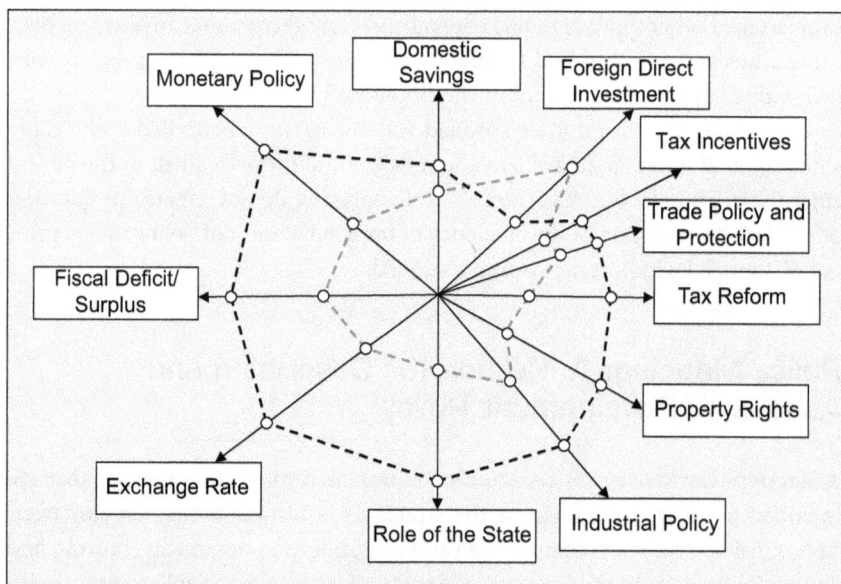

Figure 3.3 Policy map

The outer configuration reflects a policy stance that is much more aggressive where the role of the state is enlarged, reforms – for example, land reforms – are promoted along with tax reforms with distributional objectives, fiscal and monetary policies are expansive and foreign direct investment is not especially favoured relative to domestic savings.

We use the policy map to compare and contrast the stance of policy across the time periods of our review and analysis of development policy in Trinidad and Tobago.

Conclusions

Our review of the theories of growth and development, traditional and modern, as well as our review of the theory of economic policy allows us to draw five conclusions that inform the approach taken to the assessment of development policy in Trinidad and Tobago.

First, development is a process that involves the progressive enhancement of the potential of individuals and communities to command goods and services so as to expand the real freedoms that they can enjoy. These include health care, education, personal security and so on.

Table 3.1 Policy Factors Represented in the Policy Maps

Domestic savings	The extent to which policy encourages more or less domestic savings (public or private) compared to a reliance on external financing
Foreign drect investment	The extent to which policy encourages more or less foreign direct investment (FDI)
Tax incentives	The extent to which policy utilizes tax incentives to encourage particular investments or behaviours
Trade policy and protection	The extent to which tariff and/or nontariff barriers are deployed to influence the composition and direction of trade and/or the development of particular industries
Tax reform	Changes in the structure of taxation (as distinct from changes in tax rates); this would include new forms of taxation or removal of certain forms of taxation. Movement away from the centre indicates greater use of changes to the tax structure.
Property rights	The preservation and enforcement of property rights; at the extreme property may be nationalized or expropriated. Movement away from the centre indicates abridgement of property rights.
Industrial policy	Identification of particular industries that the policymakers wish to support or particular industries that will no longer qualify for state support. Movement away from the centre indicates greater use of industrial policy and "picking winners".
Role of the state	The extent to which government seeks to directly influence the pace and direction of economic activity using state enterprises. Movement away from the centre indicates a more active role of government in the economy in directly productive activities.
Exchange rate	Active or passive use of the exchange rate in economic stabilization and adjustment or as an aspect of industrial policy. More active policy is represented by positions farther from the centre.
Fiscal surplus/deficit	The overall level and composition of government spending and revenue so as to influence aggregate economic activity and influence particular industries or activities.
Monetary policy	The use of interest rate policy, money supply variations to influence liquidity and/or investment activity

Second, growth in output and income is a *sine qua non* for development. In order to achieve growth, societies need to raise the savings rate, the investment rate and total factor productivity through technical progress and innovation. Growth also requires a profit rate that encourages capital accumulation.

Third, the "initial conditions" are critically important. The state of the society and its institutions, labour force, use of technology, and the values and attitudes of citizens are important to the policy choices made and hence to the path of development. It makes a difference whether a society begins life as a slave plantation economy, a frontier economy or a settlement of free men and women.

Fourth, special considerations apply to petro-states or rentier economies in respect of policymaking because of the fluctuations in income over the commodity cycle, the appropriation and disposition of the rents, and the corruption and resource misallocation that arises from perverse price structures. These considerations are arguably inimical to sustained growth and development over the long term.

Fifth, ethnicity, class and regional factors may influence policy formulation, but are more likely to influence the implementation of policy.

4

Colonial Economic Policy

Introduction

Until self-government and independence, it would be entirely valid to question whether it is either sensible or appropriate to talk about the formulation and implementation of policies for the development of the colony of Trinidad and Tobago, or the British West Indian colonies as a whole, or indeed any colony at all. A colony was after all merely an appendage of the mother country. John Stuart Mill, writing in the middle of the nineteenth century, had said:

> Our West India colonies, for example, cannot be regarded as countries, with a productive capital of their own. If Manchester, instead of being where it is, were on a rock in the North Sea, (its present industry nevertheless continuing,) it would still be but a town of England, not a country trading with England; it would be merely, as now, a place where England finds it convenient to carry on her cotton manufacture. The West Indies, in like manner, are the place where England finds it convenient to carry on the production of sugar, coffee, and a few other tropical commodities. All the capital employed is English capital; almost all the industry is carried on for English uses; there is little production of anything except the staple commodities, and these are sent to England, not to be exchanged for things exported to the colony and consumed by its inhabitants, but to be sold in England for the benefit of the proprietors there. The trade with the West Indies is hardly to be considered as external trade, but more resembles the traffic between town and country, and is amenable to the principles of the home trade.[1]

There are, however, two perspectives that make "colonial policy" relevant and important to the evolution of development policy in the post-independence period. First, by the mid-twentieth century, the colonies had evolved a creole class that, even though it acknowledged Britain as the "mother country", also saw the territories in which they were born as "home", and the members of this creole class were interested in the growth and development of their home territories. This did not necessarily mean growth and development for all residents equally, nor did it necessarily mean that the working classes in the colonial territories should also develop and prosper. However, it transpired that over time the interests of all the various elements of creole society were more closely bound together, than the interests of the local elite with those of the Colonial Office.[2]

Second, by and large the colonial elite remained firmly within the Western intellectual tradition, whether Capitalist or Socialist, and as a result, even when they rebelled against colonialism and sought political independence, the possibilities for action were defined or circumscribed by the inherited intellectual tradition.[3] Colonialism had brought not only economic and social discrimination and exploitation, but had also brought with it notions of democracy based on the Westminster system of representative government, the idea of the rule of law, independence of the judiciary, fundamental rights and freedoms including freedom of the press and freedom of expression. The local colonial elites repudiated colonialism as discrimination and exploitation, but embraced and indeed sought to master the Western (English) intellectual traditions, laws and habits.[4]

International Context

The onset of the Great Depression in 1929 led to a global economic meltdown impacting severely the Caribbean colonies that were dependent on primary agricultural exports – sugar, cocoa, bananas – and in the case of Trinidad and Tobago, petroleum and asphalt exports as well. The cocoa industry, which was dominant in Trinidad's exports up to 1920, had been in decline since prices peaked in 1920. Expansion of the supply of cocoa in Africa and elsewhere would ensure that prices would not return to the levels attained in the early part of the century.

The International Sugar Agreement negotiated in 1937 sought to provide greater price stability for sugar producers by instituting a quota system. During the war years and for several years afterwards, however, Britain consolidated supplies of sugar from Commonwealth countries, buying all of their exportable surpluses and in 1951 the Commonwealth Sugar Agreement came into force, which established the system of preferences for sugar exports to the United Kingdom. Imperial preference as it came to be known also governed exports of bananas, important for other Caribbean countries, though not for Trinidad and Tobago.[5]

Crude oil production increased steadily from initial commercial production in 1907–8 to reach twenty million barrels by 1939. Trinidad's oil production was critically important to Britain's war effort, accounting for 65 per cent of production in the British Empire by 1946. By the time of the Moyne Commission, Trinidad and Tobago had moved from an economy once dominated by cocoa and sugar to one in which petroleum was dominant in terms of exports, though not employment. The international trade regime for petroleum was quite different from the system of imperial preference that governed cocoa and sugar. The increasingly vertically integrated international oil companies dominated global oil production, and the complexities of negotiating with these companies was to become vital to the formulation of development policy for Trinidad and Tobago. Two of the international majors were established in Trinidad's oil industry – British Petroleum and Shell – and the American oil major, Texaco, entered the refining and distribution sector with the acquisition of Trinidad Leaseholds Limited in 1956. Texaco was also involved later on in the Soldado field offshore Trinidad's south west coast.[6]

Perhaps more important than the international trading arrangements was the process of decolonization that, led by India, had gained impetus in the interwar years. The "white dominions" – Canada, Australia – had long been granted self-government, and the nonwhite colonies in Asia and Africa, with an emerging elite educated at the best schools in England, agitated for self-government and independence.

A war-weary Britain was keen to relinquish its imperial reach and the political and economic costs that empire entailed. India was the first to go immediately after the war in 1948, and the British colonial dominoes fell steadily thereafter.

The intellectual currents in the postwar period were also fed by the victory of Communist forces in China under Mao Tse Tung, the rise of Communist Russia as a nuclear and space-age power, and the spread of socialist ideology in Asia and Africa. The Afro-Asian Conference in Bandung, Indonesia, in April 1955 gave form and substance to the idea of the "Third World". New leaders strode onto the world stage – Nehru from India, Nasser from Egypt, Nkrumah from Ghana, Nyerere from Tanzania, Lee Kuan Yew from Singapore and later on, Fidel Castro from Cuba. International politics shifted from imperial to ideological disposition. The atrocities perpetrated on the Jews by the Nazis prompted parallels in the discrimination and persecution of nonwhite peoples over centuries of colonialism. The United Nations Declaration on Human Rights in December 1948 was seen to apply to all peoples everywhere and inspired movements for equality within countries and between countries.

Domestic Context

Politics in Trinidad and Tobago in the pre–World War II period had been characterized by the appeal for greater local representation in the legislative process of the autocratic crown colony system. The appeal had been articulated in the main by Arthur Cipriani's working-class movement, fired to action by the realization, engendered during the course of World War I, that the British imperial system had imposed gross inequities on nonwhite colonial peoples.

The British response to the appeal was the appointment of the Wood Commission of Enquiry in 1921, which concluded that the territory needed to be granted some measure of government reform, but ruled out immediate responsible government on the ground that there was no independent leisure class that could effectively aggregate the interests of all communities impartially, and for the time being, only the officials in the colonies' administration could perform that role.[7] The twenty-six member legislature was then to have seven elected members. Cipriani himself was co-opted into the establishment of parliamentary and mayoral politics and effectively emasculated.

Unemployment soared in the 1930s, and low wages and poor working conditions precipitated labour unrest in the oilfields led by Tubal Uriah Butler. Butler, a Grenadian-born oil worker, took over the reins of the movement and carried it into the streets. His agitative street politics culminated in rioting and the strike of June 1937. The rioting, which left several dead in its wake, had the effect of calling the attention of the imperial authorities to the plight of the West Indian worker, and prompted the dispatch of the Forster Commission in 1937 and the Moyne Commission to the West Indies in 1938.[8] The West India Royal Commission, chaired by Lord Moyne, investigated the social and economic conditions of all the British West Indian territories. The Commission held public hearings throughout the region, and recommended sweeping economic, social and political reforms. The Moyne Commission was forced to acknowledge the desperate conditions in the West Indies, while assuaging the concerns of the plantation owners and oil companies that their interests would be protected and law and order would be maintained. The full findings of the commission were not published until 1945. The British government decided to make substantial increases in the amount of money available for colonial development, but this was delayed until after the war.

Like the Wood Commission before it, the Moyne Commission was reluctant to recommend responsible government, but thought that more "representative" government was needed, meaning thereby that the elected members should participate in the executive branch of government, though only in an advisory capacity. The question of universal adult suffrage was referred to a special franchise committee which recommended that universal adult suffrage be granted, although the voting qualifications were restrictive.

The early prewar reform movement of Cipriani and Butler was characterized by a strong reaction to the undemocratic and arbitrary nature of colonial rule, and to the basic assumption that black peoples were not "fit to rule" themselves. But there was no challenge to the idea of empire, or to the superiority and excellence of British culture and the Westminster system of government. Gordon Lewis said of Cipriani: "[H]is chief error was to believe in the ultimate moral rightness of the British Empire and of the English governing gentleman class. He fought them on their terms, not on his, with the result that he never called the massive moral bluff of English colonial rule . . . It seemed at times indeed that he was not so much against colonialism as such but merely unenlightened colonialism."[9]

Adult suffrage, limited by property qualifications, was attained in 1946 and a large number of political parties were formed, many based on the trade unions, which had mushroomed since 1937 including the powerful Oilfield Workers Trade Union (OWTU), the Seamen and Waterfront Workers Trade Union (SWWTU), and the All Trinidad Sugar Estate and General Workers Union. The party political leadership overlapped with the trade union leadership in the persons of Adrian Cola Rienzi, T.U. Butler and Albert Gomes, among others.[10]

The War Years, 1939–45, were something of a mixed blessing for Trinidad and Tobago. Economic stringency intensified with rationing and wartime restrictions. However, the establishment of the American bases at Chaguaramas and Wallerfield and the presence of American servicemen brought new jobs, which paid well for those who got them, and also led to some improvements in infrastructure through road-building and other public works. The alienation of the Chaguaramas peninsula to the American naval base was, however, to become a political cause célèbre later on during the period of independence.

A hybrid "quasi-ministerial" system operated after 1950 with five elected ministers operating alongside the governor and financial secretary in the exercise of executive power, but with no premier or chief minister. The new constitutional arrangements, which came into force in 1956, provided that there would be only two ex-officio members in the legislative council in the persons of the attorney general and the colonial secretary. There were, in addition, twenty-six elected members and five nominated members of the legislative council. The governor continued to preside over the legislative council.

Colonial Development Programmes

Economic planning in the restricted sense of a programme of public expenditure designed to accelerate or shape the economy in some preconceived way was not unprecedented in Trinidad and Tobago, though it is by no means clear that planning under responsible and independent government was motivated or influenced as to form and content by the previous colonial development programmes since precedents for five-year plans could also be found in the Soviet Union as well as in India.

In October 1938, the legislative council approved a $14 million programme for the period 1939 to 1944 of which $11 million was to be financed from loans.[11] This programme was to address slum clearance and working-class housing, improvements in hospitals and health facilities, water supply, new school buildings, extension of railway services and a new aerodrome, irrigation of agricultural lands, extension of electricity supply, and expansion of roads. World War II disrupted this programme since no loans were made available until 1946. In 1946, a ten-year programme was initiated under the Colonial Development and Welfare (CDW) organization.

This was partly the result of the recommendation of the Moyne Commission of Enquiry that a Welfare Fund be established, financed by an annual grant of £1 million from the Imperial Exchequer for a period of twenty years, and aimed at the improvement of education, health, housing and slum clearance, as well as the creation of labour departments, the provision of social welfare facilities and land settlement schemes.[12]

Here is the first reference we have to the idea of long-term programming: "The need is not for the immediate grant of a large lump sum, but for a programme of development over a period of years, according to well-thought-out policies and administered by an organisation in a position constantly to control and review the execution of such a policy."[13] Hence the CDW organization was established in 1940. It was headed by a comptroller who, with his staff of experts, was to work out the long-term programme of social reform to be submitted to the secretary of state, and to consider similar schemes submitted by the local governments on their own initiative and to control and supervise the funds and grants made from it.

The CDW Act did not work as intended. It provided £5 million annually for the entire empire for a ten-year period. However, it required the colonies to submit plans without knowing how much finance would be available, while the funds were not to be disbursed without a comprehensive programme. It has been observed that colonial development finance was characterized by underspending; that is, actual development expenditures fell short of parliamentary appropriations, and this was due to the fact that the exigencies of Britain's domestic economic policy in almost every instance outweighed considerations of colonial economic development.[14] It was in fact Britain's economic climate that determined the pace of development spending in the colonies.

Trinidad and Tobago's 1946–55 economic programme was, however, initiated under the new CDW Act of 1945, which permitted greater flexibility in the administration of funds. The ten-year programme was initially estimated to cost

$65.5 million, $5 million coming from CDW, $12 million from surplus balances and the rest from loans. The programme was divided into two quinquennia: 1946–50 and 1950–55. By December 1949, $27.6 million had been spent, with only 30 per cent being financed from general revenue. The 1950–55 programme was initially estimated to cost $38.8 million, but this was revised to $67 million. By December 1955, $41.7 million had been spent, with over 50 per cent of it being externally financed.[15]

Significant pieces of legislation driving economic policy were passed in this period. The Aid to Pioneer Industries Ordinance and the Income Tax (in Aid of Industry) Ordinance were passed in 1950. These pieces of legislation emerged from the work of the Shaw Committee appointed by then governor of the colony J.V. Shaw and included local luminaries such as Gerald Wight, Chanka Maharaj, Victor Bryan, Errol Dos Santos and Albert Gomes. In order to foster import substitution, the committee had recommended income tax exemptions, customs duty exemptions, release of foreign exchange for imports from hard currency areas, and establishment of an industrial board with executive powers to give financial assistance to pioneer enterprises.[16]

In May 1956, a new public investment programme was approved at an estimated cost of $90.5 million. However, the programme was overtaken by political events and scrapped by the new PNM administration, which then initiated the first programme (1958–62) under self-government.

Policy Instruments under Colonial Rule

The development strategy of the colonial administration was predicated on infrastructure development and on limited import substitution. The Moyne Commission report had mandated that the social infrastructure of the West Indian colonies be improved, that is, education, health and housing.

As a British colony, Trinidad and Tobago could have no independent monetary policy. There was no central bank. Notes and coins were issued from 1951 (notes) and 1955 (coins) by the British Caribbean Currency Board, with the British West Indies (BWI) dollar equivalent to four shillings and two pence. BWI dollars were fully backed by sterling reserves.

In the colonial economy, there was little or no scope for an active countercyclical fiscal policy since, with limited capacity to borrow locally, deficits would lead to the decumulation of foreign exchange reserves, contraction of the supply of local currency and hence a fall in domestic spending. Moreover, because the decline in economic activity in the first place was likely to arise from a fall in exports rather than a decline in private investment, the ability of government expenditure to stimulate real output growth in a colonial economy was questionable.[17] Active fiscal policy would relate to the level of capital expenditure, which the budget could accommodate. With limited scope for deficit budgets, the critical policy issue was the allocation of available revenues between recurrent expenditure and capital expenditure. At the microeconomic level, indirect taxation and subsidies as well as tax concessions could be used to influence the output and/or prices of certain goods and services and hence influence the structure of production at the margin.[18]

Trade and commercial policy was largely in the hands of the Colonial Office rather than the local administration. The conditions of access to external markets could not be influenced by the local administration, nor could tariffs be employed that might lower exports from the mother country. In respect of commercial policy, foreign direct investment was encouraged and foreign firms were dominant in certain industries such as banking, insurance, petroleum, oil refining, cement, petrochemicals, paints, and medicinal and pharmaceutical products.[19]

While it might be tempting to dismiss the account of colonial economic policy initiatives and to begin the history of development policy in Trinidad and Tobago with the PNM's rise to power under responsible self-government and the first five-year plan, there was not, in fact, a complete discontinuity between the previous policies and those that were formulated later.[20] Indeed, the policy of the encouragement of pioneer industries through tax concessions was retained until the end of protection in the 1970s, and these tax concessions continued to be used for the encouragement of the large-scale resource-based industries thereafter. The central bank was not established until 1964, and active monetary policy only became possible sometime afterwards. Countercyclical fiscal policy continued to be constrained until such time as a local capital market could develop.

It is, however, difficult to connect the strong growth of the economy in the postwar period to the policy and planning initiatives undertaken by the local colonial administration. The implementation capacity of the colonial government was weakened and dissipated by the factions and fragmentation that characterized the political and trade union scene in the years after the war. Moreover, the British governor and colonial administrators continued to seek the interests of foreign capital and the local plantocracy over the interests of labour and were fearful of the ethnic divide that was emerging in Trinidad's politics.[21]

Growth and Structural Change in the Postwar Period to 1957

No data are available for GDP in the period before 1951. However, the GDP (market prices) grew at 13.3 per cent per annum over the period 1951 to 1957,

Table 4.1 Sectoral Origin of Gross Domestic Product, 1951–1954
      ($ Million and Percentage Shares)

Sector	Sectoral Origin of Gross Domestic Product 1951–1954 ($M)				Average Annual Growth Rate 1951–54	Sectoral Origin of Gross Domestic Product 1951–1954 (%)			
	1951	1952	1953	1954	1951–54	1951	1952	1953	1954
Agriculture, fishing and quarrying	55.6	61.0	69.3	76.9	11.4%	18%	18%	18%	19%
Oil and asphalt	93.5	98.3	121.2	120.1	8.7%	30%	29%	32%	30%
Manufacturing and construction	51.8	56.1	58.8	64.2	7.4%	17%	17%	15%	16%
Other, including government	107.4	121.9	130.3	143.0	10.0%	35%	36%	34%	35%
Total GDP at factor cost ($ million)	308.3	337.3	379.6	404.2	9.4%	100%	100%	100%	100%

Source: Central Statistical Office, *The National Income of Trinidad and Tobago, 1966–1985*,
appendix 3, "The National Income 1951–1954".
Note: $ here refers to British West Indian dollars which circulated throughout the Eastern Caribbean.

a remarkably strong rate of growth under any circumstances. Economic growth after the war was driven by several factors. First, the postwar expansion of the petroleum industry saw steadily increasing production of crude oil and expansion of refining capacity. Crude petroleum production rose from 21.4 million barrels in 1952 to 34 million barrels in 1957, while fuel oil, the dominant product from the oil refinery, increased from 16.5 million barrels in 1952 to 21.6 million barrels in 1957.

Second, the country's infrastructure of roads, airport and ports had been improved by the wartime activity of the Americans as well as the growth of the oil industry. Third, agriculture also expanded as cocoa rehabilitation reaped benefits for cocoa producers and coffee and sugar production also increased. Cocoa production increased from 14.3 million pounds in 1952 to 22.0 million pounds in 1957. Coffee production increased from 2.3 million pounds in 1952 to 5 million pounds in 1957. Indeed Agriculture, which included Forestry, Fishing and Quarrying, was the fastest growing sector between 1951 and 1954 (table 4.1).

The economy accelerated from a growth rate of 9.4 per cent per annum between 1951 and 1954 to 12.6 per cent per annum between 1954 and 1957, reflecting strong growth in the petroleum, construction and distribution sectors. The petroleum sector, which grew at 18.5 per cent per annum over the period, accounted for 36 per cent of GDP in 1957, and distribution increased its share

Table 4.2 Sectoral Origin of Gross Domestic Product, 1954–1957 ($million and Percentage Shares)

Sector	Sectoral Origin of Gross Domestic Product 1954–1957 ($M)				Average Annual Growth Rate 1954–57	Sectoral Origin of Gross Domestic Product 1954–1957 (%)			
	1954	1955	1956	1957	1954–57	1954	1955	1956	1957
Agriculture, fishing and quarrying	76.9	83.6	84.1	93.6	5.0%	18.7%	17.6%	15.1%	14.2%
Oil and asphalt	120.1	138.9	187.1	237.1	18.5%	29.3%	29.2%	33.6%	36.0%
Manufacturing	54.6	59.4	61.2	77.9	9.3%	13.3%	12.5%	11.0%	11.8%
Construction	10.1	14.1	17	20.7	19.6%	2.5%	3.0%	3.1%	3.1%
Public utilities	13.5	14.9	16.2	18.7	8.5%	3.3%	3.1%	2.9%	2.8%
Distribution	37	54.3	72.6	85.9	23.4%	9.0%	11.4%	13.1%	13.0%
Banking insurance real estate	7.2	9.6	10.7	12.2	14.1%	1.8%	2.0%	1.9%	1.9%
Transportation	11.3	14.6	16.8	18.3	12.8%	2.8%	3.1%	3.0%	2.8%
Government	47.9	48.6	51.2	52.6	2.4%	11.7%	10.2%	9.2%	8.0%
Personal services, other	31.9	38.1	39.4	42.1	7.2%	7.8%	8.0%	7.1%	6.4%
Total GDP at factor cost ($ million)	410.5	476.1	556.3	659.1	12.6%	100%	100%	100%	100%

Source: Central Statistical Office, *The National Income of Trinidad and Tobago, 1966–1985*, appendix 4, "The National Income 1952–1962".
Note: $ here refers to British West Indian dollars which circulated throughout the Eastern Caribbean.

Table 4.3 Investment Performance, 1952–1957

	1952–1957
Gross capital formation/gross domestic product	23%
Foreign direct investment/gross capital formation*	42%
Government capital expenditure/Gross capital formation	15%

Note: Some care is needed here as not all government capital expenditure is properly really capital formation. However, government's role in investing activities is certainly understated since investment by state enterprises and other government agencies is not accounted for here.
*1955–1957

from 9 per cent to 13 per cent, on the basis of an average annual growth rate of over 23 per cent. There were corresponding declines in the shares of manufacturing and agriculture (table 4.2).

Investment over the period 1952 to 1957 was moderate, averaging 23 per cent of GDP. Foreign direct investment over the period 1955 to 1957 for which data are available averaged 42 per cent of gross capital formation, a proportion that was not exceeded until the 1990s. Government capital expenditure was modest over the period reflecting the constraints on any form of active fiscal policy.

Over the period 1951–57, relative income shares are more nearly equal, although from 1955, the share of profits, proxied by the operating surplus, began to increase relative to the share of wages in total GDP (figure 4.1).

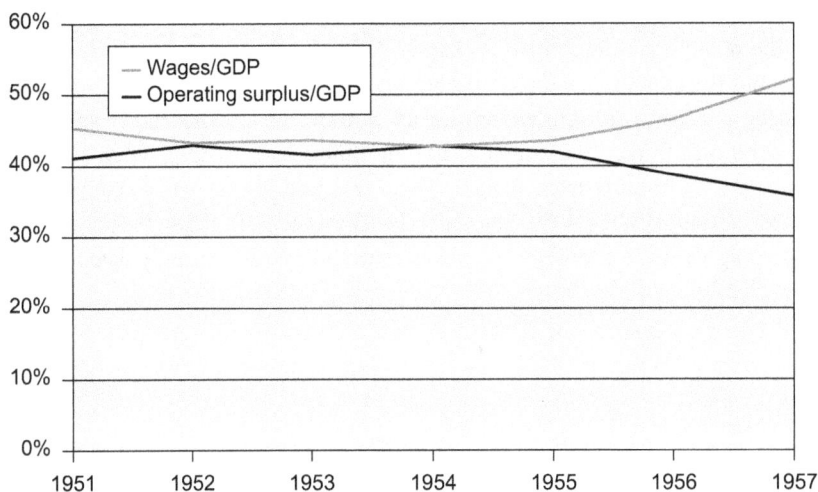

Figure 4.1 Relative income shares, 1951–1957

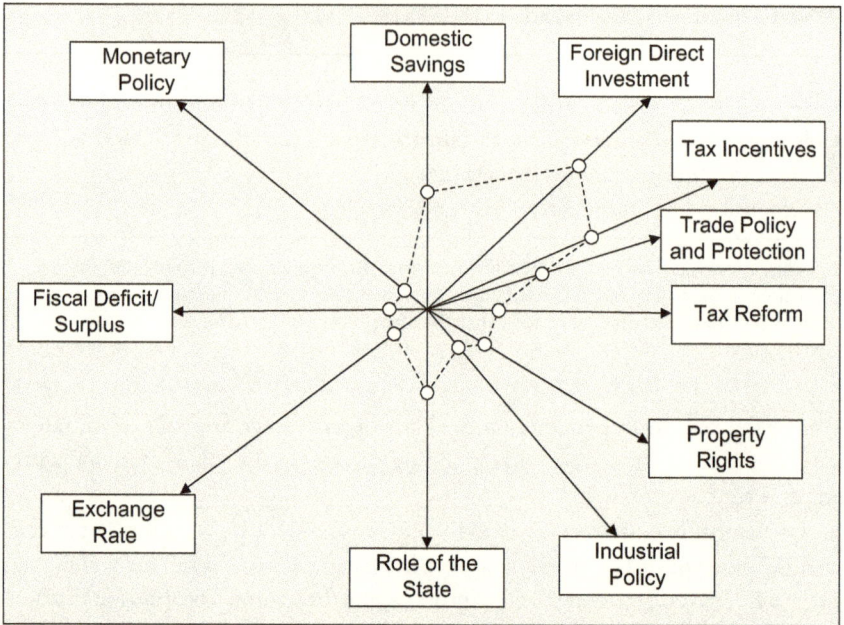

Figure 4.2 Colonial economic policy

This was the structure of the economy that the new administration operating under self-government would be inheriting and that it would seek to transform through a series of five-year plans beginning in 1958.

Figure 4.2 depicts graphically the orientation of colonial economic policy using the policy map developed in chapter 3. Emphasis was placed on tax incentives and the encouragement of foreign direct investment. Industrial policy was nascent in the proposals for an industrial board (later the Industrial Development Corporation). In fact the industries to be promoted were those which could not compete with imports from Britain. There was nothing by way of conventional macroeconomic policy – monetary, fiscal and exchange policies. Property rights, in keeping with the country's Westminster traditions, are strongly defended and preserved.

Part 2

Import-Substituting
Industrialization, 1958 – 1973

5

Development Strategy in a Newly Independent Economy

International and Regional Developments

Historians now recognize the decade of the 1960s as being in some sense quite special. The United States had come off best after the war and determined to assert its power and prestige in world affairs. Russia for its part was equally determined that, despite its huge losses during World War II, its hegemonic ambitions and socialist agenda would not be derailed by American hubris, and set about forging a strategic alliance with Maoist China and intervening actively through Marxist movements in the developing countries that were keen to remove the yoke of colonialism. The Russians would be the first in space, a feat that enhanced its perceived technological prowess in the eyes of the developing world and raised the spectre of intercontinental nuclear war. It was a decade in which the Cold War, with roots in the stand-off in occupied Berlin and America's use of atomic weapons against Japan, played out in the conflict on the Korean peninsula, the Bay of Pigs fiasco and the interdiction of Soviet arms to Cuba, and later on in the long and bloody conflict in Vietnam.

A war-ravaged Europe, boosted by the Marshall Plan for the reconstruction of the continent, determined that such conflict as occurred in World War I and World War II must never happen again on European soil and that the best way to achieve that was for Franco-German détente and economic integration, pulling the rest of Europe along in its wake. The Treaty of Rome in 1959 set the stage for the eventual creation of the European Community. For its part, Britain knew that it could no longer hold on to its empire, but was concerned that the retreat had to be orderly and face-saving.

As far as the West Indies were concerned, orderly retreat for the British Colonial Office meant an attempt at federation, which was proposed and implemented from 1958. The arrangements provided for a federal parliament and a prime minister, with the capital of the Federation located in Port of Spain, Trinidad. The first federal prime minister was a Barbadian. In 1961, the Jamaican electorate rejected the federation and precipitated Jamaica and Trinidad and Tobago seeking independence from Britain as early as August 1962, followed thereafter by Barbados and Guyana. While the failure of federation left scars on the territories of the region, arguably up to the present time, the region was, however, prompted to form a free trade area, the Caribbean Free Trade Association (CARIFTA), which came into existence in 1966, and progressed to a customs union with the Treaty of Chaguaramas in 1973.

The 1960s was a decade in which the children of the postwar baby boom were beginning to articulate their preferences for personal liberty without responsibility in the "hippie" movement, for universalistic values and respect for other peoples, rather than the particularistic values of WASP America and upper-class Britain, and for the conspicuous consumption and enjoyment of income and wealth.[1] The arms race gave tremendous impetus to industrial production of steel, aluminum and plastics, and the space race saw the incorporation of new technologies developed for the space programme into everyday products, including information technology and communications technologies.

The United Nations Declaration on Human Rights gave impetus, if impetus was needed, to the American civil rights movement led by Martin Luther King Jr as well as to the assertion of black power by Malcolm X and the Trinidad-born Stokely Carmichael, who had changed his name to Kwame Ture.

These powerful global social and cultural forces impelled the Catholic Church to convene Vatican II, leading to the most significant reforms in the church for decades, including the use of local language instead of Latin in the rituals of the church and the emphasis on social justice and the "preferential option for the poor". Liberation theology emerged from Latin America and gave powerful support to movements for agrarian reform, reform of income and wealth distribution, and improvements in the condition of the poor and the powerless.

The Emergence of the PNM, Self-Government, Independence and Aftermath

Whatever its weaknesses and failings, the prewar reform movement of 1919 to 1937 had laid the basis for the postwar assault on direct colonialism. It had promoted the emergence of local political figures ranged, if at times ambivalently, against the arbitrariness of the Colonial Office and its commissions of enquiry. It had stirred the working class into effective organization for agitation and action in defending and protecting its interests. The postwar period ushered in a new, higher phase in the development of the nationalist movement, distinguished by the proliferation of political groups, and a new style of political leadership summed up in the apparently charismatic appeal of Eric Williams. Williams and his PNM governed Trinidad and Tobago from 1956 until his death in 1981, and without question, Williams's personality and policies dominated the life of the country over that period and indeed for a long time afterwards.[2]

Much of literature on the emergence of the PNM has emphasized the virtual transformation of the political culture that appeared to take place between 1956 and 1961. Whatever may have been the reasons for the heightening of political activity and consciousness, it certainly was not to be found in the economic and social programmes articulated by the new party that came to power in 1956, for in this respect, Williams was of a piece with the earlier nationalists.

The PNM's economic programme differed from those of its predecessors only in the extent and vigour of its intended industrialization programme. The moribund British capitalism was to be replaced by a vigorous and assertive American Capitalism, and it was therefore logical for Williams to hail the takeover of Trinidad Leaseholds Limited by Texaco whose anticipated investment expenditure would generate significant increases in government revenue, wages and output, "not under the red banner of nationalization . . . but under the red star of the Texas Company".[3] This warm embrace of foreign capital and American capital in particular, must be contrasted with the rather more radical rhetoric of previous parties and groups such as the Trinidad Labour Party and the West Indian National Party.[4]

The PNM, Williams declared, was nonsocialist, although its programme was similar to the avowedly "socialist" programmes of Manley in Jamaica and Adams in Barbados. Williams averred that socialism was no different from the welfare state and the principle of distributive equity, and the real choice in the world at that time was between private centralized control and public centralized control. As far as the worker was concerned, it was "six of one and half a dozen of the other".[5] For Williams, the development programme was not to be sidetracked by pointless ideological issues. Williams and the PNM can therefore be characterized as "pragmatic".

The political and social programme articulated by the PNM promoted the need for immediate self-government in internal affairs; morality in public affairs, a reaction against the corruption and "bobol" that characterized Trinidad's politics; the promotion of an enlightened and self-confident public opinion; West Indianization; and interracial solidarity. The party's constitutional proposals argued against the retention of the unicameral system proposed by the 1955 Constitutional Reform Committee on the ground that it perpetuated the colonial system of politics.

Instead a bicameral legislature was proposed to "check and balance" the popular opinion of a still politically uninformed people. This measure, would, paradoxically, give the local vested interests in the plantocracy, who had been in retreat since Butler, a place of continuing influence in the political system. The *People's Charter* also proposed a labour policy to promote effective democratic trade unions and to improve working conditions; an education policy to end metropolitan influence in respect of school curricula and to promote highly trained workers and responsible citizens; and policies in respect of housing, health and water.[6]

Williams is to be distinguished from his predecessors in the learning and intellectual authority with which he vested his speeches and pronouncements, and the style and strategy by which he finally won political power. Unlike Cipriani and the early reforming nationalists, Williams was quite prepared to call the "moral bluff" of British colonial rule, but a Britain that was already weary of the colonial burden, having suffered heavily from previous assaults made by its colonies in India and Africa.[7] The abolition of the system, Gordon Lewis has noted, "was not so much the single-handed victory of the nationalist assault movement as it was the fruit of British retreat from empire".[8] Williams was able to win constitutional issues, and gain cabinet power for the elected ministers and the selection of party nominees for the upper house. All that happened in three years, where before the Colonial Office had vacillated in its insistence on "fitness to rule". Independence came in August 1962 and there came thereafter a series of events that culminated in the Black Power Movement in 1969–70, an army mutiny and the declaration of a state of emergency in April 1970.

The Development Strategy, 1956–1973

A development strategy is constructed essentially from four elements: (1) a statement of goals, or in some cases, a long-term "vision" for the economy and society, which may be ideologically based; (2) a theory of how the economy works or "way of seeing" the economy and which defines the policy instruments that are to be used to achieve the goals; (3) the specific tactical objectives to be achieved over a defined period whether a budget year or a plan period; and (4) the specific policies implemented to achieve the objectives. The first three elements are discussed in this chapter, and the policies and instruments are discussed in chapter 7.

Goals

Despite the then strong view among developing countries following the winning of independence in the aftermath of World War II, the Bandung Conference, and the Cuban revolution in 1959, the political leadership that emerged in the Caribbean – Eric Williams, Norman Manley, Grantley Adams – was never tempted to embrace socialism even though the political rhetoric and discourse, in keeping with the *zeitgeist*, seemed at times to flirt with quasi-socialist notions and prescriptions. Their struggle was to bring an end to colonial rule in the region but also to function within the British Commonwealth, with an understanding that the Caribbean fell within the American sphere of influence and that accommodation with Washington was necessary. Thus while ideological debates raged around the developing world, with many governments drawn to the Soviet Union as an alternative to Western capitalism, the region's leadership, including Williams in Trinidad and Tobago, adopted a very pragmatic approach to these ideological questions, and tended to place more emphasis on the tactical objectives, which were unexceptionable, than on grand ideological pronouncements either pro-capitalist or pro-socialist.[9]

The closest therefore that the government in Trinidad and Tobago came to a clear statement of fundamental goals was in the third five-year development plan, where it was noted that the long-run economic tasks outlined must be carried out within a framework of certain goals for the society, and these goals were described as "the creation of a more equal society which has its own political, cultural and psychological identity; which sets its own goals and values for itself rather than taking them from other societies, and more important, which gives the ordinary people a sense of dignity and worthwhile participation in the society". The echoes of the anti-colonial struggle resonate in this statement, more so than the achievement of equality in some socialist sense.[10]

In eschewing an ideological position, however, the government opened itself up to acting on the basis of sheer political expediency, and as the ghost of colonialism faded from view, economic policy and the development strategy seemed more and more to be driven by political expediency.

Theory of the Economy

The theory of the economy espoused by the policymakers over the period 1956 to 1973 focused essentially on the lack of resources (raw materials and minerals to support manufacturing), lack of skills, and lack of capital. The one apparent abundant resource, labour, was seen to be more of a problem as this was expressed in rising levels of unemployment.[11] The high fertility rate in the postwar years was now throwing a large number of people into the labour market each year and the absorptive capacity of the labour market was limited by the increasing mechanization of plantation agriculture and the slow growth of jobs in the capital- and skill-intensive petroleum sector. Unemployment was the critical problem. Another problem identified was the changing system of preferences for the country's export crops, mainly sugar, and it was perceived that the erosion of the preference system would demand structural change in the economy to accommodate the decline in the export of agricultural goods under preferences.

It followed that the development problem was to find a set of activities that would absorb the labour surplus, as well as provide the basis for sustainable growth over the long run. While the analysis of the fundamental problem might have been the same or similar, depending on their particular interests, different interest groups evolved and articulated different policy prescriptions for the Caribbean territories. Three sets of interests can be identified: the British Colonial Office; the local colonial administration; and local professionals and politicians, such as, and most notably, Arthur Lewis.[12]

The Colonial Office and its agents, like Moyne, while sharing the prevailing conception of the economy, were of the opinion that, a few activities apart, large-scale industrialization was impossible or undesirable in the British West Indies as a whole.[13] The local colonial administrations, which by then had some representation from locals in the legislative councils, were inclined to an expanded industrial development effort based on import substitution and encouraged by pioneer and other incentives for industry. Arthur Lewis's strategy was different from both these approaches, and indeed revolutionary in the context of the times.[14]

Lewis argued that the islands were overpopulated and that agriculture could absorb no more people. In fact agriculture was shedding labour under pressure of mechanization on the plantations. Lewis presented statistics to show that the numbers engaged in agriculture had declined absolutely since 1911 throughout the West Indies. The growing labour force had adjusted by a declining female participation rate, increasing open unemployment and the growth of unproductive jobs. The prospect he perceived, was for even further decline in the agricultural labour force, since rationalization of the peasant sector would only be accomplished on the basis of larger, more viable, more capital-using farm units.

Making projections of the gap between the demand for and the supply of labour, Lewis concluded that new jobs would have to be created for 413,000 persons throughout the British West Indies. Apart from emigration and the tourism industry, it was the manufacturing sector that would have to go a long way towards bridging the gap between demand and supply. Once this had been established, the crucial questions were: what would be produced and with what resources, for which markets and by whom, that is, with what enterprise and management. These were the questions which Lewis sought to address.

On the question of markets, Lewis concluded that local incomes were too low to sustain and develop a manufacturing sector, and the small size of the local market militated against large-scale production, which would be necessary in some cases if production was to be economic. For both these reasons, Lewis concluded, production had to be for export.[15] The problem then was one of how to promote exports in a hostile, competitive world market for manufactured goods. According to Lewis, this required specialization in those products for which local resources were most appropriate, and the avoidance of others.

In a labour-surplus economy, labour is the abundant resource, and therefore the level of wages becomes a critical variable in the selection of industries for export promotion. The index used was the ratio of wages to value-added. Capital, by contrast, was a scarce resource, and industries where capital per person was relatively low were to be isolated for consideration. Using these and other related indices, Lewis listed those industries that he thought could be established in the West Indies.[16] The potential target markets were the local market (in the form of a customs union), Latin America, North America and Britain itself.

The most significant and difficult question for Lewis was then: who was to undertake the business of penetrating the markets of North America and Britain? Lewis thought that manufacturers who were already established in those markets should be invited to set up branch plants in the West Indies, attracted by the low wage incentive. But the initial inertia had to be overcome by active government intervention to bring the West Indies to the attention of those manufacturers. There had to be, he argued, a period of "wooing and fawning" upon foreign manufacturers, who might be discouraged by the absence of industry (since industry is gregarious), and would therefore require a premium to become pioneers in the form of incentives such as temporary monopoly rights, subsidies, tax holidays or tariff protection. Foreign capital would be needed because industrialization "is a frightfully expensive business. . . quite beyond the resources of the islands". He argued that even the governments were not capable because penetrating foreign markets required an experience and expertise that they did not possess.

Lewis envisaged that the process would be cumulative. Foreign capital in manufacturing would increase national income and given a higher marginal savings rate and acquisition by locals of the "tricks of the trade", the industrialization process would eventually be self-sustaining and become largely locally driven. Institutional support in the form of a development agency and wage restraint were also seen to be necessary to the successful prosecution of the strategy.

Tactical Objectives

The development strategy actually followed was not the radical prescriptions of the Lewis approach, the centrepiece of which was export promotion. Rather, the strategy pursued was import replacement, influenced by the position of the local colonial administration. In the 1950–55 period, the Gomes administration in Trinidad and Tobago worked with a five-year programme developed by the colony's financial secretary.[17] The Eric Williams administration from 1956 promised to do a better job than the "economic bungling" of its predecessor administration. But the institutional structure – tax incentives, pioneer industry legislation, and so on – were already all in place for the pursuit of import replacement industrialization. The effort of the Williams administration was to be wider in size, scope and ambition, but there was no explicit embrace of the idea that import substitution had to lead to export-promoting industrialization. The reason for this was perhaps that the imperative for generating foreign exchange through manufactured exports was muted by the strong performance of the dominant petroleum industry that had expanded refining capacity significantly.[18] The problem was, however, that while foreign exchange was not a problem, unemployment was rising.

By 1964 and the second plan, the conception of the economy had been modified, reflecting the thinking of William Demas. The rethinking was probably provoked by the seeming intractability of the unemployment problem. The notions of "structural dependence" and "structural unemployment" were introduced. Dependence is understood not only as "openness", but also as incorporating an examination of the structure of and the markets for the output of the export sector, mainly petroleum. Thus the second plan identified the dominance of petroleum in the economy and the "uncertainties of the world market situation" as a major source of concern. The small size of the economy contributed to its structural dependence and conditioned the possibilities for the manufacturing sector.

The unemployment problem began to be seen as due not only to rapid population growth, but also to the rising expectations of the population that led to an increase in the demand for jobs of a certain type. Another consideration was the technology employed by modern industry, which was generally biased against labour. The solution to the unemployment problem was seen to be more difficult and more remote. In rather arcane language, the Second Plan noted: "So fundamental and involved a problem cannot . . . be solved in a very short period, nor can any lasting improvement of the situation be obtained on the basis of ad hoc stop-gap measures. It is for this reason that the employment problem of developing countries is inevitably seen as part of the whole complex of underdevelopment and its solutions inseparable from the process of overall economic development."[19]

The closing of the employment gap was subsumed into the wider, vaguer objective of "overall economic development".

While there was no explicitly stated change in the development strategy, initiatives aimed at short-run employment generation began to gain prominence.

Agriculture and construction are noted, primarily because their labour-absorptive capacity was seen to be greater than that of manufacturing and growth in those sectors would help to satisfy the pressing needs for more adequate housing and domestic food supplies.

By the time of the preparation of the third plan in 1968, pessimism about the prospects had increased along with a growing concern about the vagaries of the dominant petroleum sector. The achievement of full employment was postponed to 1983–85 and, while foreign investment was still welcome, there was greater emphasis on the need for "more positive steps to promote tastes for local goods and services, local technological research, local engineering and other skills, local enterprise . . . and the mobilization of local capital".[20]

Lewis's clear clinical analysis and prescriptions of 1950 had given way by the late 1960s to a preoccupation with short-term problems and policies that were not guided by an overarching development strategy, consistently pursued, but a series of initiatives conceived and implemented in response to various mounting social and political pressures.

In the next chapter, we examine the construction and implementation of the three five-year plans that were employed in pursuit of the development strategy.

6

Plan Organization and Implementation

The Idea of and Rationale for Economic Planning

In the 1950s and 1960s, the production of development plans was *de rigueur*, inspired by the acceptance of government intervention in the economy after the Great Depression, the apparent economic and technological success of the Soviet Union and the attribution of that success in part to central planning. However, in most developing countries with ties to the West, planning was not seen as superseding market forces. Planning and the market mechanism were not mutually exclusive, but one supplemented the other. According to the United Nations writers: "[plans] . . . are intended to guide and coordinate public policies and supply coherent production and investment targets for the major branches of the economy, but they seldom supplant the decisions of the individual enterprise managements".[1] Governments intervene to ensure that resources are allocated in accordance with the long-term goals of the country.

Under central planning, the state through its Central Planning Office sends down directives to the producing enterprises with detailed instructions in respect of output, wages and bonuses, disposition of investible resources, and so on, and also regulates the enterprise's relationships with other enterprises. Under indicative planning, the state works through the market to effect changes in the allocation of resources. Here consultation between the public and private sectors is crucial to the process, and the government makes full use of the instruments of incentive and control at its disposal.

We find nowhere in the plan documents a rationale for planning. However, William Demas, who defined planning as "the formulation and execution of a set of interrelated measures designed to achieve certain specific economic and social goals", argued that the most important goal for a developing country was "transformation". He went on to argue that planning comes into its own because: "The market mechanism working unaided will by the very definition of underdevelopment be unable to generate structural and institutional changes at the pace required by development."[2] This is exactly the same idea as expressed in the traditional literature in development economics at the time.

Eric Williams provided a rationale for planning that, if it did obtain, would make more sense than the conventional rationalizations and comes surprisingly close to the rationale for the "visioning" approaches that emerged at the end of the twentieth century. He observed that "the purpose of planning in an underdeveloped country is internally to impart discipline and enthusiasm to the pursuit of the development effort by both the public and private sectors of the economy. Externally, its purpose is to enable the developing nation to exercise a greater degree of control over its external environment."[3]

Williams goes on to point out that viewed in this way, planning "is from start to finish a political process". There is no question that the Williams rationale is entirely sensible and realistic in the context of a capitalist society where the achievement of social and economic objectives depends on the relative strengths of the private and public sectors and the extent therefore to which the public sector is able to influence the private sector. Where the private sector is dominated by foreign multinational companies, and the relative strengths of the parties are more nearly equal, the ability of the government to exert meaningful control over its external environment becomes much more moot.

Plan Organization

Planning is a multistage process whose success depends on the interaction of many people and institutions. Engineers, technocrats and administrators must work closely together. Politicians direct and evaluate, and in a market economy under indicative planning, the private sector is brought into the exercise and its cooperation is important to the plan's success.

Many writers on development planning have argued that no matter how sophisticated the concepts and techniques, no matter how comprehensive or how well-intentioned, the eventual success of a plan depends on effective plan organization and implementation.[4] To put it differently, proper organization and effective implementation are necessary to translate the rhetoric of the plan into the bricks, mortar and steel that are one set of indicators of successful planning.

It will be useful to distinguish conceptually the two aspects of planning dealt with here. "Plan organization" refers to the set of actors involved in formulating the plan and the relationships between and among them. "Plan formulation" encompasses the definition of goals, construction of models, identification and appraisal of projects, integration of acceptable proposals into a consistent framework, and the assessment of the financial requirements of the plan. The activity of plan formulation may take place at one level (centralization) or it may take place at several levels, possessing differing amounts of decision-making power and responsibility.

The basic input for plan formulation is information. The process of plan formulation may be looked at and judged as a system of information flows where efficiency is maximized by the existence of maximum flows of relevant information to the Central Planning Office from as few sources as possible. As the number of direct sources of information increases, the Central Planning Office will be hard put to digest and analyse the many bits of information presented to it, some of which may be irrelevant to its final decision-making.

The case of "information overload" is far less important here than the case of "information deficiency", which arises when either the private sector is left out of the exercise of plan formulation (partial planning) or, though involved, withholds or distorts information in its own interest. Plan implementation on the other hand begins when the plan has been formulated and accepted. This stage involves the communication of the decisions of the planning authority to the agencies and institutions carrying out the plan, in the form of a set of projects, targets and tasks, the phasing of investment in the various projects, and the evaluation of progress in the execution of projects.

While it is conceptually easy to distinguish between plan formulation and plan implementation as activities taking place at different points in time, in practice, both activities are closely bound together. The organization of plan formulation may well determine plan implementation to the extent that participants in the process come to see the plan as their own and the achievement of the targets as being in their own interest. In addition, since plan formulation is a more or less continuous process, implementation and evaluation will take place with a lag, but the activities feed upon each other.

Planning may therefore be rendered ineffective by a breakdown in one or other of these activities – plan organization, plan formulation, or plan implementation and evaluation. If plan organization is poor, the output of the planning effort will be poor and the achievements are likely to be inconsequential. If a well-formulated plan is poorly implemented, the results will also be bad. Weak evaluation will also contribute to poor formulation and implementation.

The failures of planning in many developing countries have been blamed on the breakdown of one or another of these activities. In what follows, we examine these activities in Trinidad and Tobago since 1958 and attempt some assessment as to how they have influenced plan performance.

The Organization of Planning: 1958–1973

Plan organization for the 1958–62 five-year development programme (first plan) reflected the rudimentary level at which planning necessarily began, given the limited technical resources then at the disposal of the government. The programme was prepared by the Economic Planning and Development Department (EPD), which was attached to the Ministry of Finance. The department had a staff of twelve and was assisted as advisors by W. Arthur Lewis and Teodoro Moscoso of the Puerto Rico Economic Development Administration (Fomento). The presence of these two men in particular was a clear indication of the direction in which the newly elected PNM administration intended to take the economy, as well as an expression of confidence in West Indian talent finding solutions to West Indian problems. Eric Williams had pronounced some years before: "The sooner the British West Indies dispenses with imported economists the better. We have sufficient West Indian economists who can apply their academic knowledge for the good of the West Indies."[5]

The EPD worked in collaboration with the various ministries under the economic advisors in preparing the programme, which in the end was a synthesis of the policy statements of each minister. In 1959, the EPD was removed from the Ministry of Finance and placed in the Office of the Premier. The reason for so doing was stated in the 1961 budget speech:

> In any system of democratic Parliamentary Government, the Cabinet is the ultimate planning authority. Since planning is a process involving coordination between the various Ministries of Government, it is both logical and appropriate that the member of Cabinet under whose portfolio Planning should fall should be the Premier. This is why with the introduction of Cabinet Government in July 1959, the subject of Planning and Development was transferred from the portfolio of the Minister of Finance to the Premier.[6]

At the same time it was observed that the EPD had become too involved in controlling development expenditure and supervising project execution, and planning had virtually ceased. These functions were transferred to the budget division of the Ministry of Finance to free the EPD to carry out basic plan formulation.

The quotation above makes it clear that the idea of planning held high status in the thinking of the government at that time and in fact seemed to be personally supervised by the premier, Eric Williams, himself. This is also reflected in the enthusiasm with which the government went about its task in the early years, as measured by the size and scope of the development programme relative to previous efforts.

The second plan (1964–68), which claimed to be more than just a public sector programme in that it specifically noted the need to use "sticks and carrots" to achieve the plan objectives, boasted a more complex organization structure than the previous plan. In January 1963, the National Planning Commission was created to formulate "long-term, medium-term and annual plans for the improvement and expansion of the country's material resources; for the fullest development and utilization of its human resources, and for the economic and social betterment of its people".[7] The commission comprised the prime minister (chairman), the minister of finance, ministers of economic ministries – agriculture, industry and petroleum – the minister of labour, the director of statistics, a representative of the then proposed central bank and the head of EPD, along with two others: the general manager of the Industrial Development Corporation and the permanent secretary to the prime minister. The EPD was to function as the secretariat of the National Planning Commission. The EPD operated from the "stables", offices at the back of the Whitehall office of the prime minister. It attracted to its ranks some of the more outstanding economists and public servants to have served in Trinidad and Tobago including William G. Demas,

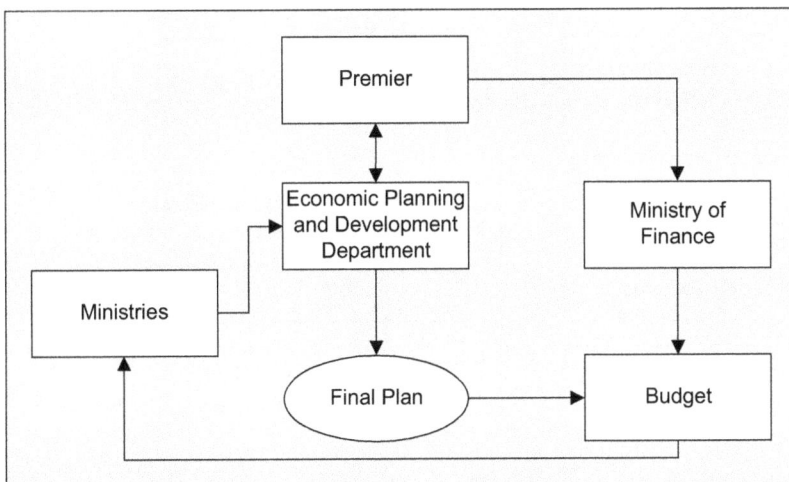

Figure 6.1 Plan organization under first five-year plan, 1958–1962

Frank Rampersad, Patricia Robinson, J. O'Neill (Scotty) Lewis, Eugenio Moore, Doddridge Alleyne and Frank Barsotti. In the early years, the National Planning Commission met monthly, again reflecting the seriousness with which planning was approached.

The procedure for plan formulation provided for "consultation" with the ministries and "where necessary" with the private sector, in assessing the country's human and material resources and setting up mutually consistent quantitative targets. It would appear that the planners did not perceive the private sector and labour as having anything like a major role in plan formulation. The private sector and labour had no representation on the National Planning Commission itself, and the private sector was to be consulted only "where necessary".

The ministries were invested with both a plan formulation and plan implementation role. The allocation of responsibilities was clearly stated: "sectoral and project plans should originate as much as possible within the Ministries. The National Planning Commission and its Secretariat will be more concerned with overall planning, coordinating Ministerial plans and developing them into a coherent whole in the light of the economic and social objectives of the Government and of available financial resources, and evaluating the extent to which the implementation of the Plan is proceeding satisfactorily."[8] There was to be horizontal communication between ministries, but based on a clear demarcation of responsibilities.

Coordination with the private sector and labour in plan formulation took place through the National Economic Advisory Council to which the draft plan

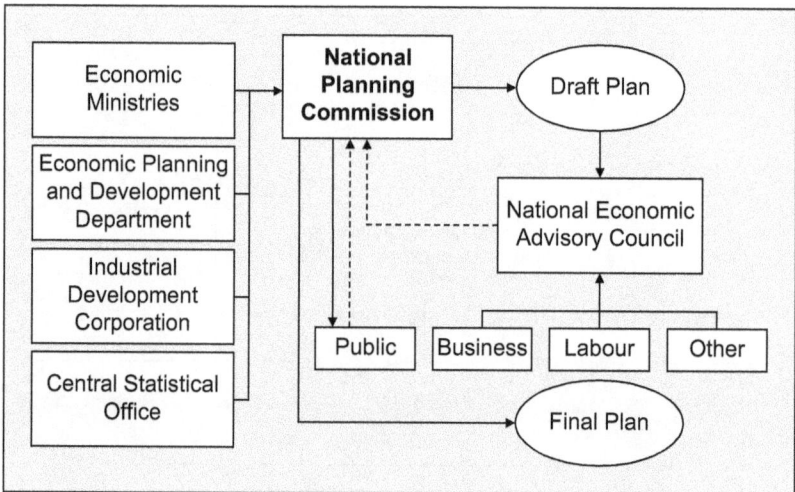

Figure 6.2 Plan organization under the second five-year plan, 1964–1968

was submitted. The council consisted of twelve persons – five representing business, five representing labour and two chosen by government to represent other economic interest groups. Each chapter of the draft plan was reviewed by the National Economic Advisory Council. The general public was brought into the picture when the draft plan was submitted for public comment.

It should be noted that the involvement of the private sector, labour and the public in plan formulation was *ex post facto* and restricted to review and commentary, rather than actual formulation of proposals, setting goals or stating plans and intentions for the next plan period. It is thus difficult to assess the influence of these actors on the final plan. There was also no explicit role for parliament and the parliamentary opposition in the process of plan formulation.

The Chamber of Commerce, spokesman for part of the private sector, noted somewhat acidly of the planning process:

> [I]n this exercise, it is important to preserve not only the form but also the substance. Although the Draft Second Five Year Development Plan 1964–68 was . . . offered for comment, and although much well-intended comment was made by the various organisations which now constitute the Federation, we were never privileged to see the substantive Plan, and . . . we remain to be convinced that our comments were, at the time, given the serious consideration we think they deserved.[9]

In fact, a final second plan was never published, so that the supposed feedback simply evaporated.

Some changes were effected in the machinery of planning for the third five-year plan. The EPD was removed from the Office of the Prime Minister in 1967 and made into a separate ministry. Its functions were broadened to include physical and regional planning, and social planning was subsequently added to its portfolio of activities. Sectoral planning units were established in the ministries of Health and Education. Other planning units were located in the Industrial Development Corporation, the Economic Studies and Planning Division (ESPD) in 1968, as well as the Electricity Commission and in the Ministry of Agriculture. The basic structure developed for the second plan, however, remained intact for the third plan.

Assessment of the Organization of Planning to 1973

Given the outline of the organizational structure of planning to 1973, some appraisal of its efficacy is possible. The process of plan formulation was located entirely within the public sector and within that, in the Economic Planning and Development Department (later Ministry of Planning and Development). The private sector and trade unions and the public at large were never integrally involved in the process of plan formulation.

The consequences of this were several. First, the relationship between the private and public sectors was not such as to achieve the "concertation" effect, which is the basis of indicative planning. The private sector was not required to divulge its plans, and the sectoral projections made by the planning division were too highly aggregated to be of much use to the individual enterprises within the private sector. As a result of this, the information flows to the planning centre were weak and unreliable. Most of the information provided by the private sector flowed through the Central Statistical Office whose own organizational problems made efficient, useful data collection difficult. Information flows from the ministries were also weak, since as noted, they did not have the required expertise to formulate projects properly or to determine priorities. The lack of data led to a verbosity of the plan documents, described disparagingly as "oratorical planning".

The organizational structure set up for plan formulation had largely broken down or atrophied by the early 1970s. The National Planning Commission and the National Economic Advisory Council had ceased to function. No new planning units were created. The ESPD within the Industrial Development Corporation shifted into project identification and appraisal on its own and increasingly sat apart from the rest of the planning structure. The planning unit in the Ministry of Agriculture focused on project implementation and did little planning. The Ministry of Planning and Development in the early 1970s was headed by a junior minister who also had responsibility for housing, a sea change from the days when the prime minister took personal responsibility for planning.

Two reasons may be adduced for this breakdown. First, planning had lost its "mystique" and its status in the thinking of government, the turning point being around 1969. The economic difficulties of the 1960s and mounting social unrest probably contributed to the shift in thinking about how to proceed and what priorities needed to be addressed. The second reason was most likely the dispersion of the key public servants who led the initial planning efforts. William Demas, the head of the EPD and economic advisor to the prime minister, left to take up a position in Georgetown with the newly formed CARIFTA. Patricia Robinson went to the newly established central bank. Frank Rampersad, Eugenio Moore and Frank Barsotti were elevated to senior positions in the Ministry of Finance and other ministries.

Plan Implementation in the Public Sector

Each of the three public sector programmes – 1958–62, 1964–68 and 1969–73 – outlined in broad terms the projects that were to be undertaken by the various ministries over the plan periods. For each financial year, the various executing ministries submitted their projects in detail, and a capital provision was made for each approved project. Between 1958 and 1964, these annual projects were outlined in a published document that also, in a few cases, contained a review of the previous year's expenditures, achievements and problems.[10] The practice of publishing the annual development programme seems to have been discontinued after 1964, and the annual budgets began incorporating greater detail on capital expenditure.

Actual expenditure on the development programme increased from $218 million for the first programme to $299 million for the second plan and $488 million for the third plan, an increase of over 100 per cent over the ten-year interval. The following analysis seeks to assess implementation of the public sector programmes by comparing the annual capital provision with actual expenditure in that year. This is not an entirely satisfactory measure since wage and price increases could raise expenditure without projects being completed; it assumes that the initial cost estimates and the capital provision accurately reflect what is possible to achieve in the course of the year; and excesses may indicate neither increased cost nor inadequate provision but simply the addition of new ad hoc projects. The alternative to the monetary measure would be a detailed listing of project achievement (miles of road constructed, school places provided, and so on), which would be impossible here.

The picture of the five-year development programme for 1958 to 1962, and for 1963, is outlined in the following table. The average shortfall over the period was 30 per cent, ranging from 41 per cent in 1960 to 16 per cent in 1963 (the year in which expenditure was directed to address the effects of Hurricane Flora in Tobago). Thus although actual expenditure of $218 million exceeded the initial

Table 6.1 Capital Provision and Expenditure, 1958–1962 and 1963 (TT$M)

Year	Provision	Actual Expenditure	Ratio of Actual to Provision (%)
1958	44.4	28.4	64
1959	55.3	38.2	67
1960	65.0	38.6	59
1961	70.0	52.6	75
1962	82.0	60.7	74
1963	68.4	58.0	84
Average (1958–1963)	64.2	46.1	70.5

Source: Government of Trinidad and Tobago, *Projects for 1959, 1960, 1961 and 1962; Projects for 1963* and *Five-Year Development Programme 1958–1962.*

estimate of $191 million, the implementation performance was not good. A number of projects could not get off the ground.

The 1959 Report of the Premier noted the problems of implementation and attributed the difficulties being experienced to obtaining suitable sites for certain projects; poor communication with the public, particularly the farming community; and unavailability of adequate supplies of local building materials.

Implementation improved considerably in the course of the second plan period. The average shortfall was 19 per cent, and there were no large variations from year to year as in the first programme, suggesting that the capacity to implement projects had probably grown since 1960.

The picture changed completely over the third plan period due to the unrest in 1969 and 1970 and the response it provoked from the government as reflected in the sharp increase in development programme expenditure.

Table 6.2 Capital Provision and Expenditure, 1964–1968 ($ million)

Year	Provision	Actual Expenditure	Ratio of Actual to Provision (%)
1964	74.5	62.6	84
1965	76.2	57.9	76
1966	71.5	60.3	84
1967	71.0	54.9	77
1968	78.0	66.8	86
Average (1964–1968)	74.2	60.5	81

Source: Government of Trinidad and Tobago, *Estimates of Expenditure* (various issues) and *Budget Speeches, 1965–1969.*

Table 6.3 Capital Provision and Expenditure, 1969–1973 ($ million)

Year	Provision	Actual Expenditure	Ratio of Actual to Provision (%)
1969	78.1	60.2	77
1970	75.1	97.1	129
1971	100.3	103.5	103
1972	110.3	123.1	112
1973	112.3	104.4	93
Average (1968–1973)	95.2	97.7	102.8

Source: Government of Trinidad and Tobago, *Estimates of Expenditure* (various issues) and *Budget Speeches, 1970–1974.*

We can identify three reasons for the problems experienced with plan implementation in the public sector: (1) administrative inadequacy; (2) shortage of technical and professional capacity; and (3) extraneous political factors. The problem of public administration in postcolonial society has been well documented.[11] In respect of plan implementation, weak administrative capability was reflected in delays in negotiating external loans and aid; delays in tendering and in securing the services of consultant engineers and architects; obtaining the required permissions to go on site; and even after project completion, finding the staff to make the project operational.[12]

A more serious problem lay in the shortage and misuse of technical and professional capacity, which afflicted all ministries. Projects were often inadequately formulated, tending to evolve in response to specific demands rather than being identified, formulated and appraised on the basis of clearly stated objectives and using well-established criteria. The planning units established in the ministries of health, education and agriculture might have reflected the insistence of foreign financing providers who demand proper planning and evaluation of projects.

The effects of these lacunae were significant. Project estimates tended to be inaccurate, erring on the high side in order to avoid financial delays in the execution phase. There were no clear consistent criteria used to vet projects and the ministries urged all their projects on the Ministry of Finance on the ground that they were all equally important. This shifted the burden of project selection onto the shoulders of the EPD who, having no criteria itself, developed a method of project selection that gave priority in the following order: (1) incomplete projects from the previous year; (2) foreign financed or aided projects; (3) special works projects; and (4) new projects. The ultimate criterion in project selection turned out to be the financial control exercised by the Ministry of Finance.

It is noteworthy that the implementation problems in the public sector persist up to the present time and project selection criteria are today more nearly the same as in the 1960s.

7

Policies and Their Effectiveness

This chapter examines the sets of policies employed by the government over the period 1958 to 1973 in pursuit of the strategy of import substituting industrialization. In addition to examining the various policies and assessing their effectiveness, it would be useful to address the question of whether or to what extent policy in economies in which the private sector is large and powerful can be really effective.

Fiscal Policy

Three phases in the operation of fiscal policy can be distinguished. Between 1958 and 1965, policy was focused mainly on the reorganization of the system of tax collection on a pay as you earn (PAYE) basis, and the restriction and reorientation of consumption expenditure through increased indirect taxation, which also helped to raise revenue. In 1962, tariff adjustments were effected with increased taxation of manufactured consumer goods thought to be substitutable, but exempted essential foodstuffs such as rice, milk and flour. In 1963, purchase taxes were imposed on imported consumer durables as well as on locally produced goods. In that year also, corporation tax was raised from 40 per cent to 42.5 per cent, and personal income taxes were increased. There were no increases in 1964 and 1965.

Table 7.1 shows that between 1958 and 1961 recurrent expenditure was growing at 13.6 per cent per annum, while revenue was growing much slower at 4 per

Table 7.1 Fiscal Operations, 1958–1973 ($ million)

Year	Recurrent Revenue⁺	Recurrent Expenditure	Surplus	Surplus/Revenue (%)	Capital Expenditure*	Surplus/Capital Expenditure	Revenue/GDP (%)	Average Annual Rates of Growth
1958	129.8	95.6	34.2	26.3	28.4	120.4	18.0	Revenue
1959	133.2	105.2	28.0	21.0	21.6	70.1	16.6	1958–1961: 4.02%
1960	148.7	118.9	29.8	20.0	36.2	77.2	17.1	1961–1963: 12.6%
1961	145.5	140.2	5.3	3.6	45	10.0	15.2	1958–1963: 12.5%
								Recurrent Expenditure
1962	166.7	154.1	12.6	7.5	56.1	20.1	16.5	1958–1963 : 11.9%
								1958–1961: 13.6%
								Capital Expenditure
1963	185.4	168.9	16.5	8.8	55.3	26.8	17.2	1958–1963: 16.7%
1964	202.9	189.5	13.4	6.6	52.5	19.7	17.6	Revenue
1965	206.2	193.1	13.1	6.3	52.3	20.7	17.3	1964–1967: 3.8%
1966	214.3	203.6	10.7	4.9	60.3	17.0	16.1	1967–1968: 18.0%
								1964.1968: 7.3%
1967	226.8	216.6	10.2	4.4	48.1	16.6	16.4	Recurrent Expenditure
								1964–1968: 5.5%
								Capital Expenditure
1968	268.0	232.4	35.6	13.2	61.8	46.1	17.5	1964–1968: 3.1%
1969	303.6	254.8	48.8	16.0	70.8	68.9	19.1	Revenue
1970	313.2	280.4	32.8	10.4	109.1	30.0	18.8	1969–1971: 6.0%
1971	341.9	349.3	-7.4	-2.1	115.8	-6.3	19.2	1971–1973: 18.0%
								1969–1973: 11.9%
1972	398.3	417.5	-19.2	-4.8	136.4	-14.0	20.1	Recurrent Expenditure
								1969–1973: 14.8%
								Capital Expenditure
1973	476.0	452.9	23.1	4.8	120.6	19.1		1969–1973: 14.3%

Sources: Government of Trinidad and Tobago, *Estimates of Revenue* (various issues); *Estimates of Expenditure* (various issues), Central Statistical Office, financial statistics, 1967/68; 1971; Auditor General's Reports (various years); Review of Fiscal Measures in the 1974 Budget (Port of Spain: Government Printery).

Notes: ⁺ Revenues include loans and grants to statutory authorities; recurrent revenue is as stated in the auditor general's reports.
*Capital expenditure excludes loans and grants to statutory authorities.

cent per annum over the same period. There was a consequential drop in the recurrent surplus from $34 million to $5.3 million, and, by 1961, the recurrent surplus could finance only 10 per cent of capital expenditure.

The fiscal changes effected in 1962 and 1963 helped to correct the revenue position. Revenues increased 12.6 per cent over the period 1961 to 1963; the surplus climbed to $16.5 million in 1963 and was able to finance 27 per cent of expenditure on capital account in that year. This was the time, however, when independence was gained, bringing with it new expenditure obligations for defence and external affairs. The recovery from Hurricane Flora, which struck Tobago in September 1963, added its share to the government's expenditure burdens.

The years 1966 to 1970 marked the second phase in the operation of fiscal policy and was characterized by reform of the system of direct taxation. This was brought about by the Finance Act of 1966 (Act no. 23 of 1966). The rationale for the act as outlined in the 1967 budget speech was simple enough. The minister of finance pointed out that for some purposes a company was treated as a legal entity separate from its shareholders and for other purposes, it was not. The act sought to regularize this so as to treat a company consistently as a legal entity. Also it was proposed that the tax rates on personal income be less steeply graduated and that a capital gains tax be instituted.

The changes wrought on the fiscal structure by the act were an increase in the corporation tax from 42.5 per cent to 44 per cent, though allowances were granted for export performance, except for re-exports, sugar, mineral oil and the products of pioneer industries – the tax rate on insurance companies was set at 15 per cent; imposition of a 30 per cent withholding tax on distributions and other specified payments to nonresidents, except where a double taxation treaty provided otherwise; a dividend income allowance of 70 per cent on distributions accruing to residents; and a tax on capital gains accruing on the disposal of an asset within one year of acquisition, though certain gains (such as on securities) were exempt.[1]

The finance bill was unfavourably received by the business community. The Chamber of Commerce observed:

> The proposals of the 1966 Finance Bill were an almost crippling body blow to the effectiveness of the private sector. Were it not for the subsequent introduction of the 70 per cent Dividend Income Allowance, after tax income in the pockets of local shareholders would . . . have been almost cut in half. The provisions of the Withholding tax came as a shock to West Indian and other foreign shareholders who, finding their investment in our country less profitable than investment at home began to sell their holdings.[2]

Though a modified bill was eventually passed, the government was prompted to appoint a fiscal review committee in April 1967, comprised of representatives of business, labour and government, to review the country's fiscal policy and make recommendations that would suggest modifications to the fiscal system "which would influence a much greater volume of investment decisions in favour of this country and which in turn would result in greater government revenues needed for the development programme".[3]

Despite proposals that tax concessions should be made more selectively, the tripartite committee's report reinforced the traditional emphases of fiscal policy, to wit, provision of incentives and indirect rather than direct taxation, but its proposals accepted and partly implemented in the 1968 budget, took much of the sting out of the proposals in the finance act.

Some of the measures implemented in the 1968 budget were: (1) the corporation tax was increased from 44 per cent to 45 per cent; (2) the rate of personal income tax was lowered for chargeable incomes in excess of $4,000, while rebates were granted for incomes below that level – the highest marginal rate of tax fell from 90 per cent for incomes over $60,000 to 70 per cent or an average rate of 50 per cent of total chargeable income, whichever was lower; (3) withholding tax was lowered from 30 per cent to 15 per cent for remittances from subsidiaries to parent companies, from 30 per cent to 20 per cent for other nonresident investors and from 30 per cent to 20 per cent for all other noncorporate nonresidents. The 1968 budget also effected changes in import duties, and increased purchase taxes, excise taxes and motor vehicle taxes.[4]

These changes immediately impacted the government's fiscal position. Revenues increased 18.0 per cent over 1967 and halted the decline in the surplus-revenue, surplus-capital expenditure and revenue-GDP ratios. The surplus reached a peak of $48.8 million for the fifteen-year period 1958–73, and in that year the revenue-GDP ratio reached 19 per cent.

The period 1970 to 1973 may be considered the third phase in the operation of fiscal policy in Trinidad and Tobago over the planning years, and as in so many other areas of the social and economic life of the country, those changes were provoked by the black power demonstrations and ensuing social upheaval in 1969 and 1970. First, the government imposed an unemployment levy of 5 per cent of chargeable income in excess of $10,000, which effectively raised the corporation tax rate from 45 per cent to 50 per cent, although the levy was not paid into the consolidated fund but into a special unemployment fund. Second, there was a spurt in recurrent and capital expenditures, which turned the previous year's surpluses to deficits.

Recurrent expenditure in 1971 was 24.5 per cent higher than in 1970, while revenues had increased by only 9 per cent. The surplus position was restored in 1973 as revenue increased by 20 per cent over 1972, while the increase in recurrent expenditure had fallen to a more modest, and normal, 8 per cent, over

1972. The improved revenue position was again due to increases in indirect taxation.

There is evidence to suggest that from 1970 on, the thinking of the government had shifted in that it no longer seemed to view corporate profits as the prime mover in the economy, but had tentatively invested itself with that role. The government's ability to assume that role was boosted by rising oil prices from 1973, which freed government from the tight revenue constraint it had operated under during the planning years. This is explored further in part 3.

Monetary Policy

The Central Bank of Trinidad and Tobago was established in 1964, and its full powers were not granted until August 1, 1966, and therefore came into existence and operation during the second-five-year-plan period. Among the stated purposes of the central bank was "the promotion of such monetary, credit and exchange conditions as are most favourable to the development of the economy".[5]

The bank was invested with a range of powers including discount rate, cash reserve requirement (set initially at the statutory minimum of 5 per cent), other special reserve ratios, open market operations, selective credit controls and the power to determine the foreign currency working balances of the commercial banks.

At the time of its establishment, the bank had to control a financial sector that was, with the exceptions of the Post Office Savings Bank and the Trinidad Cooperative Bank ("Penny Bank"), wholly owned and controlled by seven foreign-owned commercial banks and foreign-owned nonbank financial intermediaries. These institutions had developed to service the operations of the export sector, to finance imports and to tap the savings of a fairly well-monetized community.

Another aspect of the circumstances in which the Central Bank began to formulate monetary policy was the government's firm intention to remain pegged to the pound sterling. Free and full convertibility was maintained with the establishment of the central bank. No more than 50 per cent of the currency could be backed by local government securities, and, in fact, the 1968 Sterling Area Minimum Sterling Proportion Agreement made the sterling backing for the currency effectively 80 per cent, even though the pound was declining as an international reserve currency and at a time when the country's trading pattern was already swinging decisively away from its previous orientation towards the United Kingdom.

Other institutional changes that took place in the financial sector over this period were the Commercial Banking Act of 1965, the Insurance Act of 1966 and the establishment of a call exchange in 1967. Also in 1967, the Central Bank took responsibility for the government's Treasury Bill operations. In 1968, the Agricultural Development Bank was established to replace the Agricultural Credit Bank, and the Development Finance Company was also created to cater to the needs of the nascent manufacturing industry.

There was little that could be considered as an active monetary policy from 1965 to 1973. The cash reserve ratio was maintained at the statutory minimum of 5 per cent, until 1973 when it was raised to 7 per cent and then to 9 per cent in 1974 in order to remove excess liquidity from the system. Changes in bank rate were made several times to keep the local interest-rate structure in line with interest rates externally so as to forestall the outflow of interest-sensitive funds.

Credit policy was shaped in the early years by the concerns that given strong deposit mobilization by the commercial banks (table 7.2), the banks were underlending. This was evidenced by the low ratio of loans and advances to deposits (table 7.3), and lending more to foreign-owned enterprises and more for consumption than for investment or production.

Table 7.2 Commercial Bank Deposits, 1960–1973 ($ million)

Year	Demand Deposits	Savings Deposits	Time Deposits	Total
1960	83.1	86.3	24.5	193.9
1961	78.1	94.7	17.1	189.9
1962	81.3	96.9	24.6	202.8
1963	99.6	106.9	33.9	240.6
1964	103.2	114.8	29.6	247.7
1965	109.1	121.0	37.5	267.6
1966	98.6	128.6	45.9	273.1
1967	96.9	140.9	55.2	293.1
1968	92.3	158.1	77.0	327.5
1969	89.4	180.7	109.3	379.4
1970	102.5	199.8	152.7	455.0
1971	123.6	248.5	200.3	572.5
1972	126.6	297.2	222.6	646.4
1973	115.8	282.8	333.0	731.6
Growth Rates 1960–1971 (% per annum)	3.7	10.2	20.8	10.4

Source: Central Statistical Office, financial statistics, 1967–68, 1971; Central Bank, *Handbook of Key Economic and Financial Statistics*, 2005.
Note: Data for 1972 and 1973 are from the Central Bank source and not strictly comparable with the data for previous years.

Table 7.3 Ratio of Loans and Advances to Deposits (Selected Years)

Year	1963	1965	1967	1969	1971	1973
Loans and advances/ deposits (%)	49.1	62.3	65.3	73.6	65	87

Source: Central Statistical Office, financial statistics, 1967–68, 1971.

In 1967, some attempt was made at credit control by fixing the down payment and repayment periods on instalment credit for consumer goods. This was done in collaboration with the Chamber of Commerce, which claimed that the initiative in this regard came from the private sector. Notwithstanding these initiatives, lending for personal consumption rose from 18 per cent to 30 per cent of total loans, with government borrowing shifting to the Central Bank. Lending to the manufacturing sector also increased from 12 per cent to 19 per cent over the period (table 7.4). In 1973, the Central Bank took other more direct measures to control consumption. The bank rate was raised independently of external interest rates for the first time so as to force up commercial bank lending rates and thus restrict loans for consumption purposes.

Table 7.4 Distribution of Loans and Advances by Sector (Selected Years, 1963–1973) (%)

	1963	1965	1967	1969	1971	1973
Agriculture	1.6	3.9	2.8	1.8	2.0	1.9
Petroleum and asphalt	0.9	0.3	0.7	3.0	2.5	2.7
Construction	4.7	3.1	5.1	3.9	2.1	2.8
Manufacturing	11.9	13.9	13.1	18.2	19.3	18.5
Distribution	23.1	23.2	30.4	27.3	23.2	18.1
Transport and communication	3.7	4.3	2.6	3.0	3.7	1.9
Financial institutions	4.6	3.1	4.5	1.5	2.8	3.7
Business and professional	3.2	6.1	2.8	1.9	3.4	2.4
Public sector	26.9	19.4	8.3	5.4	5.1	13.0
Personal	17.9	21.2	28.8	28.7	30.4	29.7
Other	1.5	1.5	0.9	5.3	5.5	5.3
Total ($ million outstanding at year end)	118.0	167.4	191.3	279.8	375.1	636.1

Source: Central Statistical Office, financial statistics, 1967–68, 1971; Central Bank, *Statistical Digest*, 1973.

Further policy initiatives came in 1970 when a Regulated Borrowers Policy was instituted, which was intended to restrict borrowing by foreign-controlled enterprises so as to channel financial resources into the domestic activities of locally owned firms. In 1970, the pound sterling was declared a foreign currency and free convertibility was suspended. This was introduced to prevent excessive capital flight following the 1970 unrest.

Following the disturbances in 1970, several commercial banks and insurance companies were encouraged to localize their operations by selling part of their share capital to local individuals and enterprises. The government itself bought the business of the Bank of London and Montreal and created the National Commercial Bank.

Incomes Policy

Of the policy measures thought to be necessary to the successful implementation of the Lewis strategy, perhaps the most important was an incomes policy, or more appropriately, a wages policy.[6] This measure was thought to be necessary for four reasons: (1) on the classical assumptions, rapid capital accumulation necessitated a rate of growth of profits higher than that of wages; (2) rising wages would directly check the expansion of employment where those already employed (and unionized) could increase their own incomes at the expense of the unemployed; (3) wage increases (in excess of productivity increases) could push up costs, and this was undesirable particularly in the case of exports where it is critically necessary to hold on to preferential markets or to penetrate markets for manufactures; and (4) rapidly rising wages in the public sector would seriously upset the budget and the government's labour absorptive capacity.

The first attempt at implementing an incomes policy, though not directly or formally, was the Industrial Stabilization Act of 1965. The stated purposes of the act were to provide for the compulsory recognition of trade unions by employers, and the establishment of an expeditious system for the settlement of industrial disputes and the regulation of prices. The act established an Industrial Court to deal with these matters. In discharging its duties, the court was to be guided, *inter alia*, by the necessity to maintain a high level of capital accumulation; to maintain and expand the level of employment; to ensure workers a fair share of increases in productivity; to prevent the erosion of wages by unjustified price increases; and to preserve the competitive position of the country's products.

The intended effect of these guidelines was to link wage increases to productivity growth and to the overall community interest as expressed in the guidelines. Profits, however, were excluded from consideration since the government "thought it best to treat (the) question of profits as a matter of . . . monetary and fiscal policy".[7] As a corollary of this, trade unions were not to demand wage increases based on the company's profit position or "ability to pay".

This first attempt at incomes policy failed because the court could not and did not apply the guidelines, and the Industrial Stabilization Act itself was attacked by the militant trade unions since it virtually removed the right to strike. Within three years the act had become a dead letter, until replaced in 1972 by the Industrial Relations Act (IRA).[8]

The Industrial Stabilization Act may have had a short-term repressive effect on wage increases as wages grew more slowly than prices between 1966 and 1968, although the sharp increase in prices in 1968 was due in part to the devaluation of the pound sterling in November 1967 as well as increases in indirect taxation (figure 7.1).

In 1968, a tripartite committee was appointed to consider the feasibility of the introduction of an incomes policy. In addition to the four considerations mentioned above, the committee identified as further reasons for the adoption of an incomes policy: the alleged "pull effect" or "demonstration effect" of wages in the highly capital-intensive sectors on wages elsewhere; and the critical role played by the public sector in labour absorption, particularly of unskilled and semi-skilled workers who were in excess supply. The committee, however, noted that technology was inappropriate to existing factor proportions, that increases in incomes leaked abroad through increased imports to create employment elsewhere, and that wage restraint by itself did not guarantee expanded investment because of foreign ownership and the shortage of entrepreneurial, managerial and technical staff.[9]

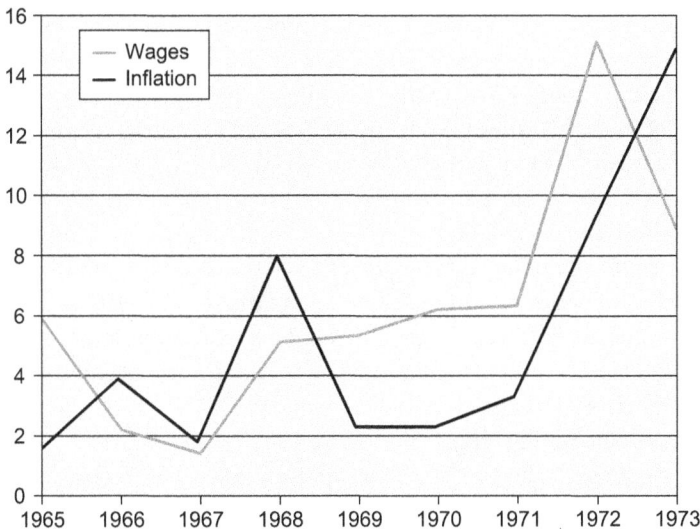

Figure 7.1 Wages and inflation (percentage change), 1965–1973

The committee recommended that voluntary guideposts be developed for wage increases, based on expected rate of growth of labour productivity, with exceptions being made in the case of skilled workers who might be in short supply; workers who earned substandard wages and worked in substandard conditions in relation to the capacity of the employer to pay and conditions prevailing in similar occupations; and wage increases in highly capital-intensive foreign-owned industries where it was recognized that wage restraint would reduce the national income. Profits were to be left to monetary and fiscal policy to encourage maximum reinvestment.

Recommendations were also made in respect of prices, technology (the development of suitable "intermediate" technologies), taste patterns and fiscal incentives, in acknowledgement of the fact that a wages policy by itself could not secure expansion of employment opportunities and that other complementary measures were needed.

In the event, the recommendations were never implemented, and the subject of wage restraint was dropped until it rose again forcefully in 1974. The Industrial Relations Act of 1972 dispensed with the guidelines for the arbitration of industrial disputes. Wages policy therefore was never allowed to bear meaningfully on the development process, contrary to the conditions required for the success of the Lewis strategy.

Trade, Exchange and Commercial Policy

Trade and commercial policy in Trinidad and Tobago has been distinguished by the maintenance of a more or less open economy. The maintenance of openness on the export side is explained by the employment and income generation expected of manufacturing industries producing for export and the continued export of agricultural staples under preferential trading agreements necessary to maintain the large labour force employed in export agriculture. On the import side, there was much more policy conflict. It was thought that "inessential" imports needed to be shut out as far as possible and that domestic industry required some measure of protection. In addition free repatriation of profits on the services account was needed if foreign capital was to be attracted and made welcome at all. Finally, certain imported inputs – raw materials and capital goods – would be essential to both export and domestic production.

The importance of the export-stimulating policy was evidenced in the government's decision to devalue by 14.3 per cent in November 1967 in order to maintain parity with the pound sterling and preserve export agriculture and manufacturing exports. It was argued that if parity was not maintained, export receipts from the sugar, cocoa and citrus industries would fall, leading to a loss of thousands of jobs in those activities. Other trade considerations dictated the decision to devalue passively with the British pound sterling – the competitive disadvantage that Trinidad and Tobago's exports would suffer in the nascent CARIFTA and the enhanced competitiveness of imported manufactures vis-à-vis locally produced goods.

In the area of commercial policy the main thrust was to protect local industry from competition from imports. To this end, a negative list was consolidated in 1966 to which items were added as local import-replacing manufacturing enterprises came into operation. Items not on the negative list were subject to open, general licence. Import protection would have also had an adverse effect on government revenues, not compensated by the imposition of sales or purchase taxes on locally produced goods as that would have adversely affected sales and profits of the local manufacturer.

The Private Sector and the Plans

In an economy like that of Trinidad and Tobago during the "planning years", the "private sector" was not a homogeneous category. In fact, three constituent parts of the private sector can be distinguished: (1) the large foreign corporations in petroleum, sugar, manufacturing and finance, particularly banking; (2) the local business sector engaged mainly in wholesale and retail trades and in some light manufacturing, whose voice was mainly the Chamber of Commerce; and (3) small "residentiary" businesses in agriculture, retail trade and miscellaneous personal and commercial services. These three categories differed substantially in their economic and political strength.

During the "planning years" from 1958 to 1973, the private sector, taken as a whole, was by far the more dominant sector, accounting for over 80 per cent of output and investment in the 1960s, although its share declined as the public sector (government and public utilities) grew relatively faster. The government acknowledged this dominance but intended to apply both moral suasion and market instruments in achieving the plan targets.[10] The second five-year plan boasted that

> the Government has a fairly wide array of measures at its command which could be used to influence, encourage and where necessary, discourage the private sector from doing certain things. Such measures include the granting of tax incentives on a selective basis, fiscal and monetary measures designed to affect the flow and direction of savings and investment, commercial policy measures designed to encourage the production of local manufactures, etc. Moreover, the announcement effect of the Plan is bound to be of some efficacy in that it could be demonstrated to individuals in the private sector that the attainment of certain targets and objectives is in their

interest, . . . the Government expects that the large private companies which dominate the economy, especially in sugar and petroleum, will cooperate in achieving the
development goals of the nation.[11]

Moral suasion was hortative since the private sector was not integrally involved
in plan formulation. During the planning years, market regulation or competition policy was not considered, nor was nationalization or direct government
participation ever in contemplation.[12]

At this juncture we can examine the nature of the "targets" or objectives that the
private sector was supposed to achieve. These were in fact made only in the second
plan, and related only to manufacturing and agriculture.[13] They were based on the
projections of sectoral output as well as the identification of possible new products
that could be produced. Insofar as there was no private sector consensus in setting
the targets, they could not properly be considered targets at all, but at best, hopes
and forecasts. The second plan seemed to recognize this problem in noting that
" 'targets' represent what is considered to be feasible in terms of both the physical and organizational production possibilities of the economy as well as in terms
of market factors . . . they are meant to draw the attention of the private sector to
certain production possibilities considered to be broadly feasible".[14] The "target-
setting" was really then a preliminary project identification exercise that would
supplement the project identification exercises of foreign and local entrepreneurs.

It is these two factors – the intention to use the instruments of policy and
the setting of private sector "targets" – that led the planners to claim that the
second and third plans were more than just partial plans or mere public sector
programmes, but in fact constituted "overall" or "comprehensive" planning.

Moral Suasion and the Private Sector

The efficacy of moral suasion depends on the morally superior position of the
government, which is related to its legitimacy and the respect with which government is regarded by sections of society. The superior position of government is enhanced by greater social cohesion and by the ability of the government to actually
exercise its power over the private sector. The private sector in the Trinidad and
Tobago economy during the planning years was, as already noted, fairly powerful.
There were large foreign-owned enterprises in petroleum, sugar manufacturing,
and banking and finance, and the distribution sector through the Chamber of
Commerce was vocal in the defence of its interests. The trade union movement
was also quite powerful, being independent of the major political parties and well-
entrenched in the key sectors of the economy.

Generally, the posture of the government towards foreign enterprise was to be accommodating. Concessions were provided, profits were freely repatriated and they were able to operate without significant restrictions or qualifications. The power of these enterprises was reinforced by the government's ignorance of their operations. Between 1963 and 1969, several mechanisms were set up for consultation with the private sector. These were the National Economic Advisory Council whose private sector component was the Business Advisory Council. Another mechanism was the Tripartite Committees [on Employment (1965), Fiscal Policy (1967) and Incomes Policy (1968)], which brought together representatives from business, labour and government to tackle specific problem areas and to inform policy.

After 1969 the relationship between the private and public sectors tended to become strained. There were two reasons for this. First, by the time of the preparation of the third plan, the public sector technocrats were beginning to critically review the development strategy, acknowledged its failures, especially the failure to generate employment, and sought to place the blame on the private sector. Reviewing the private sector's performance over the period 1964–68, the third plan pointed out that the private sector did not appreciate the need for the negative policy instruments such as the Finance Act and only reluctantly took advantage of the positive instruments such as tax and other incentives.[15]

Having concluded that the private sector was weak, the public sector was geared for a new and more dynamic role by entering into directly productive activities in partnership with foreign or local private capital, or even alone. The third plan stated: "Any attempt to make a sharp distinction based on ideological preconceptions between the respective spheres of the public and private sectors under the specific conditions of Trinidad and Tobago would be totally irrelevant to the real problems of economic and social transformation of the country."[16] Later on the public sector was to go further and invest itself with the role of prime mover in the economy, in preference to private capital.[17]

The second reason for the strained relationship was government's stated policy towards foreign investment set out in the final version of the third plan. It argued for a greater degree of economic independence and restriction of certain areas of endeavour to nationals, including *inter alia*, the mass media, utilities, commercial banking and distribution, but did not reject foreign direct investment. Indeed in certain areas, such as petroleum and petrochemicals, direct investment was deemed necessary because of the heavy initial capital outlay. The private sector reacted strongly to these statements and protested to little or no avail the erosion of the role of the private sector.[18]

8

The Record of Economic
Development, 1958–1973

I n this chapter we describe the record of economic development over the period 1958 to 1973. We examine the record in each of the three plan periods
under three main heads: objectives; the means employed to achieve the objectives, including institutional changes and the level and financing of public sector expenditure; and achievements and results. The economic and sociopolitical
context at the time of formulation of the plans has been discussed in chapter 5.

The First Five-Year Development
Programme: 1958–1962

The 1958–62 programme had come at a time when the economy was riding the
crest of a boom period, which lasted from 1954 to 1957. At the beginning of
the decade the rate of growth of GDP (factor cost) was relatively slow, averaging 3.6 per cent per annum over 1951–54.[1] Between 1954 and 1957, two factors
were mainly responsible for creating boom conditions: strong external demand,
and a high rate of investment particularly in the petroleum sector.[2] Indeed, this
period displays in classical fashion the synchronous gearing of the fortunes of
the economy as a whole to developments in the petroleum sector. Between 1951
and 1954, the annual growth rate of the petroleum sector averaged 3.7 per cent

(cf. 3.6 per cent for the whole economy), but between 1954 and 1957, the average growth rate in petroleum was over 13 per cent per annum, while the growth of the economy as a whole was also over 13 per cent per annum.

The development programme, which was only a multiannual public sector programme, sought to harness the prosperity of the then prevailing boom conditions, by providing the economic and social infrastructure within which private capital, local and foreign, could thrive and expand and promote economic development. This self-imposed restriction on the role of the public sector in promoting economic development was based on a clear division of labour between the private and public sectors in terms of what each should provide for the development effort. That division of labour was founded on a pragmatic rather than ideological commitment to private enterprise, based on the view that national resources and capabilities were not as yet fully up to the task, and that what was required was a period of "wooing and fawning" of foreign private capital who would be attracted by a "favourable economic and political climate".[3]

Despite the rapid growth of output during the mid-fifties, unemployment remained a problem, and the main objective of the programme was relief of the unemployment situation.[4] The programme indicated a need to find 35,000 jobs over the plan period. It was hoped that the "basic" industries – agriculture, manufacturing and tourism, as well as petroleum – would provide about 17,000 jobs, with services, a catch-all sector, employing another 17,000. These were not targets to be achieved, and the government noted that it could not guarantee that all the jobs needed would be created. The programme emphasized the need to provide infrastructure that would, in turn, provide employment by encouraging investment. The other objectives of the programme were increased productivity and "better amenities for the workers", that is, increased and improved provision of social services.

The programme for agriculture, forests and fisheries was relatively modest. The need to expand production and increase productivity was noted. The protection enjoyed by sugar and bananas in metropolitan markets and the favourable prices being enjoyed or projected for coffee and cocoa were acclaimed. Scientific research was to be directed to the traditional tree crops, coconuts and cocoa, as well as rubber, corn and grass and to seek to control diseases and improve yields. Subsidies were to be granted to lands planted in rubber, coffee, bananas and grass, and to livestock farmers and small farmers for mechanization and disease control. Improvements were also to be made in production and marketing of domestic agricultural output, and extension services were to be expanded and improved.[5]

However, the main thrust of the development effort was to come from manufacturing, which at the beginning of the programme contributed 10.6 per cent to GDP, having shown little increase from the 1951 figure of 10.1 per cent. The cutting edge of the programme was to be the Industrial Development Corporation, which was to be established with the expressed aims of establishing contacts with industrialists; locating adequate factory sites and buildings; and providing incentives to private capital, local and foreign. Two million dollars was initially allocated to the Industrial Development Corporation. The corporation was invested with 345 acres of land for the development of industrial sites, of which it developed and partially developed 272 acres at a cost of $1.7 million.

The importance that the government attached to industrial development was not reflected commensurately in the distribution of government expenditure because as noted above, the government saw its role at that time as a provider of the necessary infrastructure for the expansion of the private sector, rather than engaging in directly productive activities itself. Initial planning expenditure amounted to $191.3 million, a sum unprecedented in the financial history of the public sector, and reflective of the ambition and assertiveness of the new PNM administration. The distribution of planned and actual expenditure is shown in table 8.1.

The distribution of expenditure reflected a heavy emphasis on the provision of economic and social overhead capital. Of the total actual expenditure, 11 per cent went to roads and bridges ($23.9 million), 17.8 per cent to electricity ($38.7 million) and another 11 per cent went to health, mainly for sewerage facilities and construction of additional hospital space. However defined, expenditure on infrastructure was well in excess of 50 per cent of total expenditure, and at the end of the plan period, the stock of social overhead capital had increased appreciably. The classification of activities in table 8.1 is highly aggregated and therefore arbitrary to some extent. However, it gives a useful indication of the main directions of expenditure. "Agriculture" and "Industry and Tourism" are self-explanatory; "Transport and Communications" covers roads and bridges, harbours and ports, airports, bus transport, BWIA (the national airline), telephones and mass media;

Table 8.1 Distribution of Development Programme Expenditure ($ million), 1958–1962

	Initial Planned	Actual	Percentage of Total Actual
Agriculture, forests and fisheries	9.5	4.8	2.2
Industry and tourism	18.3	18.8	8.6
Transport and communications	45.7	35.9	16.4
Public utilities	63.2	72.5	34.6
Social services	54.6	81.5	38.2
Total	191.3	218.5	100.0

Source: Government of Trinidad and Tobago, *Five-Year Development Programme 1958–1962 (First Plan)* and *Second Five-Year Plan 1964–1968 (Second Plan)*.

"Public Utilities" covers electricity, drainage and reclamation, water and sewerage and public buildings; "Social Services" covers education and training, housing, local government, special works (the public works programme) and urban and rural redevelopment.

The financing of this extraordinary outlay of public funds was unusual. Over 90 per cent of the programme was locally financed. This significant accomplishment can be ascribed to deliberate as well as fortuitous occurrences, namely, the reorganization of the system of tax payment on a PAYE basis from November 1957, which increased revenue; tariff adjustments from 1962, which taxed luxury imports and brought in $14 million in additional revenue in 1962; the underestimation of the capacity of the local economy to generate funds (the initial estimate of the contribution of local loans was just $8.0 million compared with the actual figure of $56.5 million); and increased revenues made possible by the buoyancy of the petroleum sector. The financing of future programmes was not to prove as easy.

Results of the First Five-Year Programme

We can now assess the development programme in terms of its achievements, frustrations and failures. Agriculture had a mixed performance. Export agriculture (sugar) and livestock grew rapidly, particularly the latter, which increased its share of the sector's output from 13.4 per cent in 1958 to 22 per cent in 1961. Domestic agriculture, however, grew much more slowly, and its share of sector output declined from 33 per cent in 1958 to 27 per cent in 1961.[6]

Statistically, the industrial sector performed very well, though its share of GDP remained at 10.6 per cent due to the much larger increases registered in the petroleum

Table 8.2 Financing of Development Programme Expenditure, 1958–1962

Source	Actual	Per Cent
Current budget surplus	91.0	41.6
Local loans	56.5	25.7
Other local receipts	53.0	24.1
Foreign loans	15.7	7.1
CDW grants	2.9	1.3
Total	218.5	100.0

Source: Second Plan, 1964.
Note: "Other local receipts" includes use of surplus balances, sale of concessions and savings of statutory bodies.

and sugar sectors. Industry grew at 9.4 per cent per annum and output increased from $59.7 million in 1956 to $99 million in 1961.[7] The operations of the newly created Industrial Development Corporation were also successful. Forty-three pioneer factories were launched between 1959 and 1963 with a total investment of $44.4 million and employed 1,952 workers, an investment cost of $22,000 per worker. Forty-seven other nonpioneer companies were assisted by the corporation.[8]

In respect of overall growth of the economy, however, after the exceptionally strong growth recorded in the period up to 1957, the economy slowed appreciably to 4.7 per cent between 1957 and 1958. GDP growth accelerated again to reach 10.2 per cent in 1959–60 and 9.2 per cent in 1960–61, but below the rates achieved in the first half of the decade. In contrast, the petroleum sector grew 12.8 per cent in 1958 when the economy as a whole had slowed, and remained above 10 per cent per annum until 1960 before falling sharply to 4.3 per cent.[9] The fact that the rate of growth of the overall economy fell out of phase with the growth of the petroleum sector did not mean that the economy had developed its own independent growth dynamic, an inference drawn by Rampersad in his monograph.[10] It would not have been realistic to expect that the economy could have achieved structural change in so short a period, and the later history of the economy (even up to the present time) indicates that structural change in resource-based economies is not easily achieved.

While the economy did achieve strong growth in GDP over the plan period, unemployment increased from 7 per cent in 1957 to 10.6 per cent in 1963. It is more difficult to assess how successfully social needs were met by the development programme because of the lack of data on the various relevant indicators of social need, such as number of hospital beds per 100 population; doctors per 1,000 population; access to potable water; access to electricity; and access to telephone service per 100 population.

The Second Five-Year Plan: 1964–1968

Whereas the first five-year programme had been formulated and implemented at a time when the economy was experiencing rapid growth in GDP, the second plan was formulated at a time when the rate of growth of real GDP had declined to just around 3 per cent per annum (1962–64), and indeed national income was not growing at all.[11] This was due to the slowing down of activity in the petroleum sector, which, as noted previously, had begun in 1961. Socially and politically, important changes had occurred between 1961 and 1964. Constitutional independence was granted in August 1962 to a PNM government that had been returned to power in general elections in 1961. Independence meant a rise in the expectations of the population, as well as new government and administrative responsibilities (Defence and Foreign Affairs) and a somewhat different colour and flavour to political activity.

Much like its predecessor programmes, the second plan was essentially a multiannual public sector programme, but laid claim to a greater reach in prescribing targets and policy instruments to influence and measure private sector performance.[12] It also indicated government's possible entry into certain industries itself should private enterprise prove too timid, provided that those areas were "sufficiently vital to the country's economic progress". This comment is not an indication of a changing attitude towards the private sector or private enterprise, which was to come later.[13]

It was in this context that the second plan set itself the objectives of changing the structure of the economy so as to reduce dependence of the economy on petroleum; achieving a "satisfactory rate of growth"; and finding productive employment for the growing labour force.[14] Achievement of these objectives would require an increase in the level of national savings and foreign investment, with the former increasing faster at the margin so as to form the larger part of total savings over the long run; investment programmes geared to the provision of jobs; public sector programmes geared to increase productivity; and the channeling of private sector investment funds into manufacturing and agriculture rather than into commerce and real estate.[15]

If the first programme was not very sanguine about the unemployment problem being solved, the second plan admitted that unemployment could not be reduced over the plan period and indicated the need to adopt a number of short-term expedients, which included the encouragement of self-employment, shift working (or what is more appropriately termed "job sharing"), and an expanded special works programme to periodically put some money into the hands of the unemployed.[16]

The thinking of the second plan on agricultural development differed from the continued domination of the sector by export crops, which was clearly implied in the first programme, and distinguished between the "peasant" and "plantation" sectors, noting that the dominance of the plantation sector had resulted in a type of development geared to metropolitan interests.[17] Rather less emphasis was to be placed on the growth of the plantation subsector, and the plan envisaged that in order for the objectives of the agricultural programme to be realized (which were greater self-sufficiency, increased productivity and protection of the balance of payments), there would need to be established the basis for a productive small and medium-sized farm system producing large quantities of milk, eggs, poultry, green vegetables, root crops, pork and pulses for the local market, as well as for export in processed form.[18]

In contrast to the agricultural programme, there was no change in the objectives and conceptualization of the industrial development programme. In 1963, manufacturing (including sugar refining) accounted for 13.1 per cent of GDP. The intention was to raise this percentage to 15.1 per cent in keeping with the overall strategy of diversifying the structure of output and providing employment opportunities. The plan envisaged that the main obstacles to the achievement of the objectives of the industrial development programme were the capital intensity of the new industries and the inadequate indirect employment created because of poor internal linkages. The plan outlined opportunities for profitable investment in food processing, metal work, chemicals, lubricants, bagasse and a host of consumer goods. The incentives were there for the taking.[19]

Whereas the first programme addressed petroleum not at all, the second plan devoted a chapter to this sector in which it stated that the national interest required the closer cooperation of both labour and government with the oil companies in achieving national goals. A separate Ministry of Petroleum and Mines was to be created, and a commission of enquiry (Mostofi Commission) was appointed to look into the industry with reference to its organization, structure and finances; assessment of the equity of the share of product accruing to the country; and the industry's labour policies.[20]

The distribution of public sector expenditures is shown in table 8.3. Initial planned expenditure was half as large again as that planned for the first programme. This was subsequently revised upward to increase the allocation to Tobago, which had been struck by Hurricane Flora in September 1963. Actual expenditure fell short of planned expenditure by 6.3 per cent with significant shortfalls in agriculture, urban and rural redevelopment (mainly Tobago), and industry

Table 8.3 Distribution of Development Programme Expenditure ($ million), 1964–1968

	Initial Planned	Revised	Actual	Percentage of Total Actual
Agriculture, forests and fisheries	40.9	60.9	45.7	15
Industry and tourism	12.9	11.9	7.8	3
Transport and communications	72.5	57.7	60.6	20
Public utilities	94.6	96.8	113.6	38
Social services	81.7	93.4	72.0	24
Total	302.6	320.7	299.5	100

Source: Second Plan, 1964; Modifications to Second Five-Year Plan and Third Plan, 1969.
Note: Sewerage, previously classified under health, is reclassified here under public utilities, hence the relative decline in social services and the relative increase in public utilities.

and tourism. The distribution was in some respects markedly different from that of the first programme, with 15 per cent (cf. 2.2 per cent) spent on agriculture and the (absolute) drop in the amount spent on industry and tourism.

The second plan had anticipated that 69 per cent of the programme would have been financed from foreign sources – loans and grants. However, despite a fall in public sector savings, 62 per cent of the programme was locally financed mainly through a large contribution from local loans (37 per cent of total expenditure). The decline in public sector savings was due to a large fall in the current account surplus from $91 million over the period 1958–62 to $40.8 million over the period of the second plan. The important role that the Chaguaramas grant played in the financing of expenditure is also noteworthy at a time when government's fiscal position was beginning to be problematic.

Results of the Second Five-Year Plan

If by "changing the structure of the economy" is meant effecting a statistical shift in the sectoral distribution of output, this certainly seemed to occur over the period of the second plan. By 1968, manufacturing accounted for 17 per cent of GDP, up from 13.1 per cent in 1963, on the basis of an annual average growth rate of 7 per cent over the period 1963–68. However, most of this growth occurred in petrochemicals and when this industry is excluded, the rate of growth of manufacturing is a more modest 4 per cent per annum over the period compared to 4.3 per cent for the economy as a whole. Manufactured exports increased from

Table 8.4 Financing of Development Programme Expenditure, 1958–1962

Source	Planned (Revised)	Actual	Per Cent
Current budget surplus incl. public utilities surpluses	45.4	71.0	23.7
Local loans	65.5	110.0	36.7
Other local receipts	4.0	3.0	1.0
Foreign loans and aid	154.1	64.5	21.5
Chaguaramas grants	51.5	51.0	17.0
Total	320.6	299.5	100.0

Source: Second Plan, 1964; Third Plan, 1969, 418.
Note: "Other local receipts" includes use of surplus balances, sale of concessions and savings of statutory bodies.

$24.1 million to $99 million. When petrochemicals exports are excluded from these figures, manufactured exports grew from $11.9 million to $29 million.

The statistical illusion of structural change was also aided by three factors. First, the performance of agriculture over the period was poor. Export agriculture declined at –0.4 per cent per annum, while domestic agriculture and livestock grew at only 2.4 per cent per annum. Agriculture's share of GDP accordingly fell from 10 per cent to 8 per cent in 1968. Second, petroleum stagnated between 1963 and 1966 such that its share of GDP declined from 28 per cent to 25 per cent. Third, construction declined at 5.1 per cent per annum reflecting the fall in investment in the dynamic petroleum sector. The only sectors that grew faster than average were in the services sector, which includes government, public utilities, transport, and distribution and financial services.

The unemployment situation worsened as the unemployment rate rose to 14 per cent in 1968 from 10 per cent in 1962. These failings in the second plan period prompted a shift in thinking about the development challenge, which was to inform the preparation of the third five-year plan.

The Third Five-Year Plan: 1969–1973

The third five-year plan was an impressive document. In retrospect it marks a high point in the technocrats' conceptualization and understanding of the economy and its problems, and probably because of this, epitomizes both the ambivalence of the technocrats, as well as the most basic contradictions facing the nationalist, postcolonial administration in Trinidad and Tobago. It was no accident that the plan was never implemented as intended for it was interrupted by a profound social conflict under the banner of "Black Power" and which for a few tense months threatened to overwhelm the government. The black power demonstrations, which convulsed Trinidad and Tobago from February 1970 to April 1970 when a state of emergency was declared, succeeded in disrupting the business of government and threw the third plan on the dust heap, replacing it with a series of ad hoc measures designed to stabilize the social situation.

The third plan identified the "structural problems" facing the economy as: the dependence on petroleum; the poor export performance of the manufacturing sector; the stagnation of the traditional export crop sector; and the high rate of unemployment. These problems were seen to be derived from the history, geography, demographic situation and the psychological attitudes of the people.[21]

The plan objectives were the elimination or alleviation of these problems, specifically economic diversification, that is increasing the share of domestic agriculture, manufacturing and services in GDP; the elimination of structural unemployment; and a shifting of the centre of decision-making in investment, production, employment, management and marketing from overseas-controlled to locally controlled institutions. It is perhaps this last objective that serves to differentiate the third plan from its predecessors in that it acknowledged explicitly the critical importance of local control and decision-making and thereby implied that foreign control and decision-making was perhaps suboptimal. It was felt however, that the gaining of economic independence would "take time" since the country's people "do not now possess the technical and managerial skills to a sufficient extent".[22]

The plan also evinced a leaning away from purely economic measures to an increased emphasis on institutional changes. Thus, the diversification programme envisaged not only increased manufacturing exports, increased agricultural production and increased productivity of the traditional export crops, but also a "deliberate attempt to reduce the taste for inessential imported goods and services in favour of locally-produced goods and services".[23] The indigenization process also was seen to involve "a conscious attempt to build up local sources of savings; local mechanisms for mobilizing risk and loan capital, local entrepreneurship, local management, local technology, local designs and styles and the greater use of indigenous local resources".[24] The elimination of unemployment was, like the second plan, cast in a longer time frame and no solution was envisaged until 1983–85.

In its sectoral programme for agriculture, the plan stated that there would be no fundamental policy changes from that of the second plan, and reiterated the position that there was no conflict between the promotion of the traditional export crops sector and the development of the domestic agriculture sector.[25] Several pages of the plan document are devoted to spelling out the need for agricultural education, credit, marketing facilities, and so on, which were thought to be major constraints on the development of the agricultural sector.[26]

The industrial development programme also remained fundamentally unchanged from the two previous programmes, though the need for a "somewhat modified strategy" that would involve a stronger export orientation, greater use of local resources as inputs and greater local retention of value added. In addition, the incentive policy was to be reviewed and the Industrial Development Corporation was to be reorganized.[27] Government indicated its intention to become more involved in the petroleum industry in the direction of influencing company policy on retrenchment, updating of petroleum legislation, strengthening the Ministry of Petroleum and Mines and establishing a national petroleum company. The rationale provided for the establishment of a national petroleum company was that "Trinidad and Tobago was, with the exception of the USA and a few others, the only oil-producing country in the world which did not have a National Petroleum Company".[28]

The size and pattern of public expenditure over the plan period clearly illustrate, quantitatively, the effect that the 1970 social unrest had on the government. The government, at least temporarily, abandoned its tentative approach to socioeconomic problems and began to channel funds massively into directions that would hopefully appease the popular cry for social justice.

By the fourth year of the plan period (1972), planned expenditure on the development programme had already been exceeded and its distribution showed a marked increase in funds channelled into social services with corresponding shortfalls in other areas, particularly transport and communications, and public utilities. Recurrent expenditure also increased markedly (table 8.5).

Also appearing under development programme expenditure for the first time is a new item – asset acquisitions – which accounted for 9 per cent of total expenditure. Its appearance indicated that the government had unhesitatingly abandoned the formerly sacrosanct distinction between directly productive activities (the preserve of private enterprise) and social overhead capital (the preserve of the public sector). The government acquired or participated in enterprises in banking and finance, sugar and manufacturing and this process culminated in 1974 with the $93.6 million purchase of the assets of Shell Oil Company.

Financing of the Third Five-Year Plan

Since planning was effectively abandoned shortly after the third plan was published and social unrest ensued, there was no comprehensive evaluation of the financing of expenditure over the plan period as had been done for the previous plans. However, the foreign component of the financing is estimated at about 36 per cent compared to 38 per cent for the second plan. In contrast to previous sources of foreign finance, large amounts were raised as market loans and not as institutional

Table 8.5 Distribution of Development Programme Expenditure ($ million), 1969–1973

	Planned	%	Actual	%
Agriculture, forests and fisheries	61.5	16.3	69.4	14.1
Industry and tourism	32.5	8.1	45.4	9.2
Transport and communications	80.6	21.3	53.9	11.0
Public utilities	91.0	24.0	70.8	14.3
Social services	112.4	30.0	204.5	42.1
Asset acquisitions	–	–	44.8	9.1
Total	380.0	100.0	488.8	100.0

Source: Third Plan, 1969; Estimates of Expenditure, 1971–1975.

or government to government loans. The emerging Eurodollar market provided $19.8 million in 1971 and $34.5 million in 1972.

Public Sector Participation in Industry

During the course of the period of the third plan, as economic and social problems mounted, there was a major shift in policy in respect of the role of government in the economy. The government caused white papers on government participation in industrial activities to be prepared, the first of which was published in 1972.

At the time of the first *White Paper on Public Participation in Industrial and Commercial Activities* (1972), the government had participation in twenty-one companies with equity of $58.5 million. In 1972, $22.9 million was spent on acquiring seven companies, raising the total value of equity held to $80.1 million in twenty-four companies. Further, whereas in 1971, the assets wholly owned by the government were valued at $10.6 million and those majority-owned at $43.4 million, in 1972, its wholly owned equity position had increased to $38.3 million and majority-owned had declined to $37.4 million. In 1973, $4.8 million was spent on participation in or acquisition of other assets. In 1974, purchase of Shell meant that the government to that date had spent some $200 million on asset acquisitions, most of this ($170 million) after the events of 1970.

The rationale for the programme of investment in industrial and commercial businesses is stated in the *White Paper* where the statements of the third plan are quoted in support of the government's decision to enter into the field of directly productive activities, in the face of the alleged reluctance and lack of dynamism displayed by the private sector. The *White Paper* stated that government participation: "was a natural corollary of the decision of Government to move more positively in transforming the economy and in reducing the excessive domination of the economy by foreign capital and establishing a basis for a greater amount of national self-determination in economic affairs".[29]

It was argued that only the government was able to assume the role of "prime mover" in the economy since only it was "endowed with characteristics comparable to those of the large corporation in the developed societies".[30] This statement seemed to imply that development could best or most easily be achieved by institutions comparable to multinational corporations. Nonetheless, the complete reversal on the government's role from the time of Lewis is remarkable. Government's new policy was, however, not to imply that foreign capital was unwelcome but that certain areas of the economy were to be reserved for national effort; key sectors were to be subject to 100 per cent local ownership and control; and foreign enterprises were to be good corporate citizens.

The new policy of public sector entry into directly productive activities is important not only because it helped to render the third plan an academic curiosum, but because it introduced a fresh dimension to public sector activity, which bore implications for the size and pattern of public revenue and expenditure, the scope it offered, at least in theory, for a more effective planning effort, as the small size of the public sector was often cited as a major constraint in planning, and, over the long term, for the possible social and political effects of a trend towards a kind of state capitalism. The projected trend notwithstanding, the government's stated intention was to divest its holdings at future dates to the private sector, whose alleged lack of dynamism prompted the new policy in the first place.

Results of the Third Five-Year Plan

An assessment of the third plan's achievements is made difficult by the many events that interrupted its implementation – the trade union unrest in 1969, the wider social unrest and army mutiny of 1970, culminating in the declaration of a state of emergency, an acceleration in inflation from 1972, without precedent in the nation's history, and the oil boom, which began in 1973 and which rescued the balance of payments and gave a tremendous fillip to the government's revenue position. It would be true to say that the third plan was effectively stillborn.

The diversification of the economy had slowed down considerably as the growth of the manufacturing sector slowed. The share of agriculture in total GDP fell further to about 7 per cent. The solution to the problem of rising unemployment was nowhere in sight. Official figures on the unemployment rate showed a decline to 13 per cent in 1971, as public works programmes were implemented in the wake of the 1970 unrest, but returned to 14 per cent in June 1973 and an estimated 17 per cent at the beginning of 1974.

Growth and Transformation over the Planning Years

We can now examine the performance of the economy over the entire period of the planning years, 1958 to 1973, though analysis is constrained by the absence of consistent data series spanning the whole period. Over the period, the steady decline of the agriculture sector stands out, falling in current prices from 13.2 per cent of GDP in 1958 to 8.4 per cent in 1964 and to 4.3 per cent (including sugar manufacturing) by 1973, although the sector continued to employ large numbers of workers, especially in the sugar estates. The centrepiece of development policy and strategy in the planning years was the planned growth of the manufacturing sector by means of an array of fiscal and other incentives. Excluding petrochemicals and oil refining (which were classified in manufacturing at the time), the share of manufacturing in GDP in current prices increased from 8.9 per cent in 1966 to 11.2 per cent in 1973. In constant (1970) prices, the share of manufacturing rose from 9.0 per cent to 12.9 per cent based on better than average growth of several manufacturing industries. Figure 8.1 shows those industries whose growth rates (in constant prices) exceeded the average annual growth rate of non-oil GDP over the period 1966 to 1973. The manufacturing industries that displayed exceptional growth behind protective barriers were assembly and related industries; printing, publishing and paper converters; wood and related products; and food, beverages and tobacco.[31]

There was also strong growth in the construction sector, which grew in current prices at 7.6 per cent per annum between 1958 and 1964 and at 16.6 per cent per annum between 1966 and 1973. In constant (1970) prices, the construction sector

Table 8.6 Sectoral Origin of Gross Domestic Product, 1958–1964 ($ million)
(Current Prices)

Sector	1958	1960	1962	1964	Average Annual Growth Rate 1958–64	1958	1960	1962	1964
Agriculture, fishing and forestry	94.7	102.8	103.9	96.1	0.2%	13.2%	11.9%	10.3%	8.4%
Oil and asphalt	233.3	263.4	291.5	301	4.3%	32.4%	30.4%	29.0%	26.2%
Manufacturing	91.3	108.2	132.1	183.3	12.3%	12.7%	12.5%	13.1%	16.0%
Construction	32.3	40.6	55.3	50.1	7.6%	4.5%	4.7%	5.5%	4.4%
Public utilities (electricity & water)	19.6	28.4	41.5	18.1	−1.3%	2.7%	3.3%	4.1%	1.6%
Distribution	97.2	117.2	134.7	165.5	9.3%	13.5%	13.5%	13.4%	14.4%
Banking, insurance, real estate	15.1	20	21	35.3	15.2%	2.1%	2.3%	2.1%	3.1%
Transportation	22.1	32.4	39	76.8	23.1%	3.1%	3.7%	3.9%	6.7%
Government	63.4	82.5	100.5	115.2	10.5%	8.8%	9.5%	10.0%	10.0%
Personal services, other	50.4	70.4	86.2	107.2	13.4%	7.0%	8.1%	8.6%	9.3%
Total GDP at factor cost ($ million)	719.4	865.9	1005.7	1148.6	8.1%	100%	100%	100%	100%

Source: Central Statistical Office, *The National Income of Trinidad and Tobago, 1966–1985,* appendix 4, "The National Income 1952–1962".
Note: $ here refers to British West Indian dollars that circulated throughout the Eastern Caribbean and the TT dollar for 1964.

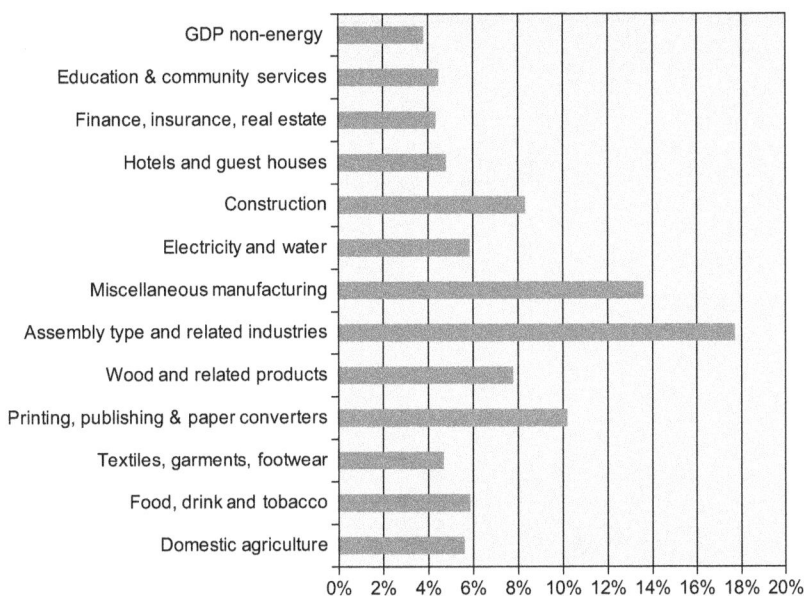

Figure 8.1 Comparative industry growth rates, 1966–1973 (constant 1970 prices)

grew at an average annual rate of 8.3 per cent over the 1966 to 1973 period. There were also very good growth performances from domestic agriculture; electricity and water; hotels and guest houses; and finance, insurance and real estate services.

Table 8.7 Structure of GDP (Current Prices), 1966 and 1973

Sector	1966	1973
Agriculture (excl. sugar manufacturing)	3.0%	1.7%
Petroleum, oil refining and petrochemicals	24.0%	25.8%
Construction	5.6%	7.9%
Government	8.4%	9.7%
Finance, insurance, real estate	7.4%	7.2%
Manufacturing	8.9%	11.2%
Distribution, incl. restaurants	19.0%	15.1%
Transport, storage, communications	13.8%	12.0%
Other services	9.7%	9.4%
Total GDP	100%	100%

Source: Central Statistical Office, *The National Income of Trinidad and Tobago, 1966–1985.*

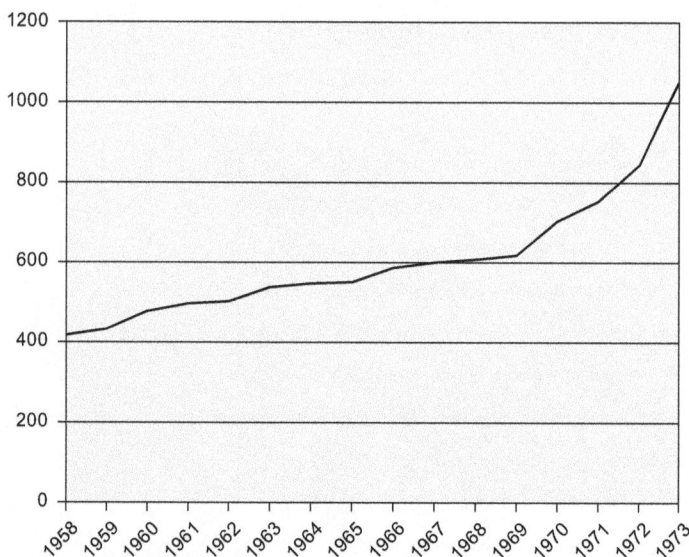

Figure 8.2 National income per capita (US$), 1958–1973

Per capita national income doubled between 1958 and 1972 from US$417 to US$844, or at an average annual rate of growth of 5.2 per cent (figure 8.2). There was a sharp increase in 1973 to US$1052 on account of the impact of the first oil shock on GDP in the petroleum sector. This rate of growth was, however, significantly lower than that achieved during the 1950s when GDP grew at over 10 per cent per annum. Growth slowed in the period 1964–68, the period of the second five-year plan, averaging just 2.5 per cent per annum, consistent with the slowdown in the petroleum sector.

The country's investment rate was high in the initial planning years due mainly to increased foreign investment in oil refining (Texaco) and petrochemicals (W.R. Grace's Federation Chemicals plant). Investment, including foreign investment, fell off between 1963 and 1968 before increased foreign investment in petroleum, this time the offshore exploration investments of Amoco boosted the overall investment rate back up to an average of 27 per cent of GDP over the period 1969 to 1973 (table 8.8).

Data on unemployment before 1963 are spotty and even the series up to 1973 is not especially reliable. However, it is clear that unemployment rose markedly from the levels of the 1950s, averaging 14.1 per cent over the period 1963 to 1973, spiking at 16.7 per cent in 1967, while data for the 1950s suggest that unemployment was then in the single digits.

Table 8.8 Investment Performance, 1958–1973

	1958–1963	1964–1968	1969–1973
Gross capital formation/ gross domestic product	27%	22%	27%
Foreign direct investment/ gross capital formation	33%	21%	33%
Government capital expenditure/ gross capital formation	19%	23%	21%

Note: Some care is needed here as not all government capital expenditure is properly really capital formation. However, government's role in investing activities is certainly understated since investment by state enterprises and other government agencies are not accounted for here.

Trade union militancy, which had prompted the passage of the Industrial Stabilization Act in 1965, had served to push wage rates up. This factor probably contributed to the rising unemployment rate and also impacted relative income shares. From 1955 to 1962, profits, as proxied by the operating surplus, accounted for a higher share of GDP than wages and salaries.[32] This changed from 1962 onward over the rest of the period such that from 1966 to 1973 when data are again available on these variables, the share of wages had risen to an average of 52 per cent while the operating surplus ratio had declined to 33 per cent. The trend over the period is shown graphically in figure 8.4.

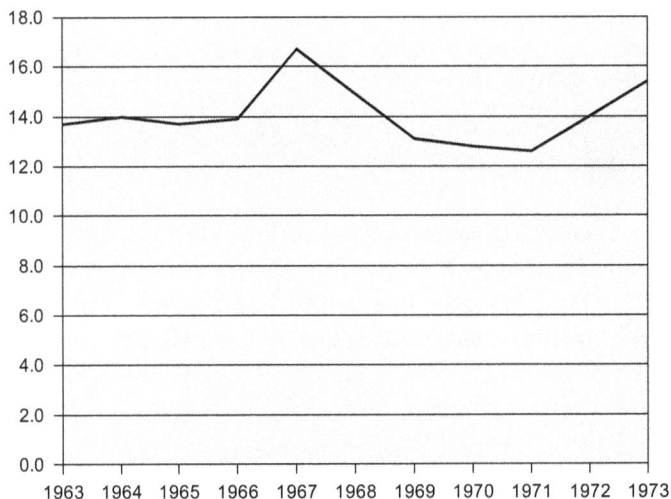

Figure 8.3 Unemployment rate, 1963–1973 (%)

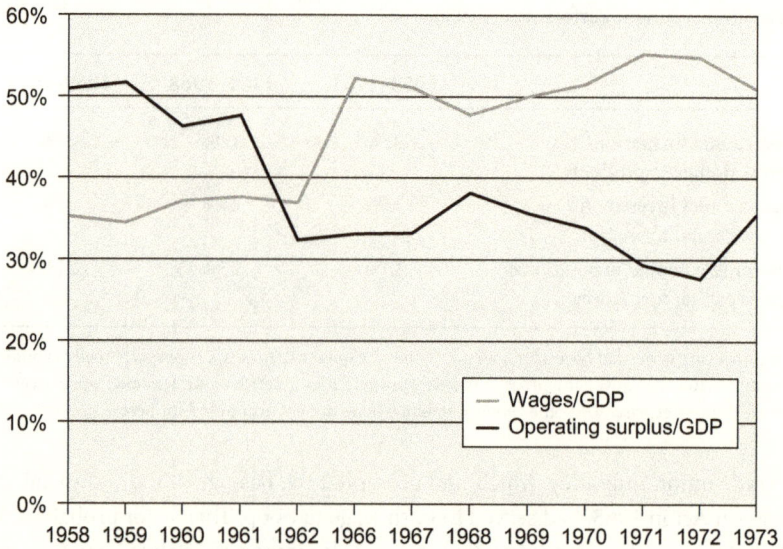

Figure 8.4 Relative income shares, 1958–1973

Table 8.9 Relative Income Shares, 1958–1973

	1958–1962	1966–1973
Wages/GDP	36%	52%
Operating surplus/GDP	46%	33%

Source: Central Statistical Office, *National Income of Trinidad and Tobago, 1966–1985.*
Note: Data for the period 1963–1965 are not available.

Income Distribution and Poverty

The data on income distribution over the period of the "planning years" comes from the seminal studies by Ahiram for the period 1957 to 1958 and Henry for 1971 to 1972.[33] The data suggest that income inequality worsened between 1958 and 1972 with the Gini coefficient rising from 0.43 in 1957–58 to 0.51 in 1971–72. Henry estimated that in 1972 over 25 per cent of the population was living below the poverty line, conventionally defined. These data, together with the data on relative income shares suggest that the incomes of the employed population – both wage and profit earners – improved relative to the unemployed population whose numbers had increased substantially over the period due in part to rapid population growth in the postwar period.

Trade Structure

The shift away from trade with the United Kingdom and towards trade with the United States accelerated over the planning years such that the United States accounted for 42 per cent of exports by 1972 compared with 25 per cent in 1962, while the share of the United Kingdom fell dramatically from 23 per cent in 1962 to just 8.1 per cent in 1972 (table 8.10). Adjusted for petroleum imports under processing agreement, a similar shift in the structure of imports is also evident.

Capabilities and Education Attainment

On some theories of development, human resource development through education is critical in building the capabilities of the labour force and promoting innovation. A significant effort had been under the plans to expand access to secondary education and the establishment of a campus of the University of the West Indies in Trinidad also opened the way for increasing the numbers of tertiary educated workers. However, by 1970, only 5.9 per cent of heads of households had attained secondary education, and only 1.1 per cent had obtained a university degree.

Table 8.10 Direction of Trade: Principal Countries Selected Years, 1962–1972 (%)

Exports (fob)	1962	1964	1966	1968	1970	1972
United States	24.5	27.8	33.8	42.2	46.4	42.2
United Kingdom	23.2	21.6	13.9	10.6	9.6	8.1
Commonwealth Caribbean	7.6	6.7	7.0	6.7	10.1	11.8
Dutch Antilles, Surinam	9.1	8.2	8.2	4.3	4.8	4.6
Sweden	3.2	3.8	6.0	7.7	6.4	7.9
Puerto Rico and USVI	n.a.	1.4	3.0	4.2	4.5	4.5
Canada	n.a.	5.3	4.1	4.3	1.4	2.8
All others	33.4	25.2	24.0	20.0	16.8	18.1

Source: Central Statistical Office, *Overseas Trade Reports*, part B, 1963, 1966, 1970, 1972.

There were steady improvements in infant mortality, the fertility rate declined, promising a slowing of the rate of growth of population later on, and the death rate also fell, as life expectancy improved.

Conclusion

There were significant changes in policy over the period of the "planning years" – 1958 to 1973. The initial faith in planning as an instrument of development gave way to more pragmatic approaches reinforced by the fiscal realities that had to be confronted in the immediate post-independence years. Taxation policy was brought to the fore in the form of increased direct taxation in order to deal with emerging fiscal deficits. The attempt at a wages policy through the Industrial Stabilization Act was not sustained in the face of trade union opposition and the wage restraint of the early planning years was reversed with adverse consequences for growth and unemployment.

The role of government as "ring-holder" gave way to the view that government needed to be more involved in directly productive and commercial

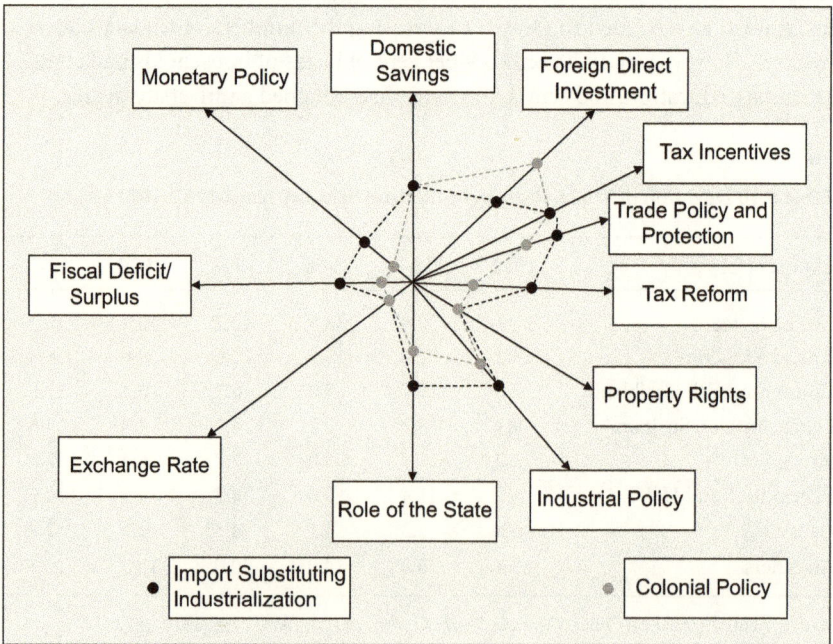

Figure 8.5 Import substituting industrialization

activities inasmuch as the private sector seemed reluctant to step up. A critical aspect of this was the perceived need to take control of the commanding heights of the economy including and especially establishing a government stake in the petroleum industry, a shift in policy that would not be fully possible despite the Petroleum Act of 1969 until the global oil market had changed after 1973 and made it fiscally possible to do so.

The posture towards foreign investment also began to shift over the period. While the Aliens Landholding Ordinance was a response to a specific immediate issue of a takeover, it reflected an increased willingness to be less supine towards foreign investment and a determination to carve out areas of the domestic economy for national endeavour and enterprise, led by the government itself.

The policy map in figure 8.5 shows graphically how policy changed between the colonial period and the planning years. The expanded role of the government in the economy is evident, along with a reduction in the role of the private sector and foreign direct investment.

Overall, the record of the economy of Trinidad and Tobago under economic planning was not at all distinguished. GDP spurted occasionally whenever the petroleum sector gathered momentum. At other times, 1961 to 1966, the growth of output has been less than impressive and, in fact, per capita national income stagnated in those years. Together with a progressively worsening distribution of income, the average Trinidadian and Tobagonian was worse off in 1973 than they were in 1958. The principal objective of development policy, employment creation, was not achieved.

Part 3

Resource-Based
Industrialization, 1974–1982

9

Reshaping the Development Strategy

Crisis

The decade after independence in August 1962 seemed to have been all downhill for the new nation. Unemployment had continued to rise inexorably. The trade unions were becoming more militant, and there were bloody confrontations between protesting workers and police. Prices were rising. The political situation was fraught. Young black men and women, university students and intellectuals marched in the streets of Port of Spain under the banner of Black Power. The marchers reached across the ethnic divide to seek solidarity with rural East Indian workers in the sugar industry. Anthony Pantin, the young, newly appointed Roman Catholic Archbishop sought at one stage to join a demonstration, but was dissuaded from so doing. The demonstrators condemned foreign ownership and control of critical sectors of the economy and demanded change. A state of emergency was declared in April 1970 when elements of the Trinidad and Tobago Regiment started a mutiny. The government of Eric Williams was shaken to the core.

The pace of economic and social change in the newly independent country had been too slow for large sections of the population. Unemployment had to be addressed along with the distribution of income and wealth in the society. Racial discrimination in employment had to be ended. The government dealt with the problem the only way it could, by throwing fiscal caution to the winds and hiking government spending from $390 million in 1970 to $556.2 million in 1973. Fiscal

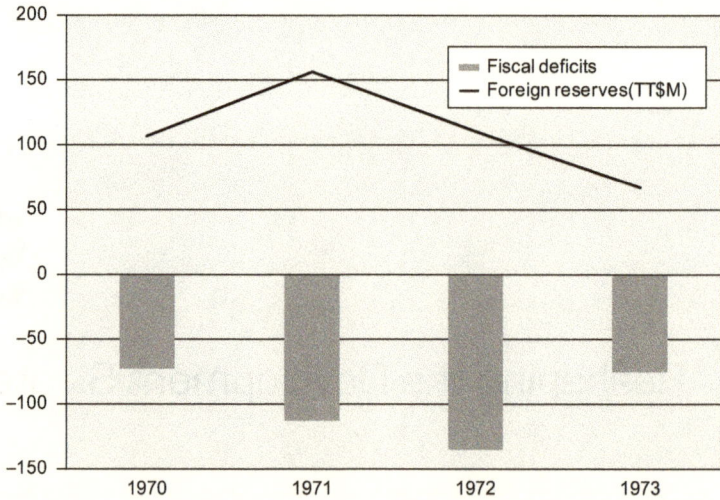

Figure 9.1 Foreign exchange reserves and fiscal deficits (TT$M), 1970–1973

deficits ensued and the country's foreign exchange reserves were exhausted, having fallen to just TT$67.1 million (US$32.5 million) equivalent to just four weeks of imports, with the IMF reserve tranche already used and the commercial banks in a large negative net foreign position (figure 9.1).

By 1973, the country was on the brink of collapse. Not only were the foreign exchange reserves exhausted, but despite the fiscal stimulus, unemployment had actually risen from 12.6 per cent in 1970 to 15.5 per cent in 1973. Inflation had jumped from 2.5 per cent in 1970 to 9.3 per cent in 1972 and 14.8 per cent in 1973, driven mainly by sharply higher import prices.

A.N.R Robinson, a former minister of finance and heir apparent to the prime minister had left the Williams cabinet in April 1970 and formed a new political party, the Action Committee of Dedicated Citizens (ACDC). The ACDC joined forces with the Democratic Labour Party to fight the 1971 general elections. However, ostensibly in protest against the introduction of voting machines, the coalition mounted a "No Vote" campaign, resulting in the PNM winning all the seats at the general election and no official opposition in parliament.

Young men armed with guns, allegedly inspired by Castro, Che Guevara and even Mao, had taken to the hills of Trinidad as "freedom fighters". Williams and those who had led the fight against colonial rule and for self-government and independence now found themselves castigated as "neocolonial" and "undemocratic".

The Chaguaramas Declaration, the revised People's Charter of the ruling party, was prepared and presented at a PNM party convention in November 1970. It was a comprehensive and well-thought-out response to the black power demonstrations that had occurred earlier that year, the concerns arising from the army mutiny and the imposition of a state of emergency. The declaration recognized that that was an "urgent cry on all sides . . . for further social and economic changes to complete the process of Independence". However, Williams and the PNM were clear that economic and social change should not come through violence. Rather, Williams advocated a process of "reconstruction" guided neither by liberal capitalism nor by Marxism, but a philosophy, *sui generis* for West Indians, and relevant to their circumstances. The political dimension of reconstruction spoke to popular participation and constitution reform. The economic dimension spoke to internalizing major decision-making and ending foreign domination (while not rejecting foreign investment) and entrepreneurial role for the public sector while encouraging the development of the national private sector, the promotion of a "people's sector" and full utilization of the country's natural, capital and human resources.

In June 1971 following the historic events of 1970 and the general election of 1971, a constitution commission chaired by Sir Hugh Wooding was appointed. The commission reported in January 1974. The republican constitution, which emerged in 1976, did not put in place a system of modified proportional representation to elect members of parliament as some had proposed, but instead retained the first-past-the-post system. It did provide for a president as head of state who had some powers of appointment in his own discretion, such as the independent senators, but in all other matters the president was to be directed by the cabinet. However, the constitutional role of president was to prove pivotal later on in respect of the appointment of the successor to Eric Williams on his death in 1981, the resolution of the attempted coup in 1990, and the appointment of persons as ministers who had lost at the polls at the installation of the UNC administration in 2000.

In the runup to the 1976 general elections, the ruling PNM found itself in considerable turmoil, with the leadership style of Eric Williams under attack from within his own party. The outcome of that struggle was the formation of the Organisation for National Reconstruction led by Karl Hudson-Phillips, a former attorney-general. The Organisation for National Reconstruction went on to contest, unsuccessfully, the 1981 general elections.

International Context

The Organization of the Petroleum Exporting Countries (OPEC) was formed in 1960 at the instigation of Venezuela, and towards the end of the decade it had begun to wrest a greater take of oil revenues from the companies, through individual and concerted action. The power of the OPEC countries over oil prices was enhanced by the increasing dependence of the United States on imported oil.

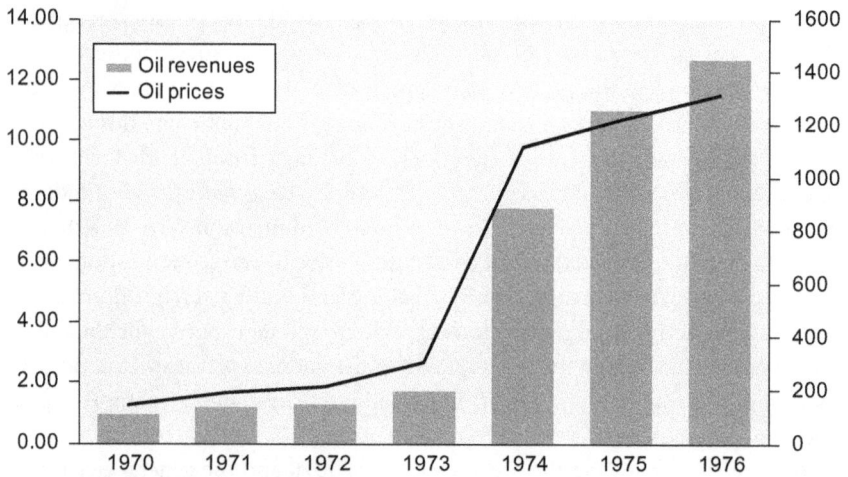

Figure 9.2 Oil prices (US$) and oil revenues (TT$M)

The Arab oil embargo of October 1973 was the action of OPEC as a response to the Yom Kippur War. At the time the Persian Gulf countries accounted for about 38 per cent of world oil production, and OPEC as a whole for about 55 per cent. The success of the OPEC oil cartel was not lost on the developed countries. It signified not just a massive transfer of capital from the developed countries to the Middle East, but the political clout which such capital carried. The Middle East countries began to recycle the petrodollars back into the international financial capitals of New York and London and to acquire assets in those countries.

Trinidad and Tobago was not a member of OPEC, but benefited hugely from OPEC's action. Oil revenues soared, mainly due to the higher oil prices, but also because production was increasing and the petroleum taxation regime had been changed to increase the government's tax take. Fiscal balances swung into surplus and the foreign exchange reserves rebounded.

The success of the Arab oil embargos in the 1970s was not the only factor that hinted that a shift in international economic and financial power might be occurring. The United States had been defeated in Vietnam by a small developing country and forced to withdraw. The Cuban Revolution had endured on the doorsteps of the United States, though Cuba had not thrived from an economic standpoint.

In 1974, the United Nations adopted a declaration for the establishment of a New International Economic Order (NIEO). The objectives of the developing countries advocating a NIEO were to redress inequalities in trading relationships between developed and developing countries; regulation and control of the activities of multinational corporations; and the establishment of a common fund that would stabilize commodity prices and mitigate the impact of adverse terms of trade on developing countries. While little was to come from the discussions that ensued, developing countries experienced a new assertiveness and following the successful actions of OPEC, became emboldened to confront these issues in their domestic policies.

In his 1981 (and last) budget speech, Eric Williams stated: "the agreement on the Common Fund has been initialed, but what exists is in fact a travesty of the US$6,000 million facility which the Group of 77 had agitated for at UNCTAD IV in Nairobi in 1976".[1] The international monetary system that had been built on American hegemony had begun to crumble. Following World War II, the Bretton Woods system of fixed but adjustable exchange rates, supervised by the IMF and with an implicit guarantee of conversion of US dollars into gold, had been put into place. The system had begun to come under stress in the mid-1960s. Sterling was devalued in November 1967, and the Caribbean countries, including Trinidad and Tobago elected to devalue passively with the pound sterling. In August 1971, President Nixon suspended convertibility into gold, and this ushered in the era of floating exchange rates.

Sterling began floating in June 1972 and the Trinidad and Tobago dollar, which was pegged to sterling, began floating relative to the other major currencies, most important, with respect to the US dollar. However, by the early 1970s, the economy of Trinidad and Tobago was firmly within the American sphere of influence. Exports of petroleum, crude and refined, flowed to the United States. The bulk of consumer, intermediate and capital goods imports came from the United States, and the United States was increasingly the major source of foreign direct investment. Students from Trinidad and Tobago opted increasingly to pursue university education in the United States and Canada.

The Treaty of Chaguaramas was signed in Trinidad in 1973 bringing into force the Caribbean Community (CARICOM), with the commitment on the part of countries to implement a common external tariff and to foster a range of areas of functional cooperation. While CARICOM did not account for a significant proportion of Trinidad and Tobago's total trade, the country enjoyed a positive balance of trade with its CARICOM neighbours mainly on account of petroleum exports, but later as well because of exports of manufactured goods.

Reshaping Development Strategy

The development strategy pursued since 1958 was assessed to have failed in that it had not created employment on the scale required, and the failure to create jobs had led to social unrest and instability, and had brought the country to the brink of economic collapse. The oil windfall presented an opportunity to review and rethink the strategy and the policies that the government should pursue to foster development. The rethinking and planning for the expansion of industry had begun earlier in the decade.[2] The 1973 budget speech had outlined three ways in which the government could secure "meaningful participation" in the development of resource-based and basic industries. The first was to make government participation a condition of licence as in the oil sector. The second was to agree with a sponsor to a certain level of government participation. The third approach would see the government "on its own initiative, and having regard to its overall priorities and plans, . . . develop projects and seek out private or official partners for joint venture operations. This is the approach which is being developed in connection with determining other possible economic uses of petroleum for the expansion of primary and secondary manufacturing in the country particularly in the field of petrochemicals and the production of synthetics."[3]

Development strategy in many of the larger developing countries, such as India and Brazil, focused on the development of "heavy industry" – iron and steel, petrochemicals, and so on – which was seen to be the basis for the growth and development of the industrialized countries. Trinidad and Tobago's petroleum industry with its major refining plants and the Grace ammonia plant operating since 1958 had differentiated this country from its Caribbean neighbours in forging a path to development through industry rather than through services, including tourism.

In his 1976 budget speech, Williams stated: "The oil revolution allowed us to aim still higher – that is to seek to transform the petroleum sector to greater linkages with the rest of the economy, particularly the industrial sector. The objectives of this effort have been and will continue to be the fuller domestic utilisation of Trinidad and Tobago's hydrocarbon resources to create greater income and employment, and to widen the industrial base of the country."[4] Williams, known for his pithy aphorisms, had said "planning seemed to have lost its mystique".[5] Williams had gone on to say:

> In the developing world, disagreement was emerging about the purpose and the broad parameters of economic development. Development was being viewed as an historical process which encompasses not only production but the entire economic and social life of a nation in transition . . . its health, education, social outlook and the dynamism of its political institutions. In addition there was lack of clarity as to whether planning would yield the best results if it was autocratic and centralized, if it was indicative . . . or if it was partial, . . . allowing for state intervention in certain sectors of the national economy to influence patterns of production, distribution and consumption.[6]

Eric Williams now turned, not to the economists who had crafted the three five-year development plans, but to engineers instead. The Coordinating Task

Force under Ken Julien, professor of electrical engineering at the University of the West Indies and deputy chairman of the Industrial Development Corporation, was appointed in 1975 to identify and evaluate the feasibility of several projects in light of the removal of the financial constraint and the availability offshore of natural gas in significant quantities. The task force was eventually wound up in 1979 and replaced with the National Energy Corporation (NEC) with essentially the same mandate as the task force. In 1993, the NEC itself became a subsidiary of the National Gas Company and its role reduced to developing industrial estates and the marine infrastructure for the energy-based plants.

In 1976, a National Advisory Council was formed under the chairmanship of Ken Julien. The remit of the council included re-examination of the adoption and utilization of national economic planning; administrative improvements in the public service; and addressing the efficiency of the utilities and state enterprises.

The elaborate planning machinery that had been put in place for the five-year plans was now effectively replaced by a project office focused on gas-based projects and located outside the mainstream public service. These arrangements apparently caused the Planning Ministry some discomfort, if not concern.

Projects and Project Financing

The projects identified by the Coordinating Task Force are shown in table 9.1. The financing of these projects was a major undertaking. However, for a country flush with petrodollars, located in the western hemisphere and historically friendly towards foreign investment, there was no shortage of supply of financing as commercial banks involved in recycling petrodollar surpluses via syndicated loans were quite willing to finance projects in Trinidad and Tobago.

Long-Term Projects Funds

The government was aware that the sharp increase in oil prices in 1973 and 1974 could quite easily and quickly be reversed. It was understood that fiscal prudence was warranted. The 1976 budget speech stated: "We cannot afford to build up recurrent expenditure in a situation in which there is always the possibility that there will be a sudden turn of events that reverses the favourable position created by the energy crisis of late 1973, or . . . to encourage new consumption and expenditures which are unsustainable under normal conditions."[7]

The inflationary impact of excessive spending was also noted especially in the light of commodity price inflation worldwide. The government developed the

Table 9.1 Energy-Based and Related Infrastructure Projects Identified for
Implementation

Project	Estimated Cost (TT$M)
Fertilizer Joint Venture with W.R. Grace (TRINGEN)*	207
Iron and Steel Complex*	653
Polyester Fibre Complex*	85
Furfural Plant*	40
Fertilizer Joint Venture with Amoco*	759
Natural Gas Pipeline*	85
TRINTOC Refinery Upgrade	300
Olefins/Aromatics Complex	2000
Aluminiun Smelter	662
Liquified Natural Gas	2310
Petrochemical JV with Texaco	122
Infrastructure Projects	
Caroni Arena Water	200
Point Lisas Power Station	265
Point Lisas Estate and Port	105
Cement Plant expansion*	70

Source: Budget speech, 1976.
Note: Projects marked with * were seen as priority.

device of the "special funds" or Long-Term Projects Funds (LTPF) whereby appropriations were made to these several funds, to be drawn on as needed as the projects associated with them required funding. By 1979, there were thirty-one different funds established even after several funds had been consolidated over the years. By 1983, when the special funds appropriations effectively came to an end, there were fifty-one funds, after consolidation. Because appropriations are regarded as (approved) expenditure, the device of the special funds distorted the presentation of government fiscal operations and government savings. The other concern related to accountability for expenditure from the funds after appropriation and the extent of parliamentary oversight of those expenditures. Those concerns prompted the government to "account" for the petrodollar periodically in publications that outlined actual expenditures from the funds, as well as measures related to tax relief and the mitigation of the impact of inflation on citizens.[8]

Table 9.2 Funds for Long-Term Development, 1974–1983 ($ million)

	1974	1975	1976	1977	1978	1979	1980	1981	1982	1983	1974–1983
Appropriations	400.7	501.7	517.6	1556.3	1013.4	1370.4	2143.0	2981.7	2671.0	1171.0	14326.8
Interest and other income	9.0	27.5	51.7	62.3	177.4	185.6	284.3	203.1	274.3	27.2	1302.4
Total receipts	409.7	529.2	569.3	1618.6	1190.8	1556.0	2427.3	3184.8	2945.3	1198.2	15629.2
Expenditure	125.2	54.8	393.0	602.9	797.5	1508.8	2204.7	2933.1	3754.0	2591.5	14965.7
Ratio (expenditure/receipts)	31%	10%	69%	37%	67%	97%	91%	92%	127%	216%	96%
Memo item Expenditure from:											
Petroleum development fund	123.1	42.5	126.8	195.9	183.1	221.0	357.1	507.0	674.2	411.7	2842.5
% of total expenditure	98%	78%	32%	32%	23%	15%	16%	17%	18%	16%	19%
Infrastructure development fund incl. roads	0	0.1	61.4	88	95.1	233.8	321.1	429.8	536.7	523.5	2289.5
% of total expenditure	0%	0%	16%	15%	12%	15%	15%	15%	14%	20%	15%
Investment in commercial enterprises	0	0	0	0	0	233.75	295.5	470.3	466.6	86.3	1552.5
% of total expenditure	0%	0%	0%	0%	0%	15%	13%	16%	12%	3%	10%
Housing	0	0	14.9	46.5	54.9	137.4	237.5	387.8	666.8	460.3	2006.1
% of total expenditure	0%	0%	4%	8%	7%	9%	11%	13%	18%	18%	13%
Education	0	0	66.8	47	53.3	66.1	41.4	65.7	113.7	133.7	587.7
% of total expenditure	0%	0%	17%	8%	7%	4%	2%	2%	3%	5%	4%
Memo item:											
Expenditure on energy-based projects (All Funds)	71.9	41.5	170.6	223.0	206.1	166.1	371.4	511.9	875.9	780.9	3419.2
% of total expenditure	57%	76%	43%	37%	26%	11%	17%	17%	23%	30%	23%

Source: Government of Trinidad and Tobago, *Accounting for the Petrodollar, 1973–1983*, 1984.

Total receipts – appropriations plus interest and other income – of the funds totaled $15.6 billion over the decade of 1974 to 1983. Total expenditure amounted to $14.96 billion. The majority of the expenditure was accounted for by the Petroleum Development Fund (19 per cent), infrastructure including roads (15 per cent), investment in commercial enterprises (10 per cent), housing (13 per cent), and education (4 per cent). Expenditure on energy-based projects from all funds accounted for 23 per cent of total expenditure from the special funds. Expenditure from the special funds started slowly as projects were developed, but by 1979, the ratio of expenditure to receipts was almost 100 per cent.

Government Investment in Commercial Enterprises

Since the 1972 White Paper, the government had determined that the state needed to play a greater role in directly productive activities and to act as entrepreneur in several industries where local or foreign private sectors were unable or unwilling. The oil windfall allowed the government to act where before it could only articulate a desire. A slew of acquisitions were made across a range of sectors and industries, and some entirely new enterprises were formed. Some investments resulted from acquisitions of foreign-owned companies such as Texaco and Tate and Lyle who wished to exit. Others were seen to be strategic and in furtherance of the industrialization of the economy based on use of natural gas as a feedstock or local control of insurance and banking. Many others were rescue operations of companies that were in chronic financial difficulty, such as BWIA. Some, for example, the School Nutrition Company or the Hospital Management Company, were formed to implement specific initiatives relating to the social sectors (table 9.3). By 1983, the government held thirty-four wholly owned state enterprises, fourteen majority-owned and one as a fifty-fifty joint venture. In addition, the government had minority interests in seventeen other companies.

Over the period 1973 to 1983 the government injected $1.6 billion into equity participation in various enterprises, although 45 per cent of this total ($740 million) was invested in one enterprise: the Iron and Steel Company of Trinidad and Tobago (ISCOTT). Another $2.2 billion was injected as loans, of which again one enterprise, Caroni (1975) Limited, accounted for 39 per cent of the total loans made ($858 million). A further $2.6 billion was injected as "advances" and $858 million as subventions. A notable recipient of government equity, loan and advances support was the national airline, BWIA, which garnered a total of $1.2 billion in funds from the government over the period.

Table 9.3 Significant State-Owned Enterprises, 1974–1983

Enterprise	Sector/Industry	Ownership	Probable Rationale
Caroni (1975) Ltd, Forres Park Limited and Orange Grove National Company	Sugar	Wholly owned	Buyout of Tate and Lyle and consolidation of sugar operations; Job preservation
National Feed Mills; National Agro-Chemicals; T&T Lime Products; T&T Forest Products; Non Pareil Estates Ltd; T&T Meat Processors; National Flour Mills; Food and Agriculture Corporation	Agriculture livestock feed	Wholly owned	Boosting domestic food production and control of food price increases.
National Fisheries Company Ltd	Fisheries	Majority-owned	Enhancing food production and export
Trinidad Cement Limited	Cement production	Wholly owned	Strategic
TRINTOC	Petroleum production and refining	Wholly owned	Buyout of Texaco; Job preservation
National Gas Company	Gas transportation	Wholly owned	Strategic – Energy
National Energy Company	Energy project management	Wholly owned	Strategic – Energy
National Petroleum Marketing	Gas stations	Wholly owned	
Fertrin	Ammonia	Majority-owned	Strategic – Energy
TRINGEN	Ammonia	Majority-owned	Strategic – Energy
ISCOTT	Iron and steel	Wholly owned	Strategic – Energy
Reinsurance Company	Insurance	Majority-owned	Strategic – Finance
National Commercial Bank	Banking	Majority-owned	Strategic – Finance
Workers Bank	Banking	Minority-interest	People's Sector
T&T Mortgage Finance	Mortgage lending	Majority-owned	Housing Support

Table 9.4 Government Participation in Companies, 1973–1983 ($ million)

Company	Equity	Loans	Advances	Subventions	Total
All Companies	1,628.5	2,209.1	2,610.6	858.0	7,306.1
Of which:					
ISCOTT	740.0	–	443.2	–	1,183.2
Caroni (1975) Limited	118.7	858.4	80.0	118.7	1,175.8
BWIA	61.0	384.0	410.3	307.9	1,163.0
T&T Telephone Company	112.1	104.3	326.6	–	543.0
National Gas Company	0.7	3.1	412.9	–	416.2
National Energy Corporation	99.8	102.0	230.8	–	432.6

Source: Government of Trinidad and Tobago, *Accounting for the Petrodollar, 1973–1983*, 1984.

Localization

The government sought to encourage the local ownership or local participation in certain industries, but especially insurance and banking. Apart from the government's acquisition and subsequent partial divestment of the National Commercial Bank, and the formation of the Workers Bank, some of the other foreign-owned banks moved to divest part of their shareholding to locals through the local stock exchange. These included Bank of Nova Scotia (Scotiabank); Barclays, which later became Republic Bank; and Royal Bank of Canada, which later became Royal Bank of Trinidad and Tobago. Citibank and Chase Manhattan resisted, even after the government had implemented ascribed capital for foreign bank branches operating in the country and restricted the opening of new branches. Citibank reluctantly agreed to issue some shares to locals after the government threatened to freeze deposit levels. Chase Manhattan, however, elected to leave, and its business was sold to the National Commercial Bank.[9]

The foreign insurance companies, mainly Canadian and English companies, progressively sold out to local investors such that the industry became almost entirely locally owned by the 1980s. However, American Life and General Insurance Company (ALGICO), a combined life and general insurer and subsidiary of the American company AIG, remained majority foreign-owned.

US Dollar Peg and the Foreign Exchange Market

In May of 1976, Trinidad and Tobago severed its link with the fast depreciating pound sterling and pegged to the US dollar at TT$2.40/US$1. The parity chosen actually constituted a revaluation relative to the level of sterling at the time.

It is noteworthy that by special arrangement with the oil companies, oil tax revenue was paid to the government in US dollars. Oil tax revenues were the largest source of foreign exchange inflows. The Central Bank credited the government account with TT dollars and retained the US dollars. This meant that the Central Bank became the largest single recipient of foreign exchange and made net sales of foreign exchange to the non-oil economy through the commercial banking system. This arrangement was to prove critically important to the conduct of exchange policy later on.

10

Natural Gas and Petrochemicals: The Point Lisas Strategy

From Oil to Natural Gas

The oil industry was always at the top of the government's agenda, although para-doxically, it was rarely addressed in the annual budget presentations. In his 1958 budget speech, Eric Williams discussed the historical development of the industry at great length beginning with the Holland report in the 1920s, although the main focus of his lengthy presentation was the grant to the foreign-owned oil companies by the outgoing administration in December 1955 of a substantial depletion allow-ance to encourage marine exploration, a decision which he roundly condemned. Oversight of the petroleum sector up until 1962 was carried out by a department of the Ministry of Industry and Commerce. The real problem in improving the coun-try's tax take from the industry was the imbalance in knowledge of the industry – technical, marketing, engineering – between the companies and the government.

In 1962, the Ministry of Petroleum and Mines was created. The Mostofi Com-mission of Enquiry, set up in 1963, submitted its report on the oil industry in 1964 and made recommendations for better oversight and management of the industry. The Petroleum Act of 1969 provided the broad legislative framework for the operation of the oil industry, replacing the previous petroleum ordinances. In 1969 as well, the Territorial Sea Act, extending the territorial sea from three miles to twelve miles, and the Continental Shelf Act, to regulate the exploration and exploitation of the continental shelf, were passed into law. Apart from these important institutional developments in respect of the petroleum industry, the government in 1969 entered into a joint venture with Tesoro Corporation to acquire the assets and operations of British Petroleum (BP), who were exiting Trinidad and Tobago for better opportunities elsewhere.

While production of crude oil had increased steadily in the postwar period, hydrocarbons (petroleum and natural gas) and industries downstream of natural gas really became the centrepiece of the development strategy in the period after 1973. There were three key factors that propelled hydrocarbons to the centre of the development strategy. These were: (1) shift towards production from the marine areas off the east coast of Trinidad; (2) discoveries of significant reserves of natural gas and the determination to make use of that gas; and (3) changes in the taxation regime to increase the government's tax take from the industry.

Offshore Production

Marine production had begun in the southwest in the Gulf of Paria in the Soldado field in the 1957, although earlier wells deviated from land had been drilled off Brighton. The Soldado field was owned and developed jointly by Texaco, BP and Shell under the company Trinidad Northern Areas, and by 1959, marine oil had begun to account for a significant proportion of crude oil production. Indeed, most of the growth in total oil production in the 1960s was due to the increased production from the Soldado field in the Gulf of Paria. Production from that field peaked around 1968 (figure 10.1).

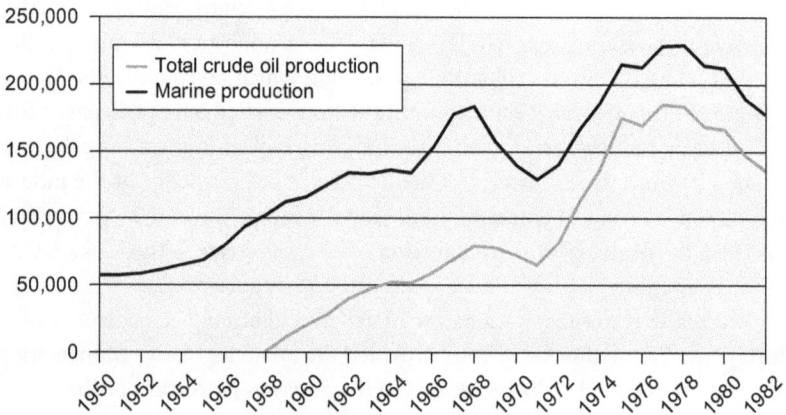

Figure 10.1 Crude oil production (bopd), 1950–1982

Amoco, a relatively small, crude-short American company, entered Trinidad in the 1960s and between 1968 and 1971 explored for, and eventually discovered, oil and gas off Trinidad's east coast. The first fields developed were the Teak, Samaan and Poui (TSP) fields. Production began in 1972 and gave a significant boost to the country's oil production. East coast crude oil, all of which was exported, was light, sweet crude, unlike the medium and heavy crudes found on land.

Natural Gas Production and Utilization

But it was the discoveries of natural gas that were truly significant for the long-term development of industry in Trinidad and Tobago. The Teak field discovered by Amoco in 1968 held about one trillion cubic feet of gas reserves, and the Cassia field discovered in 1973 held about two trillion cubic feet. Trinidad and Tobago had always produced associated gas with the production of crude oil. That gas was used either as fuel, flared or used as gas-lift for crude oil production. Up to the mid-1970s, as much as 50 per cent of natural gas production was vented or flared. The use of natural gas for gas lift in secondary recovery operations was phased out in the mid-1970s. Trinidad and Tobago's natural gas has very high methane

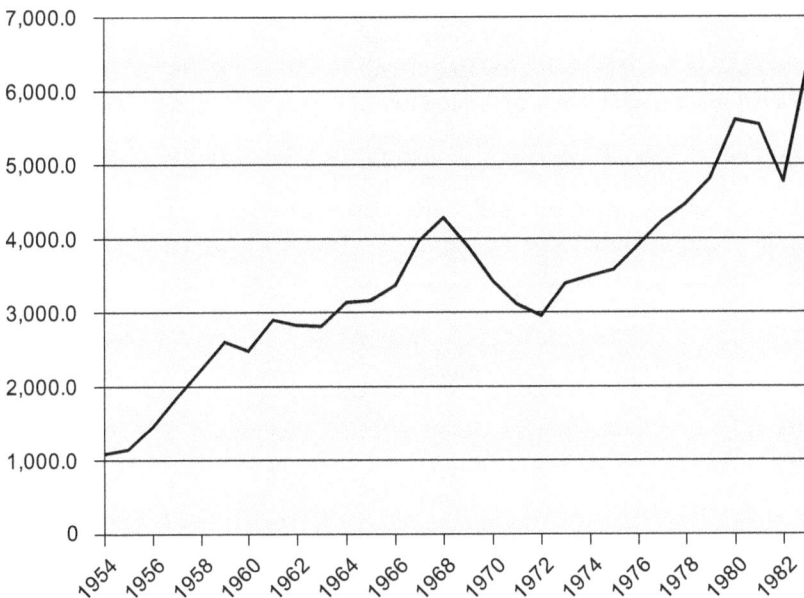

Figure 10.2 Natural gas production (million cubic metres)

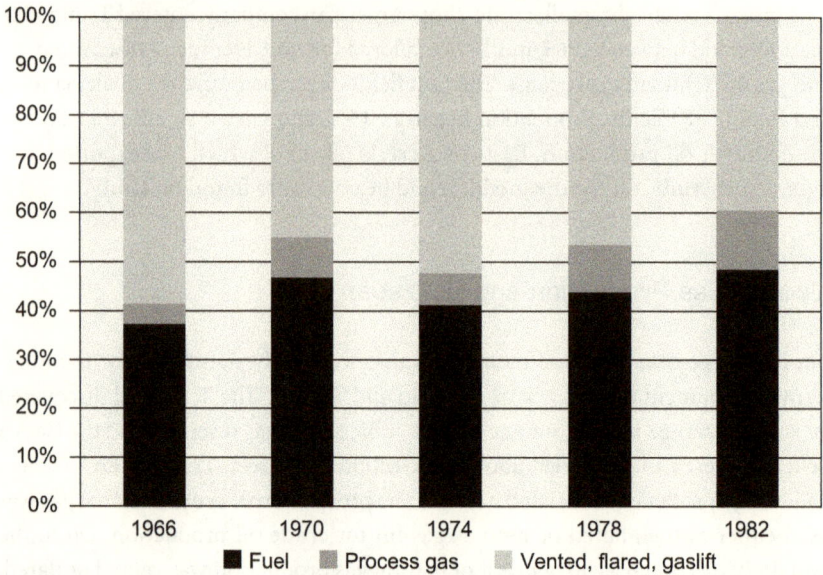

Figure 10.3 Natural gas utilization (selected years, 1966–1982)

content, 93 per cent for east coast dry gas and 99 per cent for north coast gas. High ethane content, which allows the production of ethylene, is only 2.5 per cent for east coast gas and 0.2 per cent for north coast gas.

Natural gas reserves had increased steadily over the years from the time professional independent audits of the country's reserves were undertaken in the late 1970s by Ryder-Scott, a Houston-based firm.

Table 10.1 Estimates of Natural Gas Reserves (trillion cubic feet), 1980–1997
            (Selected Years)

	Proven	Probable	Possible	Total Discounted Reserves
1980	6.65	5.68	1.68	14.0
1981	10.55	6.21	1.20	17.97
1983	10.6	n/a	n/a	17.5
1987	9.60	5.96	1.05	16.61
1997	15.85	4.9	1.47	22.3

Source: Various, including administrative reports of Ministry of Petroleum, "Demas Task Force Report".

Up to the 1970s, production of natural gas paralleled crude oil production because most of the gas produced was associated gas. However, from the late 1970s, natural gas production continued to increase even as oil production began to fall as the gas produced in the fields off the east coast reached the industrial estates on the west coast through the pipelines constructed overland.

There was a gradual reduction in wastage of natural gas over the years such that the proportion of gas production that was flared or vented fell from 60 per cent in the mid-1960s to 40 per cent in the early 1980s as increasing use was made of natural gas as feedstock for petrochemical plants and as fuel for electricity generation.

Institutional Developments in Natural Gas and Energy-Based Industries

The decision to develop industries downstream of natural gas required organizational structures for project management, gas transportation and co-investment with foreign companies. The National Gas Company (NGC) was established in August 1975 and was designated as the sole trader of gas in Trinidad and Tobago. The NGC built the gas transport pipelines in 1977 from Guayaguayare, and in 1978, the offshore lines from the Teak and Poui fields to shore were commissioned. In 2005, NGC built the large fifty-six-inch-wide pipeline across the width of southern Trinidad to deliver gas for LNG Train IV plant at Point Fortin. The NEC took on the role of project developers and managers and owned the port and industrial estates where the downstream industries producing petrochemicals and iron and steel were located.

Petroleum Taxation

The taxation of the petroleum and natural gas sector is probably the single most important policy measure that the government of any petro-state employs. It determines the bulk of government revenues and hence the amount of expenditure and borrowing the government can undertake. Petroleum taxation has to balance the maintenance of appropriate incentives to the producing and refining companies for exploration, enhanced recovery, refining and marketing in a risky, capital-intensive, globally competitive business with the interests of the government to maximize revenues and manage depletion of the country's hydrocarbon reserves.

Trinidad and Tobago had operated a petroleum taxation regime prior to 1974, which treated the petroleum business much like any other business subject to a corporation tax. Companies were allowed to consolidate their operations, write off expenses, use company transfer prices, and pay the going corporation tax rate. The net result was a low effective tax rate on oil companies operating in the country.[1] The Petroleum Taxes Act of 1974 changed the regime fundamentally. Production, refining and marketing operations were taxed separately, intangible drilling expenses were capitalized and amortized over the life of the well, and tax reference prices set by the Board of Inland Revenue were to be used for the calculation of the tax liability.

The use of tax reference prices caused significant problems, however, as the government attempted to capture the rents from higher oil prices after 1973 and 1974 by raising the tax reference prices. Those prices were not necessarily related to realized prices and did not take into account the higher costs that companies were experiencing. The companies experienced serious cash flow problems. In addition, the American companies encountered problems with the US tax authorities that altered the foreign tax credit regime to the disadvantage of the companies. By 1980 the government was forced to move away from tax reference prices to arm's length or reported prices.

The introduction of the supplemental petroleum tax in 1980 was the next most significant development in the evolution of the petroleum tax regime. The supplemental petroleum tax was levied on the company's gross income net of certain deductions. These deductions included an enhanced recovery allowance of 140 per cent for land operations, an exploration drilling expenditure allowance of 150 per cent for both land and marine operations and field size allowances to take account of marginal marine fields. As calculated, the supplemental petroleum tax was itself a deduction for the petroleum profits tax, along with royalties, depreciation and other operating costs (table 10.2).

Production-Sharing Contracts

An important adjunct to the revised petroleum taxation regime was the production-sharing contract. Production-sharing contracts began to be used in Trinidad and Tobago in 1974. Unlike the traditional licence or concession, in typical production-sharing contracts, the government owns the oil or gas if found. An agreed portion of the oil is allowed to the company as "cost oil" to enable the company to recover the costs of exploration and development, and the remaining portion – "profit oil" – is divided in an agreed split between the company and the government.

Table 10.2 Evolution of Petroleum Taxation, 1960s to 1980

Oil Taxation	Pre-1974	1974	1975	1980
Base	All local operations aggregated – production, refining and distribution	Separation of production refining and distribution; production divided into land and marine		Consolidation of producing fields permitted, but refining and marketing separate
Pricing	Company	Tax reference prices fixed by BIR varying by quality of crude	Tax reference prices revised	Actual arms length or reported prices
Expenses	All intangible drilling expenses treated as current expense	Intangible drilling expenses capitalized and amortized over the life of the well	Capitalized and amortized over the life of the well	Capitalized and amortized over the life of the well
Royalty	10%–12½%	10%–12½%	10%–12½%	10%–12½%
Corporation tax/petroleum profits tax	45%	47½% Throughput tax for refining operations (10 cents for Shell; 15 cents for Texaco)	50%	45% Supplemental petroleum tax, royalty, depreciation, operating costs are deductions for petroleum profits tax; throughput tax abolished and replaced with supplemental refining tax
Supplemental petroleum tax				Land – 35%; marine – 60% Levied on gross income net of certain deductions
Deductions to supplemental petroleum tax				Production allowance exploration drilling (150%); enhanced recovery royalty (140%)
Unemployment levy	5%	5%	5%	5%

Petrochemicals and Other Energy-Based Industries

The transformation of the industrial landscape in Trinidad and Tobago took place between 1977 and 1984 with the establishment of ammonia, urea, methanol, and iron and steel producing plants, all of which were world-scale. The Government of Trinidad and Tobago was the owner of three of these plants and a joint-venture partner in the other three plants. The government had also invested in electricity generation, water production, port and road development, and gas pipelines to support these new industries.

The other industries identified earlier, such as liquefied natural gas, aluminium smelting, polyester fibre and so on, would have a much longer gestation and indeed did not come back on the agenda until the 1990s after the "lost decade".[2]

Point Lisas

The location of the new downstream industries was a matter of great importance to the new development strategy. Federation Chemicals, the Grace ammonia plant, had been established on the west coast of the island. A private company, Point Lisas Industrial Port Development Company (PLIPDECO) had started an industrial estate and port at Point Lisas in 1966 to service southern-based businesses. The government acquired majority ownership of the company, and expanded the port and estate to accommodate the proposed gas-based industries. The cluster of world-scale plants on a modern industrial estate became the showpiece of industrial development in Trinidad and Tobago and lent its name to the strategy pursued, becoming known as the "Point Lisas" strategy.

Table 10.3 Establishment of Energy-Based Plants at Point Lisas, 1977–1983: The "First Wave"

Plant	Start-Up Year	Ownership
TRINGEN	1977	Government (51%)/W.R. Grace (49%)
Iron and Steel Company	1980	Government (100%)
Fertrin	1981	Government (51%) Amoco (49%)
Urea Company	1983	Government (100%)
T&T Methanol Company	1984	Government (100%)
Phoenix Park Gas Processors Limited	1991	Government via National Gas Company (51%); Conoco-Phillips (39%) Pan West (10%)

Source: Central Bank of Trinidad and Tobago, "Balance of Payments 2006 and 2007".

11

Economic Impact of the Resource Boom

With the background of the previous chapters, we can now assess the macroeconomic and developmental impact of the resource boom over the period from 1974 to 1982.

Boom

Trinidad and Tobago experienced boom conditions between 1974 and 1982. Oil prices were high, and oil production was rising up to 1978. Oil production peaked in 1978 at 229.6 thousand barrels per day and, following the second oil price hike in 1979, oil prices began to fall in 1981, just as the new energy-based plants were coming on stream. The sharp increase in government revenues, also stimulated by the changes in the petroleum taxation regime, allowed the government to spend massively on both recurrent and capital account. Despite the significant increase in spending, the government enjoyed surpluses on its overall fiscal operations for most of the period, with small deficits occurring in 1978 and 1979 and then a massive deficit in 1982 consequent on the fall in oil prices and oil revenues (figure 11.1).

Real GDP growth rates fluctuated upward over the period averaging 5.5 per cent per annum in 1970 prices compared to about 3.3 per cent per annum in the period from 1967 to 1972. The range of growth rates in real GDP over the period

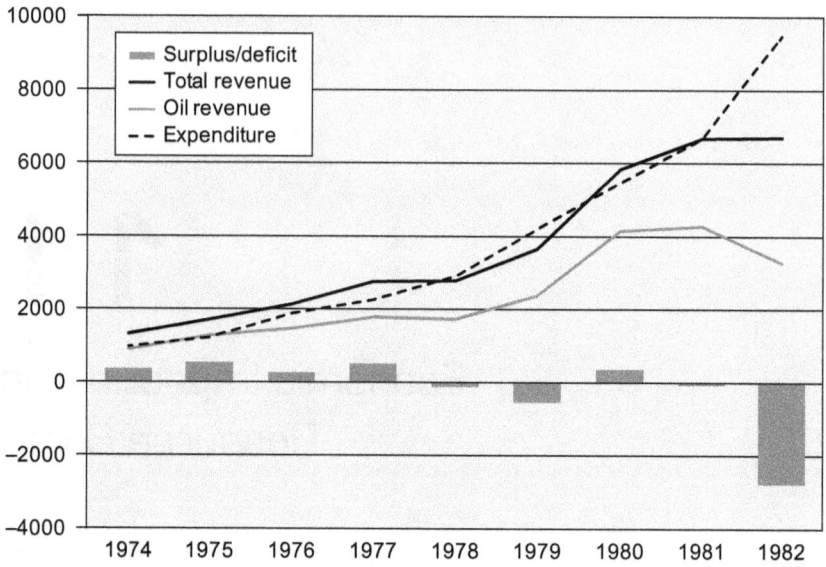

Figure 11.1 Fiscal operations, 1974–1982 (TT$M)

is striking, as is the volatility from year to year. Per capita GDP in US dollars increased from US$1,235 in 1973 to US$7,331 in 1982, an average annual rate of growth of 19.4 per cent (figure 11.2).

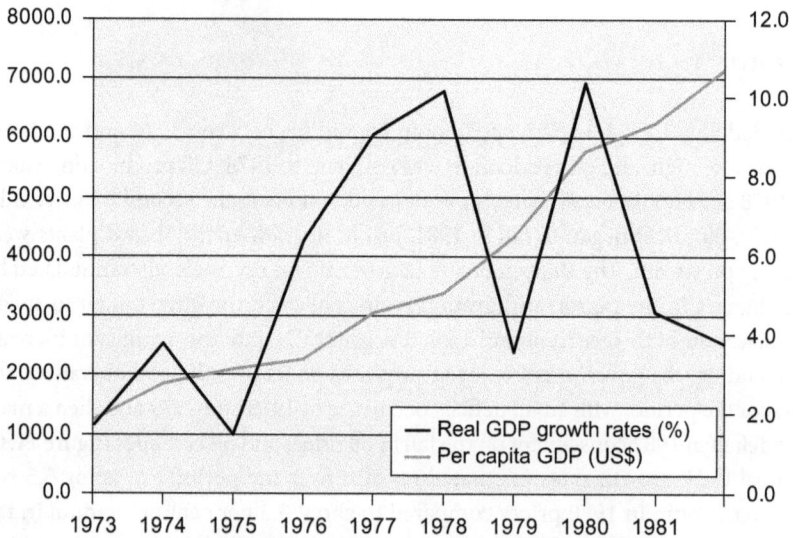

Figure 11.2 Real GDP growth rates (%) and per capita GDP (US$), 1973–1982

Under the impact of the massive stimulus of government current and capital spending, unemployment fell steadily over the period until 1982 when it reached a low of 9.9 per cent, a level not seen since the 1950s. Because the newly established industries were not significant employers of unskilled labour, a significant proportion of the increase in employment occurred in the public sector as government employed more persons and the public sector unions negotiated better wages.

However, the significant increase in aggregate expenditure caused shortages and bottlenecks in sectors such as construction. Wage rates soared and average annual inflation remained in excess of 10 per cent per annum over the period. Over most of the period, wage rates were increasing faster than inflation (figure 11.3). There was a boom in real estate prices notwithstanding government's efforts to stimulate the supply of housing units. Imports of consumer, intermediate and capital goods also rose sharply and imported inflation added to the pressure on prices.

The country's foreign exchange reserves increased steadily over the period notwithstanding the acceleration in imports, reaching over US$3 billion in 1981 from close to zero in 1973 (figure 11.4).

Assessment

There is no question that the boom conditions had improved welfare and the standard of living in the country notwithstanding an overheated economy

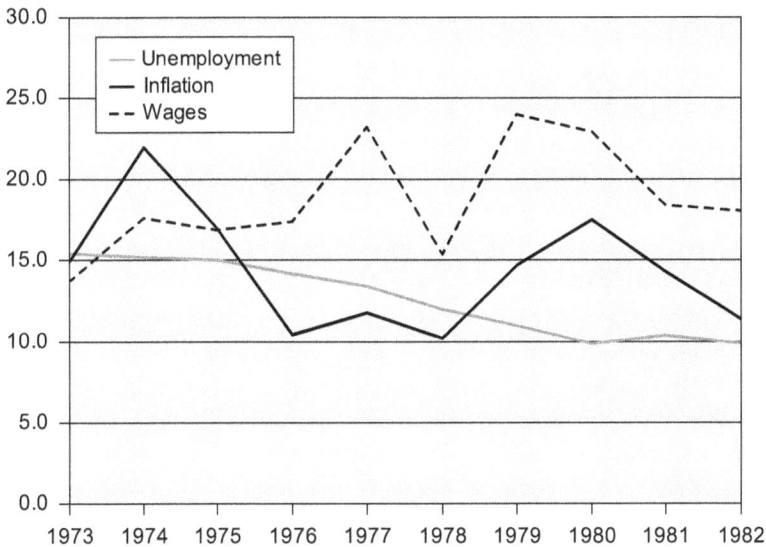

Figure 11.3 Unemployment, inflation and wage increases (%), 1973–1982

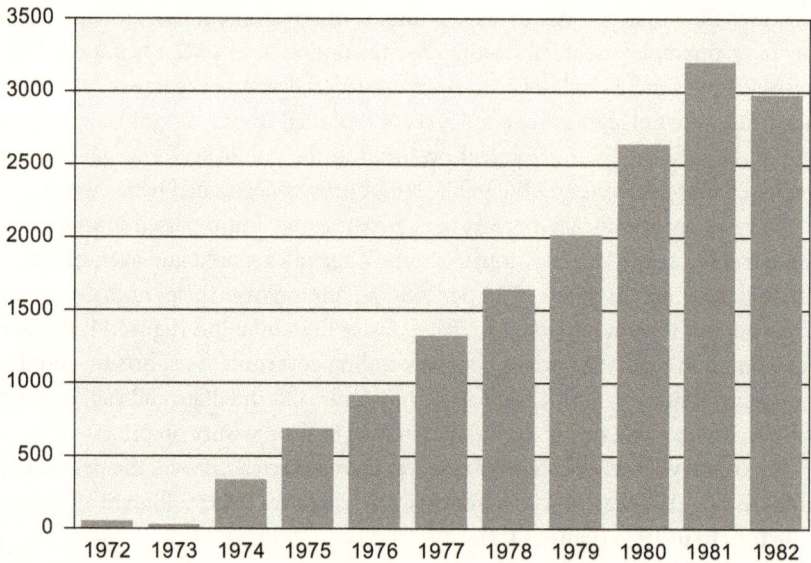

Figure 11.4 Net foreign exchange reserves (US$ million), 1972–1982

characterized by high inflation. More people were employed at better wages and the society could afford to consume imported goods and services without concern about foreign exchange availability. At the time the exchange control regime governed the services and capital accounts and, in the boom conditions after 1973, was loosely managed.

While a period of a decade is too short to assess adequately the extent of economic transformation and the sustainability of the development that occurs, there were some signs that Trinidad and Tobago was experiencing not development, but the short-lived effects of a cyclical resource boom.

The government became by far the largest employer of labour in the economy. In 1975, the government accounted for 7.7 per cent of total employment, but 18.3 per cent inclusive of government utilities and government construction. By 1982, the government accounted for 10.1 per cent of total employment, but 24.5 per cent inclusive of the utilities and government construction. These data do not include employment in government-owned (state) enterprises. Transfers and subsidies increased. Foreign consultants and workers flooded into the country, stimulating the real estate market at the high end. Conspicuous consumption was *de rigueur* among the middle and upper classes who found Miami more congenial for shopping than Port of Spain. The rents generated by the oil windfall were mediated and channeled through the government to the rest of the society, encouraging consumption rather than investment, and where there was investment, it was in distribution rather than exports of manufactures or services.

In current prices, the structure of GDP does show the effect of the boom, with significant growth in the share of petroleum and in construction. Manufacturing and agriculture, as well as "other services", which includes personal services, education, and so on, all showed declining shares of total GDP over the period. Government increased its share of GDP from 10.3 per cent to 14.3 per cent.

The changes in the relative shares of the various sectors in total GDP are not conclusive of Dutch Disease, which arises with an appreciation of the real exchange rate caused by the booming sector and incentivizes the production of home goods rather than the production of tradables. Some other indicators do, however, point in the direction of such a conclusion. The real exchange rate appreciated over the years 1976 to 1984 by 14 per cent, encouraging imports and discouraging the production and exports of manufactured goods. Between 1973 and 1982, measured in constant (1970) prices, domestic agriculture declined in five of the ten years; garment manufacturing declined in seven of the ten years; printing, publishing and paper converters fell in six of the ten years; and personal services in four of the ten years. Hilaire has shown that over the period the tradables sector was 33 per cent smaller in real terms in 1982 compared with the annual average over the 1966 to 1973 period, with agriculture suffering the largest decline.[1]

Table 11.1 Structure of GDP (Selected Years), 1973–1982 (%)

Sector	1973	1976	1979	1982
Agriculture	5.4	4.8	3.8	3.0
Petroleum and petrochemicals	28.1	43.3	39.0	27.0
Manufacturing	9.0	6.9	6.9	6.1
Construction and quarrying	7.2	8.6	11.7	14.9
Distribution	12.3	8.5	7.3	8.6
Transportation, storage communications	13.0	9.2	10.6	12.5
Finance, insurance, real estate	7.6	7.6	9.5	10.8
Government	10.3	8.4	9.4	14.3
Other services	7.1	2.7	1.8	2.8
Total GDP factor cost ($ million)	2,564.2	6,090.5	11,045.8	18,461.4

Source: Central Statistical Office, *The National Income of Trinidad and Tobago, 1966–1985.*

A New Theory of the Economy?

The development strategy pursued between 1974 and 1983 was characterized by an almost complete focus on investment in the energy sector – petroleum and natural gas and the industries downstream of natural gas; significant government direct investment in directly productive enterprises both in energy-based industries and elsewhere; and a boldness and entrepreneurial spirit the likes of which had not been seen before in the country. The simultaneous breaking of both the foreign exchange constraint and the financing constraint permitted the government to establish ambitious goals based on resource-based industrialization and to use the oil windfall to realize those ambitions.

The rate of investment in the economy rose to average about 28 per cent in the decade of the 1970s and, more important, by the second half of the decade, central government was accounting for over 50 per cent of total capital formation in the economy (table 11.2).

The potential impact on the country's development prospects was threefold. First, the gas-based industries would provide an additional source of foreign exchange earnings. Second, they would create new skilled and semi-skilled jobs in globally competitive industries using modern technologies.[2] Indeed the skills and experience built up during this first wave of gas-based industrialization would serve the industry in good stead during the second wave of resource-based industrialization from the mid-1990s. Third, these businesses, once they had become profitable, would serve to enhance the government's tax base.

There was, however, no statement of a new theory of the economy and how the economy should grow in an environment of resource abundance. Ex post, as it were, we can summarize the differences between the strategy of the earlier period and the period after 1973 in terms of the role of government versus the

Table 11.2 Investment Performance, 1966–1985

	1966–1970	1971–1975	1976–1980	1980–1985
Gross capital formation/ GDP	21%	28%	28%	25%
Government capital expenditure/gross capital formation	24%	22%	51%	56%

Note: Some care is needed here as not all government capital expenditure is really capital formation. However, government's role in investing activities is certainly understated since investments by state enterprises and other government agencies are not included in government capital formation here.

Table 11.3 Comparison of Development Policy Pre- and Post-1973

	Planning Years	Post-1973 Strategy
Strategic thrust	Import substitution	Export of output of gas-based industries
Role of government	Facilitator, enabler; provision of infrastructure and social overhead capital	Entrepreneurial; engaged in directly productive activities as well as provision of infrastructure, especially supportive of the new industries
Role of private sector	Engine of growth through investment	Partner with government bringing technical skills and perhaps markets
Policy objectives	Labour absorption; savings and investment growth balanced relative to foreign exchange constraint	Rapid investment growth; "Big Push"; income growth from government spending and multiplier effect; foreign exchange constraint is not binding.
Policy instruments	Tax incentives; protection via tariffs and quotas (negative list)	Petroleum taxation; production-sharing contracts; subsidized gas prices.

private sector, the strategic thrust, and the objectives of the policy and policy instruments employed in table 11.3. The shift in development policy between the planning years and resource-based industrialization is also captured graphically in the policy map in figure 11.5.

Conclusion

The period 1974 to 1982 marks a major shift in policy from the earlier planning period. Industrial policy, specifically the development of gas-based industries and related infrastructure, effectively supplanted the broad-based five-year plans. The government, now armed with considerable financial resources, moved to enter directly into commercial activities via state enterprises. There was a shift away from foreign direct investment and a move to localize key industries and sectors – banking, insurance and petroleum. However, this shift did not mark any change in respect to property rights or the rule of law. The acquisition of foreign assets was accomplished with due notice and negotiation, and with compensation paid for the assets acquired.

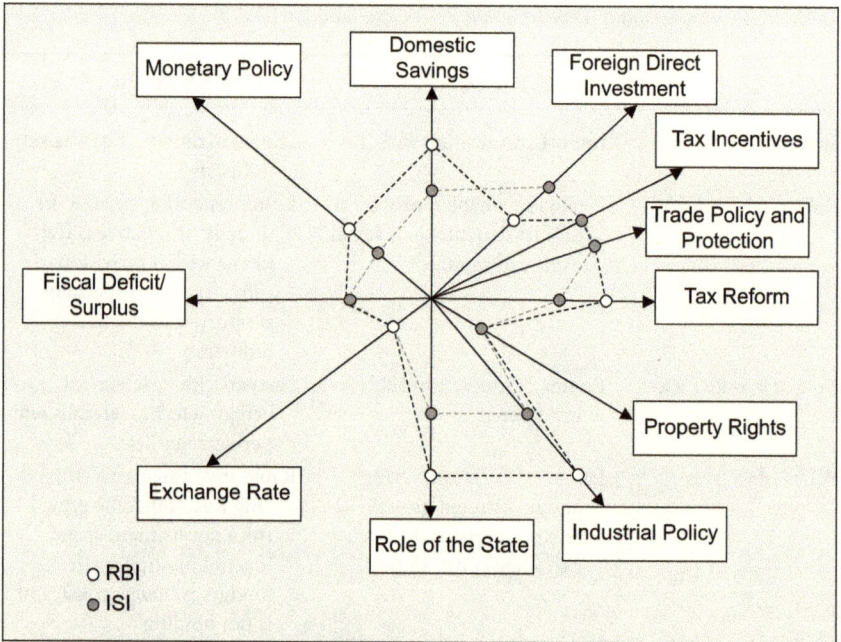

Figure 11.5 Resource-based industrialization

However, the acceleration of wage increases and increased consumption are also noteworthy in this period as it proved politically difficult to resist spending more on consumption to alleviate pressing problems of unemployment and poverty, poor housing, and amenities.

Part 4

The Lost Decade, 1983–1992

12

The Imperatives of Adjustment

The International Context

In the 1980s, history threw onto the world stage three of the most influential leaders of the postwar era. Margaret Thatcher, leader of the Conservative Party, was elected prime minister of the United Kingdom in 1979; Ronald Reagan, leader of the Republican Party, was elected president of the United States in 1980; and Mikhail Gorbachev became general secretary of the Communist Party of the Soviet Union in 1985 and president of the USSR in 1991. Thatcher, Britain's first female prime minister, set about dismantling the welfare state that had been built up in the United Kingdom since the 1960s by successive labour governments, attacking and facing down the powerful trades unions, and privatizing a range of state-owned businesses. Reagan, who succeeded the Democratic president Jimmy Carter, had seen Democratic presidents in the White House since Roosevelt in 1933, interrupted only by the Republican presidencies of Eisenhower and Nixon-Ford. Reagan attacked "big government", and his bandwagon called for smaller government, lower taxes, and allowing markets to operate freely, in complete contrast to the New Deal–era Keynesianism, which promoted active government intervention to stabilize the economy and correct market failures.

Gorbachev set out to restructure and democratize the Soviet Union in order to improve its economic performance. Perestroika (restructuring) and glasnost (openness) became the leitmotifs of Gorbachev's leadership, and it led to the relinquishing of Soviet control over Eastern Europe, the fall of the Berlin Wall in

1989, and the accelerated adoption of markets in place of central planning. By 1990–91, nationalist sentiment within the Soviet republics led to the eventual collapse of the USSR itself. The collapse of the "Second World" meant that those developing countries that were sceptical about the Western market-driven capitalist approach to economic development now saw clearly that the socialist alternative was a failed model and the leading socialist country – the USSR – was itself turning towards the market system.[1]

The embrace of what came to be known as the "Washington Consensus" had its roots in intellectual currents that had formed and begun to move long before. The protagonists within the discipline of economics were Milton Friedman and the Chicago School of Monetarists who came to prominence in the 1960s and 1970s, followed later by the Rational Expectations School, which challenged the very foundations of the theory of economic policy.[2] The political shift in the major Western countries to the right was also in part a response to the unprecedented change in global economic and financial power that the oil price shocks had brought about. Arab sheikhdoms overnight came to wield significant financial power and political influence. The concerns of the Western countries were how to secure oil supplies over the medium and long term in locations outside of the control of the OPEC cartel, and how to secure vital Western interests in the Middle East, which was one of the most unstable regions in the world.

Oil price increases had also triggered significant inflation in developed countries. In the United States, inflation soared to double-digit rates in the late 1970s. The US Federal Reserve under Paul Volcker moved to throttle back the growth of the money supply, and as a consequence interest rates in the United States jumped to double-digit levels. The Fed Funds rate reached 20 per cent in June 1981, and the commercial bank prime loan rate was at 21.5 per cent. International interest rates also increased substantially and impacted adversely developing countries that had tapped the commercial bank market for syndicated loans during the 1970s. These commercial bank loans came about from the recycling of petrodollars deposited in international banks by the oil-exporting countries. In August 1982, Mexico announced that it would not be able to meet principal payments falling due. The international debt crisis ensued with several oil-importing developing countries, already burdened by higher oil prices, unable to service their external debt obligations.

Recessionary conditions followed in both developed and some developing countries, and it was not long before oil prices peaked and then began a precipitous retreat from the highs of 1980–81. However, the recession of 1981–82 was not long lived; inflation retreated and growth resumed in the developed countries by the middle of the decade. But Latin America and the Caribbean remained in crisis.

However, there was a different story unfolding in East Asia, where those countries had succeeded in achieving higher rates of growth than any other region since 1965, especially the "Gang of Four" – Singapore, Hong Kong, South Korea and Taiwan. While Latin America and the Caribbean struggled with stabilization and adjustment, the "East Asian Miracle" was in full swing – attracting significant flows of portfolio and direct investment to the East Asian countries and increasing their share of world exports.[3] The "East Asian Miracle" prompted an extensive debate on development policy and, in particular, on industrial policy and the role of the state versus the role of the market, since the approach to policy of those countries in achieving high rates of growth along with equity in the distribution of income did not seem to conform to the neoclassical approach that was gaining ascendancy under the Washington Consensus.[4]

The Domestic Context

The domestic political context for policy also changed markedly in the 1980s. In March 1981, Eric Williams who had been premier, and then prime minister for twenty-five years, died and the reins of the government were handed to George Chambers. Chambers was a quiet, almost self-effacing man, who eschewed the conventional jacket and tie for the open-necked shirt, and whose modest educational accomplishments contrasted sharply with the Oxford-educated, celebrated historian whose oversized shoes he was now to fill. Chambers was first thrust into general elections in 1981 in which the PNM prevailed against new opposition in the form of the Organisation for National Reconstruction as well as the United Labour Front. He was then thrust into dealing with the policy crisis engendered by free-falling oil prices.

In 1986, the Chambers administration was swept from office by a massive landslide in favour of the National Alliance for Reconstruction (NAR) led by A.N.R. Robinson who had left the PNM in 1970 during the black power crisis. The NAR won thirty-three of the thirty-six seats in the House of Representatives, and for the first time in a general election since 1956, the PNM lost power.[5] The NAR was actually a coalition of the United Labour Front led by Basdeo Panday, the Organisation for National Reconstruction, and Robinson's Tobago-based ACDC. It would not be long before this uneasy alliance displayed severe cracks, and by 1988, Panday had left to form first "Club 88" and then launched the United National Congress (UNC) in April 1989. However, there were enough United Labour Front members of parliament remaining with the government to allow it to continue to hold office.

On 27 July 1990, a radicalized group – the Jamaat Al Muslimeen – attacked the police headquarters, took control on the only television station, and stormed the Red House – the seat of parliament – while the House was in session. Several persons were killed, including a member of parliament, and most of the members of the government were held hostage for five days while the regiment surrounded the parliament building and the television station, and kept the hostage-takers locked down. In the ensuing chaos, Port of Spain and other places were looted and several buildings burnt down, resulting in millions of dollars in damage. The siege was eventually ended with the release of a wounded prime minister and the rest of the government ministers. This event, without precedent in the history of modern Trinidad and Tobago, traumatized the society and effectively sealed the fate of a government that had already become unpopular.[6]

The Imperatives of Adjustment

The rapid collapse of oil prices in 1981 prompted a shift in focus from growth and development via resource-based industrialization to adjustment and stabilization. However, this shift was not immediate, and soon after the election of the new government in November 1981, Prime Minister George Chambers appointed in February 1982 a powerful team to reassess the country's development strategy, and financial management and control, along with a reappraisal of the policy measures employed in pursuit of the country's development objectives.

The task force was to formulate initially a properly articulated medium-term public sector investment programme to be followed by a more comprehensive multisectoral plan.[7] The task force was headed by William G. Demas, then president of Caribbean Development Bank, and included Patrick Alleyne, permanent secretary, Ministry of Agriculture; Eldon Warner, general manager, Industrial Development Corporation; Frank Barsotti, permanent secretary; T.A. Harewood, director, Research and Development of the Ministry of Finance and Planning; Joyce Alcantara, permanent secretary, Ministry of Public Utilities and National Transportation; Norbert Masson, permanent secretary, Ministry of Education; Trevor Boopsingh, permanent secretary, Ministry of Energy and Natural Resources; Frank Rampersad, chairman-designate of NIHERST; Patricia Robinson, director of NIHERST; Eric St Cyr and Carlton J. Bruce, senior lecturers in the Department of Economics at the University of the West Indies; Euric Bobb, deputy governor, Central Bank; and Doddridge Alleyne, permanent secretary to the prime minister.

Apart from the two university academics, the task force is notable for its dominant public sector and technocratic composition. It was also heavily weighted

with economists. At least eleven of the fourteen members were economists. Notable as well is the fact that several of its members, including of course William
Demas himself, were involved in the work on the second and third five-year plans.
It is not surprising, therefore, that the task force report emerged with much the
same structure and approach, if not the "look and feel", as the five-year plans of
the 1960s. The task force was referred to as the "Demas Task Force". The report
writing had a distinctly more robust style and tone than the older five-year plans.
It posed questions and then answered them, and all in all seemed to want to com-
municate better with its audiences than the dry technocratic style of earlier plan
documents, while at the same time striving to maintain professional integrity.

The draft plan listed twenty-eight long-term objectives for the economy and
society in the year 2000. There was no prioritization or classification of the objectives listed. Table 12.1 seeks to classify the objectives listed, partly to enable a
better grasp of what the task force envisioned for the economy and society and
partly to point to the evolution of the idea of development since the 1950s and
1960s.

The classification reveals a much greater willingness on the part of the authors
to engage social, cultural and even political issues as a part of the approach to
development policy. The draft plan castigates "materialism", and enjoins the national community to exercise the right to vote and to refrain from "major social
transgressions" such as tax evasion, illegal export of currency, lack of integrity
in public, professional and business life, crude profiteering through excessively
high markups and low-quality goods, and engaging in real estate speculation. The
reference to regional and spatial planning is also new, and this included the shift
of the population centres away from Port of Spain to the eastern counties. The
explicit reference to the relationship with Tobago is also new and reflected the
emergence of a strong movement for self-government within Tobago.

Development Strategies: 1983–1986

The Demas Task Force put forward eight development strategies for Trinidad
and Tobago for the plan period 1983 to 1986. The first strategy involved effecting change in the patterns of production and consumption by increasing crude
oil production through deeper drilling, and secondary and tertiary recovery
methods, as well as upgrade of the refinery slate to produce lighter ends; reducing
acreage devoted to sugar, cocoa and coffee, and expansion of the production of
tropical woods, flowers and fruit; downstream manufacturing from the output of
the heavy industries, development of the "residentiary" sector, and export promotion; and expansion of the tourism sector.

Table 12.1 Classification of Plan Objectives, Demas Task Force Report, 1983

Economic	Social/Political	Cultural/ Managerial
Economic diversification	Preservation of political, economic and cultural independence	Sound management and technology adaptation processes for efficient production
Greater local food production and efficient farms – small, medium and large scale	Improved income distribution	Private sector more disposed to risk-taking and innovation
Well-managed and -maintained economic and social infrastructure, including public utilities	"Health for all"	Greater sense of national and Caribbean identity and self-respect
Mixed economy with public and private partnerships, and regional partnerships	Decentralization and people participation in both government and enterprise	More efficient and motivated public service
Deeper and wider Caribbean integration	Increasingly participatory democratic system with improved social discipline and work ethic	
Numerate labour force; higher employment, especially skilled employment	Free secondary education; on-the-job training; expanded tertiary education (10% of age cohort)	
Better spatial location of population and economic activity and improved public transportation	Greater gender equality	
A "healthy" tourist industry	Youth alienation, values and sense of direction	
Broader and more innovative banking and financial services	National cohesion with particular reference to relations with Tobago	

Second, the plan called for protection of the balance of payments and development of a realistic public sector investment programme, while achieving fiscal balance; this was seen to involve reduction of subsidies, increases in indirect taxation and widening of the tax net, buttressed by a "pause" in increases in wages and salaries.

Third, the plan would seek to effect a more equitable sharing of the burden of adjustment by focusing restraint not only on wages and salaries but also on prices and rents, while encouraging the reinvestment of profits. The fourth strategy related to the roles of the state, and the local and foreign private sectors. Unviable state enterprises "should be allowed to die", and weak private sector firms should not be rescued by government. Foreign investment was welcome, except in sectors such as petroleum, banking, insurance, mass media, certain agricultural activities and the public utilities.

The other four strategies related to criteria for the size and composition of the public sector investment programme, reform of the public service, maintaining employment as best as possible during the period of adjustment and supporting regional integration initiatives.

Assessment of the Imperatives of Adjustment

The Demas Task Force was clearly very conscious that the economy was sliding quickly into economic trouble, if not distress. This awareness pervades the plan document, so that even though there is an eye to the long-term structure of the economy and society, the focus was definitely on managing the decline in the country's economic fortunes resulting from the collapse of oil prices and the attendant fall in government revenues. The "Imperatives of Adjustment" was therefore appropriately named. The report pulled no punches in its recommendations for fiscal responsibility, recognizing that the capital programme (the public sector investment programme) had to be scaled back, and recurrent expenditure reduced, including the very transfers and subsidies that supported the less well off in the society.

In respect of development policy, while the technocrats are still ambivalent about the capacity and commitment of local and foreign private sectors to development, there is a growing appreciation that the notion that state enterprise engagement in directly productive activities was the solution needed to be questioned, as the experience in the previous decade had not been particularly good. There is also a greater appreciation and awareness of the influence of social and cultural factors, and the values and attitudes of the population in the process of development. As before, the approach to planning was top-down and highly technocratic, even if there was a greater concern to explain the rationale for the policies advocated in the plan. Finally, there is an absence of quantification in the plan. There are no macroeconomic projections, no attempt at input-output analysis or econometric work. The plan document was very much in the literary, descriptive tradition of Caribbean economics.[8]

Development Planning under the NAR Administration

It is interesting to note that in the midst of grappling with the problems of stabilization and adjustment under the IMF and debt restructurings, the NAR administration, which came to power in December 1986, attempted to prepare a
development plan. A draft medium-term planning framework was produced in
July 1988 under a revived National Planning Commission chaired by A.N.R. Robinson, the prime minister. The National Planning Commission had been established in 1987 and comprised representatives of the government, business, labour
and three persons representing the "public". In addition to the National Planning
Commission, the government had also revived a National Economic Advisory
Council (NEAC) and a Joint Consultative Council. The Ministry of Planning and
Mobilization had prepared the plan for submission to and consideration by the
National Planning Commission. Although the draft plan sought to emphasize the
consultation process, the approach to the planning exercise was similar to those
of the second and third five-year plans.[9]

The draft plan noted that some progress had been achieved in respect of certain
indicators of development, including the physical quality of life index, nutrition,
physicians per thousand population and other health status measures. However,
the draft plan also observed that "the degree of structural transformation secured
so far falls well short of objectives so frequently reiterated in past development
plans".[10] The draft plan identified the "structural weaknesses" of the economy as:
dependence on petroleum in terms of GDP, government revenue and exports;
openness of the economy arising from the imbalance between the structure of
demand and the structure of supply such that the economy needed to be assured
of a flow of foreign exchange to support demand; absence of economic linkages
between the various sectors such that demand for inputs had to be satisfied by imports; technological dependence; the constraint of size which led to oligopolistic
market structures and limited benefits of competition; the high cost of production
due to wage-price escalation and underutilization of capacity; persistent unemployment; and widespread involvement of the government in directly productive
economic activity.

The plan objectives were identified as follows:

- economic diversification incorporating the promotion of inter-industry
  linkages
- self-sufficiency in food production
- entrepreneurship, innovation and investment
- commitment to efficiency, productivity and a positive work ethic
- capability in science, technology and management

- education system supportive of development
- social cohesiveness and social responsibility
- productive employment opportunities
- heightened national commitment and identity through public participation
- attention to the basic needs of the population
- acceptable distribution of benefits
- efficient social and economic infrastructure; avoidance of discrimination (age, ethnicity or gender)
- preservation of economic, political and cultural independence
- regional cooperation.

This laundry list of "objectives", which was very similar to the list developed by the Demas Task Force earlier in the decade, reflects perhaps a highly politicized process in its formulation rather than rational policymaking. Objectives such as "commitment" "cohesiveness" or "identity" are difficult if not impossible to define adequately much less to quantify or measure. Moreover, according to the theory of economic policy, the attainment of these objectives may require as many if not more policy instruments.

Rethinking the Development Strategy

Acknowledging that the strategy of import substituting industrialization based on protection of manufacturing geared to the domestic market had led to inefficiency, high production costs and an overvalued exchange rate, the draft plan proposes an outward-looking or export-oriented strategy that, though riskier, "offers greater opportunity for sustained growth and the emergence of a robust economy".[11] The draft plan saw the need to focus on nontraditional exports, particularly those which exploited the country's natural resource base, and those which exploited the "skills and creativity of the population".

In respect of income distribution, the draft plan eschewed the "trickle down" approach of accumulate first and distribute later. It also advocated a careful balancing of the use of external versus domestic resources to finance growth and development so as not to create unsustainable debt burdens.

Shifting from the macro level to the sectoral level, the development strategy singled out agriculture, petroleum, manufacturing and tourism for attention. In respect of agriculture, the draft plan envisaged the development of nontraditional export agriculture alongside the thrust towards food self-sufficiency. Sugar was to be rationalized by redeploying some sugar lands to other crops while improving efficiency and yields in the sugar industry itself. Agro-processing and fisheries were also discussed. The draft plan identified the set of policy instruments that would be used to achieve the objectives set for agriculture. These were: infrastructure, especially access roads; land distribution and land tenure regularization; marketing facilities; subsidies and price support; credit; research and development; extension services; and training and ensuring adequate human resource in the sector. However, although noting that the development of agriculture would require a substantial amount of resources, there is no analysis of the organization of the sector and what sets of incentives would be required to influence the behaviour of farmers and distributors to achieve the desired outcomes.

In respect of the petroleum sector, the draft plan indicated the need to intensify exploration so as to boost production and reserves of crude oil as well as natural gas. Refining needed to be upgraded to shift away from fuel oil and to produce a higher value slate of products. Additional petrochemical plants – ammonia, urea and methanol – needed to be brought on stream to permit more rapid monetization of the gas resource. The draft plan envisaged modifications to the fiscal regime, specifically the supplemental petroleum tax, to encourage additional crude oil exploration and production, implementation of a lease operatorship and farm out programme to stimulate land production, the formation of a single national oil company (combining TRINTOC and Trintopec), and the rationalization of refining capacity. In respect of natural gas, flaring was to be curtailed and "appropriate incentives" were to be given for the development of additional gas fields.

In respect of manufacturing, the draft plan proposed to effect a shift towards export manufacturing by phasing out protection and fostering increased linkages with the agriculture sector and with raw material inputs from the CARICOM region. The strategic areas identified were agro-industry and wood-based manufacturing, the downstream gas-based industries – ammonia, urea and methanol – high-technology industries based on "microprocessor technology" and labour-intensive industries with export potential. Industrial development was to be accelerated by a set of fiscal and other incentives including tax holidays, duty-free concessions, protection via negative listing (quotas), soft loans and so on. Small business was to be stimulated by the provision of concessionary finance through the Industrial Development Corporation and the Agricultural Development Bank.

The tourism thrust was to be founded not on mass tourism but on "special interest" tourism, supported by expansion and upgrading of the tourism infrastructure.

Assessment of the Draft Plan of 1988

The Draft Plan of 1988 was broadly similar to the earlier development plans of the 1960s. One important difference was the emphasis given to technology innovation, research and development, and technology transfer, which had emerged in the development literature in the 1970s and early 1980s.[12] However, it lacked any semblance of a quantitative model that would either identify gaps at the macroeconomic level or the absence of linkages at the sectoral level. Targets were not quantified, nor in most cases were the indicators of social or economic change identified. Too much cannot be made of these lacunae, however, as it could be argued that the draft plan still had to go through further consultation and technical work before it was finalized as the National Development Plan, which would "elaborate on the chosen development strategies (national/sectoral/regional), the major development programmes, resource allocation (physical, financial, human), the time sequencing for implementation and the institutional arrangements".[13]

It would be fair to say that the draft plan was never implemented. The final plan was not completed. Indeed, it is somewhat surprising that in the midst of dealing with the IMF programmes, debt restructuring and fiscal stringency, the government was able to produce a development plan at all. In the event, the plan was overtaken by the attempted coup in July 1990, from which the government never really recovered and a broken party lost the 1991 general election to a resurgent PNM with the new United National Congress as the official opposition.

13

In the Embrace of the International Monetary Fund

Stabilization and Adjustment

Concern or uneasiness about the sustainability of the high level of oil prices and burgeoning government revenues and expenditures was abroad even in the late 1970s. The Bobb Committee was appointed in 1978 to review fiscal policy. The committee, which reported in 1979, pointed out that

> the pattern and rate of growth of government expenditures was unsustainable, especially as oil prices could not be expected to continue rising and oil production seemed to have peaked. The Committee recommended that new welfare programmes should not be adopted and the real value of existing programmes be maintained. Further, it suggested that there be a moratorium on further tax reduction from the 1979 fiscal year and that the scope for additional taxation and higher utility tariffs should be examined.[1]

However, oil prices surged again in late 1979, and the concerns and unease about the sustainability of government expenditures quickly dissipated and the upward march of government expenditure resumed at an even faster pace. Oil production did indeed peak in 1978 and began a relentless march downward, falling to less than 140,000 barrels per day by 1992, a rate of production not seen since the early 1960s (figure 13.1). The impact of falling oil production on government

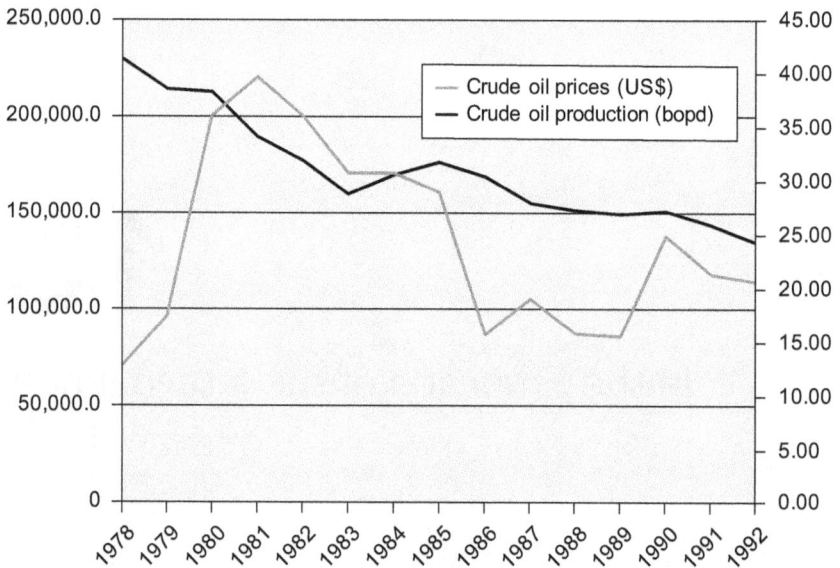

Figure 13.1 Crude oil production and prices, 1978–1992

revenues was masked in the period up to 1982 because oil prices were still high after the second oil shock in 1979. But when oil prices began to fall from 1981, the game was over and adjustment had to be undertaken.

Government expenditures are typically difficult to adjust. Capital expenditures on projects that have not yet begun can be deferred, but recurrent expenditures – wages, salaries, transfers and subsidies in particular – are hard to curtail and harder still to reduce. Moreover, increases in taxation are politically fraught. Recurrent expenditures had escalated between 1979 and 1982. Public service unions negotiated significant wage increases for the years 1981 to 1983, and the wage bill of the central government rose by 121.2 per cent in 1982 alone owing to the payment of retroactive wage increases.[2] This could not have come at a worse time. Consumption expenditures rose, as did inflation, at 17.5 per cent in 1980, 14.3 per cent in 1981, 11.4 per cent in 1982 and 16.7 per cent in 1983.

Oil revenues plateaued and then began to fall in absolute terms from 1982, even as government expenditure continued to escalate. Total revenues flatlined. The result was the opening up of massive fiscal deficits. As a percentage of GDP, the overall fiscal deficits reached 14.4 per cent in 1982, 13.1 per cent in 1983, 11.9 per cent in 1984, 7.5 per cent in 1985 and 8 per cent in 1986. The country's foreign exchange reserves began to fall precipitously from 1982 from a then historic high of US$3.2 billion to just US$493.5 million in 1986. By 1988 net reserves were negative. As the foreign exchange reserves declined, domestic and

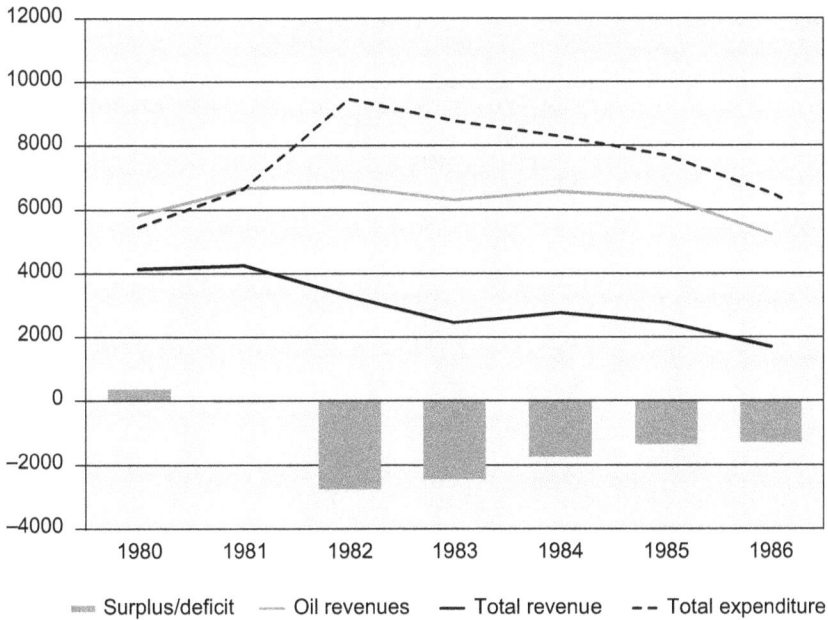

Figure 13.2 Fiscal operations, 1980–1986 (TT$M)

external debt mounted. External debt doubled from just under US$1 billion in 1981 to US$2 billion in 1986. The external debt service ratio rose from 5.8 per cent of exports in 1982 to 11.3 per cent in 1986, while the debt-GDP ratio rose from 10.9 per cent in 1982 to 43.5 per cent in 1987.[3] In the face of the tectonic external shock of collapsing oil prices and an unpropitious international environment characterized by inflation, recession and an international debt crisis, government sought to address the problem of stabilization and adjustment and achieve what was then described as a "soft landing" by a combination of fiscal, monetary and exchange measures.

Fiscal policy initially focused on expenditure reduction. Capital expenditure was halved from $3.6 billion in 1982 to $1.6 billion in 1985 and halved again to $878 million in 1986. Wages and salaries though remained at around the same level, while transfers and subsidies actually increased from $2.5 billion in 1982 to $2.9 billion in 1983, before falling slowly to $1.99 billion in 1986 (figure 13.4). This strategy did improve the overall fiscal deficits but there remained deficits, nonetheless, which increased aggregate demand and continued to pressure the balance of payments and the foreign exchange reserves. Expenditure reduction needed to be stronger, and expenditure switching also needed to be employed to halt the drain of the country's foreign exchange reserves.

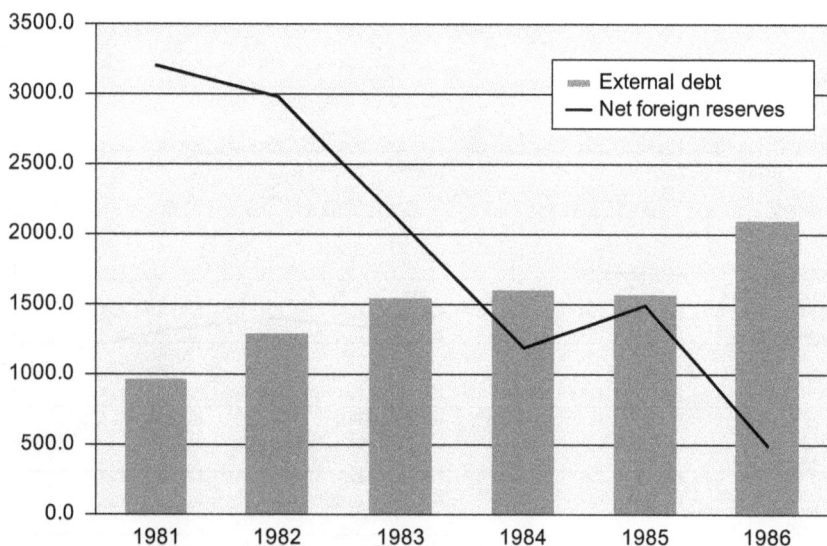

Figure 13.3 Net foreign reserves and external debt of public sector (US$ M), 1981–1986

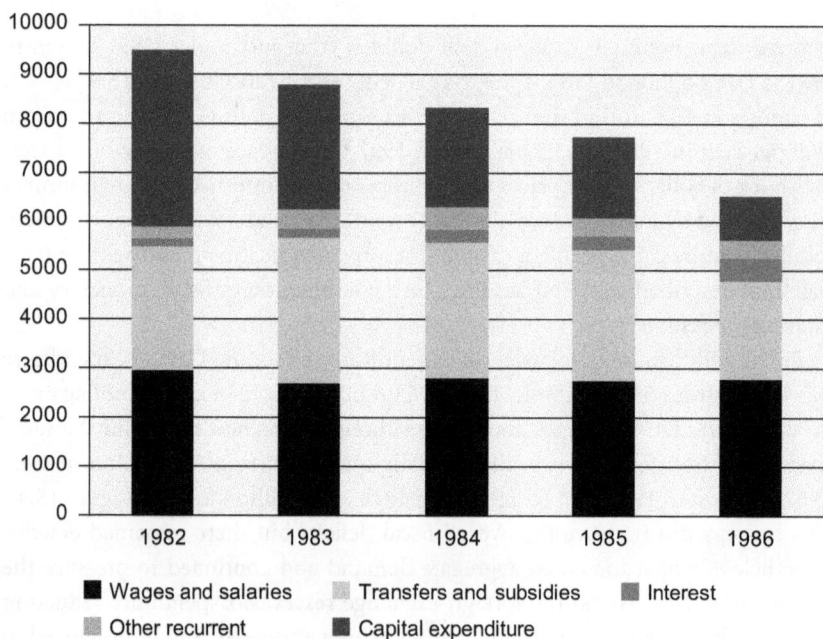

Figure 13.4 Composition of government expenditure, 1982–1986 (TT$M)

But it was exchange-rate policy that proved to be most problematic. Apart from the adjustment to the dollar peg in 1976, Trinidad and Tobago had enjoyed exchange-rate stability for most of the postwar period. The rapid decline in the foreign exchange reserves and the move to floating exchange rates in the 1970s now prompted consideration of exchange-rate adjustment to address the balance of payments deficits. Concern on the part of the trade union movement about the disproportionate impact on the working class of a devaluation, fear of further capital flight, as well as the "sacred cow" status of the exchange rate caused vacillation on exchange-rate adjustment within the government. Instead, direct controls on imports of goods and services were employed from October 1983 in the EC-Zero system. But it was clear by the end of 1984 that import compression by administrative action was not effective and indeed was counterproductive. In December 1985, the government was forced to devalue but using a dual exchange-rate system, whereby the old exchange rate was maintained for a scheduled list of items including food, drugs, school books and agricultural inputs.[4] The dual exchange-rate system was eventually abolished and unified under the NAR administration in January 1987.

However, by the time the NAR administration came into power, the foreign exchange reserves were exhausted and the country's borrowing capacity had reached its limit. Trinidad and Tobago had little choice at that stage but to begin to treat with the IMF for a standby arrangement. The IMF programme would open the door for additional external financing from the World Bank as well as debt restructuring with commercial banks, leasing companies and governments through the Paris Club. Access to the Compensatory and Contingency Financing Facility was obtained in November 1988. The first standby agreement ran from January 1989 to February 1990, followed by a second from April 1990 to March 1991. A structural adjustment loan was negotiated with the World Bank in 1990 and a business expansion and industrial restructuring loan in 1991.

The IMF arrangements opened the way for the required restructuring of the country's external debt. The period of restructuring was September 1988 to December 1992. Over this period, US$799 million was restructured, of which US$275 million was with bilateral creditors, US$452 million with commercial banks and US$72 million with leasing companies.[5] The government was required to reduce the fiscal deficit from 7 per cent in 1988 to about 4 per cent in 1989 and down further to 1 per cent by 1991. Among the measures the government took to meet the fiscal targets were reduction in the wage and salary bill in the public sector, which was accomplished with a 10 per cent cut in the salaries of public servants; and reduction in transfers to state enterprises. Several state enterprises were shut down and others divested. The loss-making Iron and Steel Company was leased to an Indian firm. The loss-making telephone company was partially divested to Cable and Wireless, and shares in the National Commercial Bank were sold to the public.

Capital expenditure was tightly controlled. Interest payments increased absolutely and as a proportion of total expenditure due to higher interest rates and the increase in the debt stock (figure 13.5). On the revenue side, a value added tax was introduced from 1990, replacing a plethora of indirect taxes that had accumulated over the previous decades. The individual and corporate taxation system was overhauled, with the number of tax brackets for individuals reduced drastically from eleven to four and the top marginal rate reduced from 70 per cent to 35 per cent. Corporation tax was similarly reduced from approximately 55 per cent to 40 per cent.[6]

The adjustment process that had begun in the middle of the decade with the devaluations and beginning of fiscal adjustment was completed over the period 1989 to 1991 under the aegis of the IMF as the fiscal deficits were reduced from over TT$1 billion in 1987 to near balance in 1991. Higher expenditure by the incoming administration pushed the deficit up to TT$628 million in 1992, but this was corrected swiftly in the subsequent years (figure 13.6). The country's foreign

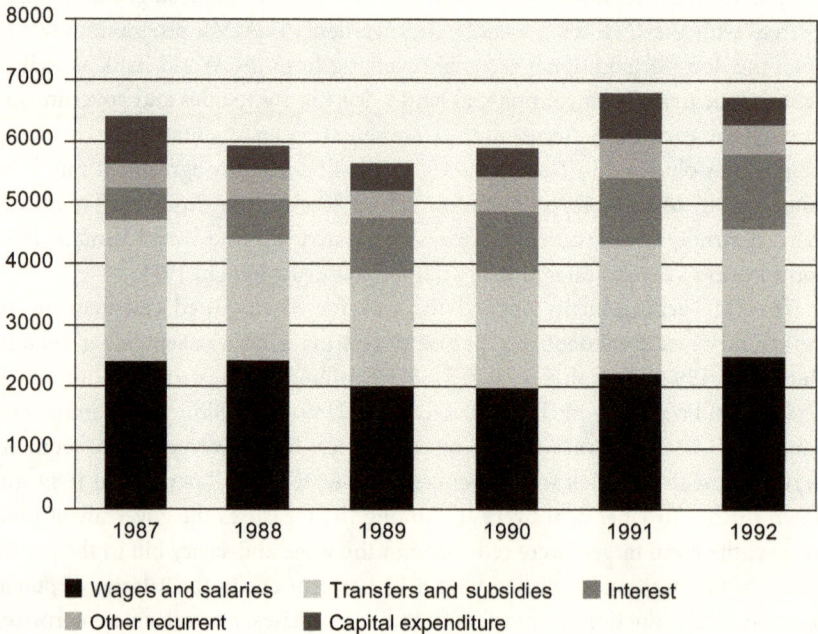

Figure 13.5 Composition of government expenditure, 1987–1992 (TT$M)

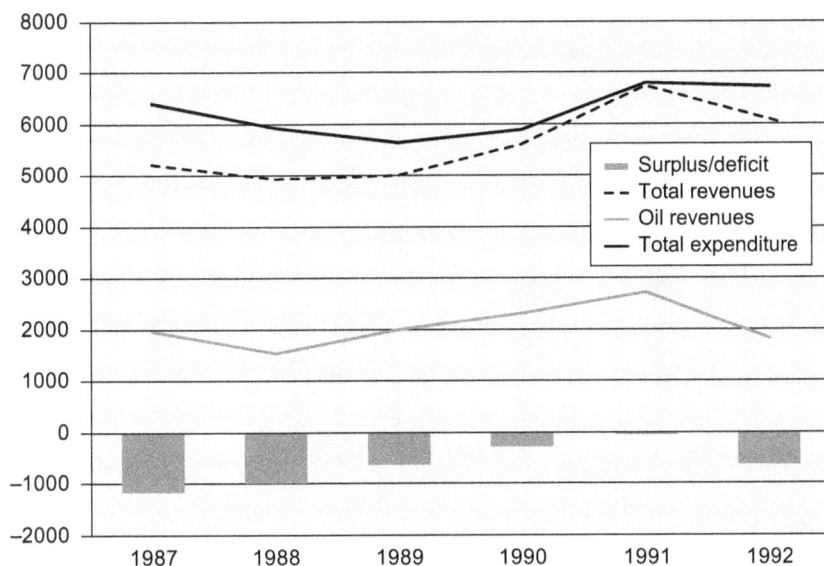

Figure 13.6 Fiscal operations, 1987–1992 (TT$M)

exchange reserves remained at precarious levels through 1992, while external debt levels peaked in 1990.

Monetary policy sought to make use of available instruments, specifically the cash reserve requirement, which was raised in effective terms from 13.6 per cent in 1981 to 17 per cent in 1985.[7] Monetary policy resulted in higher interest rates as the IMF programme limited central bank financing of the government deficit as well as commercial bank access to liquidity support from the central bank.[8] By the end of the period, treasury bill rates were twice as high as at the start, and bank prime had risen to over 15 per cent as had real estate mortgage rates, with serious consequences for mortgagors. Despite higher interest rates, banks and other financial institutions did not fare well in this period owing to increasing delinquencies and escalating loan loss provisions. By the middle of the decade, several financial institutions were in trouble and the Central Bank intervened in 1986 using newly acquired powers to take control of the Trinidad Cooperative Bank and to suspend the operations of some nonbank financial institutions. This culminated in the intervention into and merger of National Commercial Bank with the Workers Bank and Trinidad Cooperative Bank in 1993 to form the First Citizens Bank.

In respect of commercial policy, the system of import quotas implemented through the negative list began to be dismantled from 1989. Some items from which quotas were removed were afforded temporary protection by means of

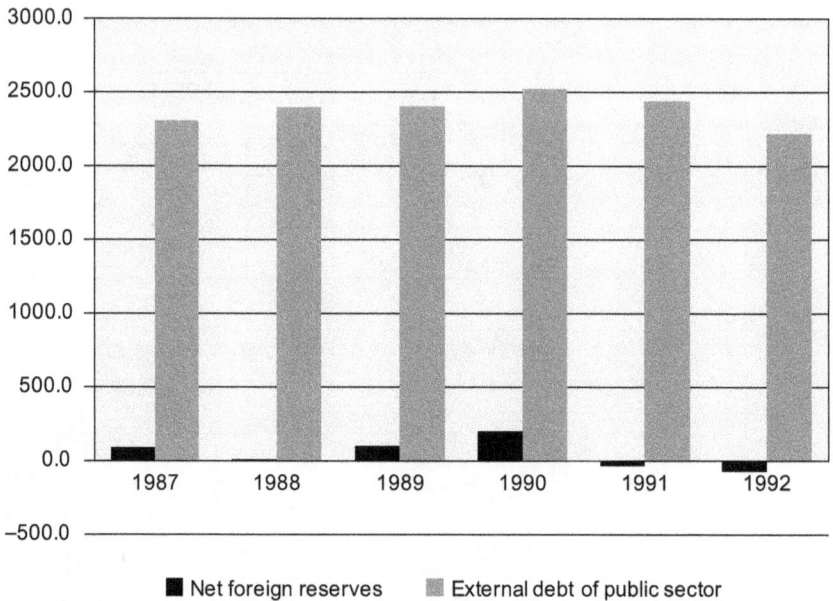

Net foreign reserves   **External debt of public sector**

Figure 13.7 Net foreign reserves and external debt of public sector US$M, 1987–1992

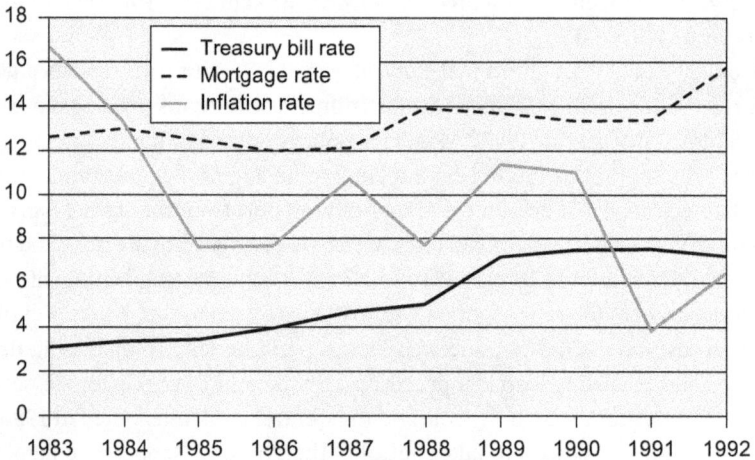

Figure 13.8 Inflation and interest rate movements (%), 1983–1992

import surcharges of 30 per cent. These import surcharges and stamp duties were eventually reduced and phased out during the 1990s.

Inflation was brought under control by the end of the period, falling from 17 per cent in 1982 to 3.8 per cent in 1991 and 6.5 per cent in 1992. The net effect

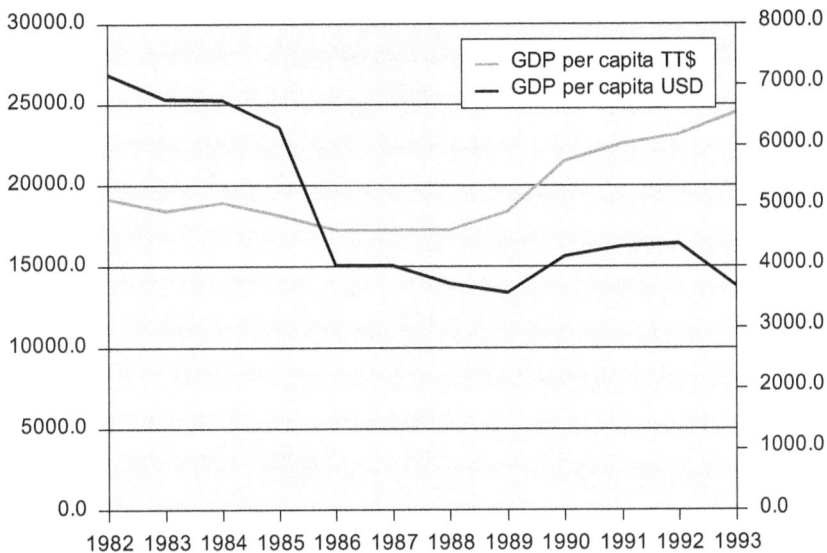

Figure 13.9 GDP per capita TT$ and US$, 1982–1993

of rising interest rates and falling inflation meant that real interest rates moved from being significantly negative at the start of the decade to significantly positive as the process of adjustment was completed at the beginning of the 1990s.

Growth and Transformation: 1983–1992

Considerations and objectives relating to economic and social development that had been harboured in the "imperatives of adjustment" multisectoral plan at the start of the decade had vanished, as did those in the abortive draft national plan of the NAR administration. As the decade wore on, policy became totally preoccupied with stabilization, adjustment and indeed economic survival.

In 1982, Trinidad and Tobago had enjoyed a level of GDP per capita of over US$7,000, making it at the time one of the richest developing countries in the world. By the end of the period of structural adjustment and stabilization in 1992, GDP per capita in US dollars had fallen massively by 45 per cent to just US$4,020.

In the ten years between 1983 and 1992, real GDP had fallen in eight of the ten years, with consistent annual declines between 1983 and 1989. Over the period, the structure of output did show some change. There was a significant decline in the share of construction, which employs a great deal of unskilled and semi-skilled labour. The share of government also shrank, reflecting the fiscal contraction over

Table 13.1 Changes in the Structure of Output: 1983, 1987 and 1992

Sector	1983	1987	1992
Petroleum	24%	25%	24%
Construction	15%	9%	8%
Government	14%	15%	12%
Finance, insurance, real estate	12%	12%	14%
Manufacturing	7%	8%	9%
Distribution	12%	14%	13%
Agriculture	2%	3%	3%
Transport storage communications	10%	10%	10%
Other services	3%	4%	8%
Total	100%	100%	100%

the period. Petroleum as well as transport, storage and communications maintained their shares of total GDP, and there were increases in the share of manufacturing, and finance, insurance and real estate services. The increase in "other services" reflects the value added tax, which was introduced in 1991.

The changes in the structure of expenditure are more revealing of the effects of stabilization and adjustment over the period. Consumption expenditure, imports and capital formation as a percentage of GDP all declined, while exports as a

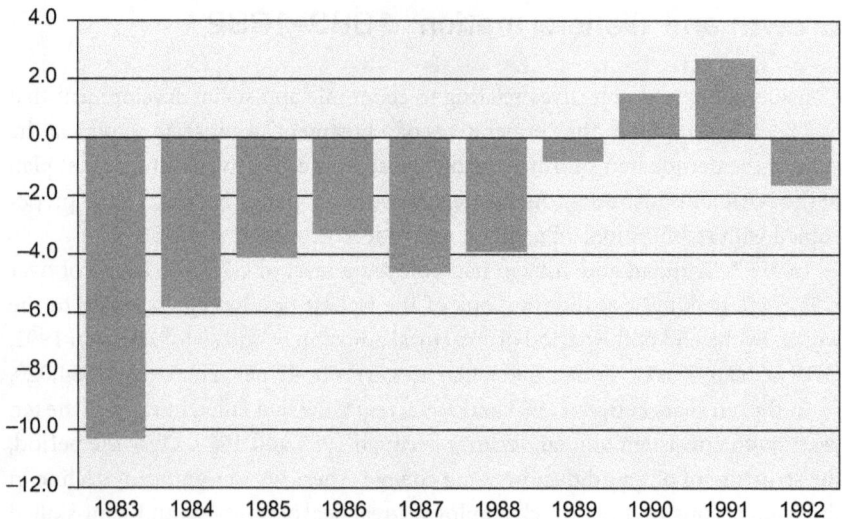

Figure 13.10 Real GDP growth rates, 1983–1992

Table 13.2 Investment Performance, 1983–1992

	1983–1987	1988–1992
Gross capital formation/gross domestic product	22%	15%
Foreign direct investment/gross capital formation	4%	17%
Government capital expenditure/ gross capital formation	39%	16%

Note: Some care is needed here as not all government capital expenditure is really capital formation.

percentage of GDP increased over the period, suggesting that the expenditure-switching impact of the devaluations had been effective.

The decline in investment expenditure (gross capital formation) was especially severe, from TT$4,790 million or 26 per cent of GDP in 1983 to TT$3,189 million or 14 per cent of GDP in 1992. Net capital formation fell from TT$3,336 million in 1983 to a paltry TT$575 million in 1992. Foreign direct investment collapsed to just TT$71.7 million in 1986 before beginning to recover to account for about 20 per cent of gross capital formation at the end of the period.

The real exchange rate had appreciated slightly between the shift to the US dollar peg in 1976 and 1984.[9] However, the devaluations in 1985 and 1986 and the effective devaluation that occurred with the floating of the TT dollar in 1993

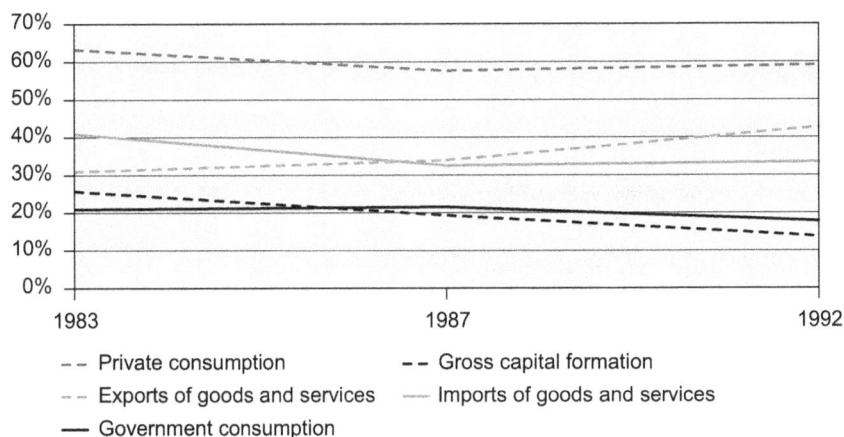

- Private consumption
- Exports of goods and services
- Government consumption
- Gross capital formation
- Imports of goods and services

Figure 13.11 Expenditure on GDP (% of GDP) (selected years, 1983–1992)

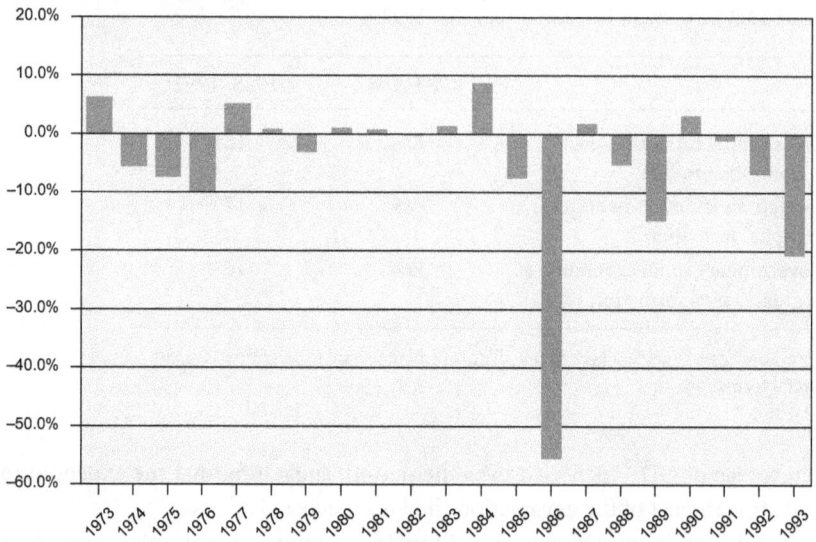

Figure 13.12 Change in real exchange rate, 1973 to 1993

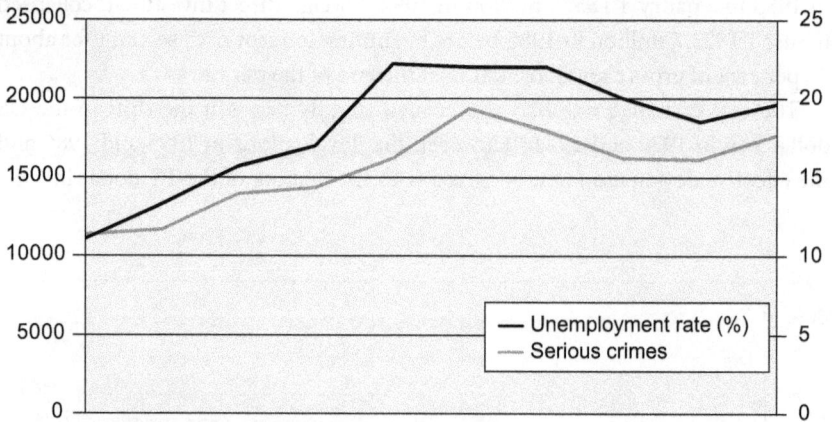

Figure 13.13 Unemployment rate (%) and serious crimes, 1983–1992

resulted in significant depreciation of the TT dollar and hence in a powerful incentive to exporters.

Unemployment rose from the post-independence low of 9.9 per cent in 1982 to historic highs of 22 per cent over 1987–89 before falling back to about 20 per cent at the end of the period. Rising inflation slashed purchasing power and real incomes, while the curtailment of government transfers and subsidies limited the relief that could be afforded to the most vulnerable in the society. A concomitant of higher unemployment was increasing poverty. Data on the change in the incidence of poverty over the period is limited, but one study using the household budgetary survey data estimated that "absolute poverty" increased dramatically from 3.5 per cent of households in 1981–82 to 14.8 per cent in 1988, then improved to 11 per cent in 1992.[10]

Income distribution worsened between 1982 and 1987, with the Gini coefficient rising from 0.45 in 1981–82 to 0.47 in 1988–89. However, the trend towards worsening inequality soon began to reverse so that by 1992, the Gini coefficient had improved to 0.42, albeit on a different measure (consumption) than the previous data.[11]

Not surprisingly, serious crimes escalated during the lost decade of the 1980s as economic and social conditions worsened, especially crimes against property such as break-ins, burglary and larceny in dwelling houses.

Conclusion

In the model of development driven by natural resources, failure to "break out" of the traditional "equilibrium" structure causes the economy to fall back into that traditional structure when the resource boom collapses.[12] This seems to have been the case with Trinidad and Tobago. The period of resource-based industrialization had not effected sufficient transformation of the structures of production and consumption so that when the boom collapsed, the economy reverted essentially to preboom conditions.

The stance of policy changed significantly over the period under review. Government retreated from centre stage as its financial resources were severely curtailed by declining foreign exchange reserves and burgeoning fiscal deficits. Industrial policy was sidelined in this period, although several plants already under construction were commissioned. Greater encouragement was again given to foreign direct investment, although private domestic savings had to be stimulated by higher (real) interest rates to enable the deficits to be financed. Exchange-rate policy became active for the first time in the country's history with devaluations followed by the managed floating of the TT dollar. Market-oriented policies required the lowering of protection on trade and tax reforms that would encourage private sector investment. Overall the stance of policy took on a decidedly neoclassical character and tone as the Washington Consensus came to dominate policy thinking. The changes in the stance of policy are indicated in the policy map in figure 13.14, which compares the stance of policy in the lost decade with the policy stances during the previous decade of resource-based industrialization.

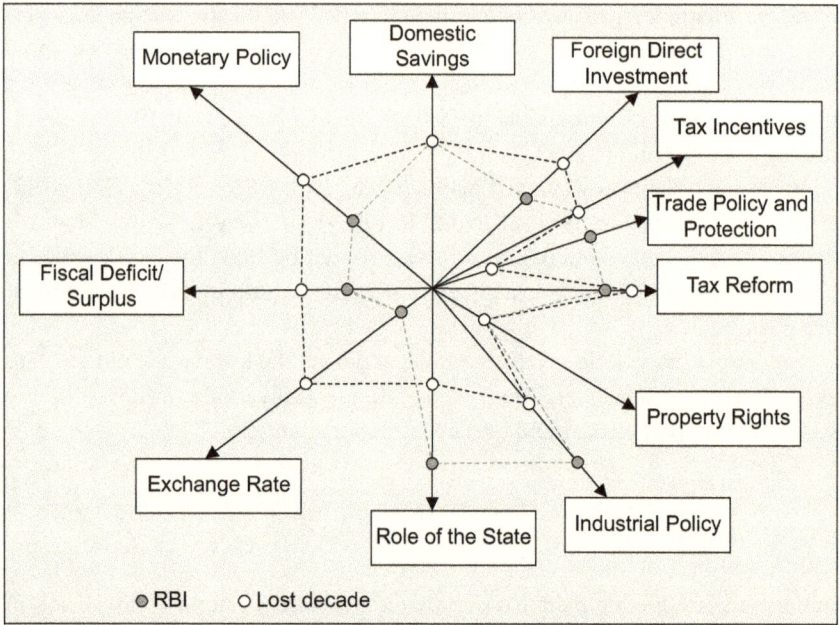

Figure 13.14 The lost decade

At the end of the period of stabilization and adjustment, however, the economy could again be poised to reestablish and resume a development agenda. But this was the era of the Washington Consensus and increasing scepticism about the development agenda. The downturn had reinforced the importance of economic diversification and reduced reliance on petroleum and the energy sector. But the new thinking was that the workings of the unfettered market would take care of the process of diversification. All governments needed to do was to establish the "enabling conditions" for investment and growth and get out of the way of the foreign and local private sectors. The pursuit of this path is discussed in part 5.

Part 5

The Neoliberal Phase, 1993–2008

14

Back to the Future

International Context

The epicentre of the international debt crisis of the 1980s was Latin America. The United States had emerged fairly well after the "Volcker Shock" in the early 1980s, and by the second half of the 1980s had returned to growth. However, by the end of the decade, the US economy was adversely affected by the "Savings and Loan" crisis. The ensuing credit crunch precipitated a recession, which helped to usher a Democrat, Bill Clinton, into the office of president of the United States in 1993. Margaret Thatcher had been cashiered by her Conservative Party, opening the door to John Major as prime minister from 1990 to 1997, but more particularly to Tony Blair and "New Labour" who won the government of the United Kingdom in 1997.

During the period of Clinton's presidency the United States experienced strong productivity-driven growth. After a small decline in 1991, GDP in the United States grew on average at 3.8 per cent per annum over the years 1992 to 2000. Personal consumption grew at an average annual rate of over 4 per cent and exports grew at over 7 per cent per year. The stock market rose almost without pause between 1993 and 2000, with the Dow Jones Industrial Average rising from 3,310 in January 1993 to 11,497 in December 1999 before retreating to under 11,000 at the end of December 2000, while the technology-heavy NASDAQ index, driven by the "dotcom" boom, rose from 696 in January 1993 to over 5,000 in March 2000 before falling dramatically to 2,470 in December 2000.

While the US economy grew at an unprecedented pace in the Clinton years, attended by low inflation, the East Asian countries that had performed "miraculously" in the previous decade went into a profound financial crisis, triggered initially in Thailand and Malaysia and spreading quickly to the rest of the East Asian countries. The East Asian financial crisis, which exploded in 1997, had been presaged by the Mexico debt crisis in 1994 and the Argentina crisis in 1995. However, the East Asian crisis was unexpected and occurred among countries that had been universally praised for good macroeconomic and development policies and that other developing countries were seeking to emulate.

The break up of the former Soviet Union led to the creation of several new states. Under Boris Yeltsin, Russia itself embraced free-market reforms and implemented these quickly and painfully, with the resulting traumatic Russian debt crisis in 1998. The new states came to be called "Economies in Transition", to distinguish them from the developing countries of the "Third World", but in recognition of the fact that they faced special and serious development challenges. The creation of these new states did have implications for countries like Trinidad and Tobago in that international capital flows, especially investment related to the exploitation of oil and gas reserves, were strongly attracted to these new emerging markets, and Trinidad and Tobago had to compete for investment as it relaunched the development and implementation of its gas and gas-based industrial development strategy.

In 1992, the Treaty of Maastricht inaugurated the European Community (EC) as successor to the European Economic Community and laid the basis for the creation and introduction of the Euro in 1999. In addition to the common currency, to which not all EC countries – notably the United Kingdom – subscribed, the EC provided for integration in respect of Justice and Home Affairs and Foreign Affairs and Security. In 1992, the North America Free Trade Area (NAFTA) was signed between the United States, Canada and Mexico, ratified by their respective legislatures in 1993, and came into force on 1 January 1994. The institution of NAFTA posed a problem for Caribbean countries that had been operating under the Caribbean Basin Initiative since 1984, and prompted efforts to extend NAFTA to the entire hemisphere in the so-called Free Trade Association of the Americas initiative.

In January 1995, the World Trade Organization (WTO) commenced operations, replacing the General Agreement on Tariffs and Trade (GATT), which had been established after World War II. The WTO initiated wide-ranging reductions in tariffs, with significant implications for the exports of manufactured goods and agricultural commodities from developing countries. More particularly, the WTO found that the Lomé IV agreement between the European Union and the African Caribbean and Pacific (ACP) countries was contrary to the WTO agreement, leading eventually to the virtual demise of the Caribbean banana and sugar industries, which had been heavily dependent on European subsidies.

The Caribbean, too, was pushed to try to deepen regional integration and accommodate the creation of new trading blocs. The Grand Anse Declaration of 1989 mandated that the Caribbean Community work towards the creation of a single market and economy in the shortest possible time. A West Indian Commission was established to help prepare West Indian peoples for the twenty-first century and in that context, to report on how greater economic and political unity could be achieved.[1] Suriname joined the Caribbean Community in 1995 and Haiti joined in 2002. The Revised Treaty of Chaguaramas was signed by Caribbean Heads of Government in July 2001, and the Caribbean Court of Justice, which would have original jurisdiction in respect of treaty matters, was inaugurated in 2005. The Revised Treaty sought to put in place the provisions for the implementation of a single market and economy as well as for competition policy and consumer protection through a new organ: the Competition Commission.[2]

The world was witnessing not only impulses for democratization and regional integration, but profound changes in technology that addressed personal productivity directly, but also corporate productivity and later on, social communication and networking. The "dotcom" boom was triggered by the emergence of the Internet in the early 1990s. Following on the PC revolution in the 1980s, and with the expansion of communications, these developments signalled not only ways of enhancing productivity within traditional industries but the development and prospects for new so-called knowledge-intensive industries such as software development, manufacture of chips and other components, and a range of services surrounding these new areas of economic activity. Broadband and mobile technologies began to become pervasive in the industrialized countries in the 2000s prompting concerns about the growing "digital divide" between the developed and developing countries and the likelihood that the gap between them would grow even wider.

Domestic Context

In 1993, the previous two decades had been a roller coaster ride for Trinidad and Tobago. In 1973 the economy had been in a parlous and perilous state. Rescued by the first and second oil price shocks, the economy boomed from 1974 to 1982. As oil prices collapsed, the economy also collapsed and worked its way through a period of structural adjustment before it began to re-emerge in 1992.

Over the fifteen-year period from 1993 to 2008, there were five general elections – 1995, 2000, 2001, 2002 and 2007; and three different parties or coalitions in power – the UNC-NAR, UNC, and PNM.[3] Despite that, we are able to characterize the overall stance of policy as "neoliberal" in that there were no shifts between these administrations in the attitude and approach to the market as the prime driver of growth, to the encouragement of foreign direct investment, to the preservation and protection of property rights, and to the role of the state as facilitator and enabler through the provision of infrastructure and development of human capital. All political parties have steadfastly and carefully eschewed ideological labels, and all have been pragmatic in the recognition of American hegemony in the Caribbean and the country's dependence on foreign investment.[4]

The PNM had regained power in 1991 after the previous NAR administration had been rent by division and secession, which led to the birth of the UNC in 1989, and then upset by the attempted coup in July 1990. The PNM had a new face under the leadership of Patrick Manning and a mixture of new and experienced ministers. Manning himself had been in government since the 1970s under Eric Williams, but with the decimation of the PNM at the polls in 1986, the old guard of George Chambers, Errol Mahabir and Kamaluddin Mohammed was ushered off the political stage. As only one of three PNM candidates to retain their seats, Manning inherited the leadership of the party and the post of leader of the opposition. Wendell Mottley, who had served in the Chambers administration as minister of industry and commerce, returned to the 1991 administration, this time as minister of finance. Lenny Saith, Keith Rowley and Ken Valley strode onto the political scene, along with Brian Kuei Tung who came from the private sector and was installed as minister of industry.

Inexplicably in 1995, the prime minister, Patrick Manning, called a snap election and the PNM saw its majority wiped away, gaining only seventeen seats in the thirty-six-member Lower House. The UNC also obtained seventeen seats, and the NAR in Tobago got the two parliamentary seats in Tobago. The NAR chose to support the UNC, which then formed the government under the leadership of Basdeo Panday as prime minister. Panday therefore became the first prime minister of East Indian descent in Trinidad and Tobago. The position of the government was further consolidated when two PNM members of parliament "crossed the floor" to support the UNC government.

The Development Strategy of the 1990s

The decade of adjustment had left the treasury in a parlous state, with already high debt service and little capacity to borrow. The government could no longer play the role of investor and entrepreneur as it had done in the 1970s, but had to assume the role of facilitator, consistent with the thinking that underlined the

Washington Consensus in a country still in the embrace of the IMF and the World Bank and still working through its restructured external debt obligations. The overriding concern of the new PNM administration was to return the economy to growth after a decade of adjustment, to reduce the high unemployment rate and to restore the foreign exchange reserves.[5]

It is difficult to discern in the annual budget statements of the period any coherent development strategy. Foreign direct investment was encouraged because the government did not have the resources to invest itself. Fiscal discipline and consolidation was emphasized because revenues were constrained, debt service was high, and the IMF and World Bank were active in monitoring macroeconomic policy. Exchange controls were to be abolished, not so much because of a commitment to free-market determination of the exchange rate, but because they had become bureaucratic, a source of corruption and a hindrance to business activity. What was clear was a shift in favour of supporting the private sector and business investment consistent with the Washington Consensus, and the notion that government regulations should be clear, simple and transparent.

However, there was no discussion of the preparation of a plan along the lines of the earlier efforts, and the government contented itself with three-year rolling medium-term policy frameworks, driven by the annual budget. Rather, the new administration picked up where it had left off in the 1970s, recalling Professor Ken Julien to head up the National Gas Company and as a member of the powerful energy subcommittee of the cabinet, and to move expeditiously to drive growth through the development of gas-based industries – ammonia, methanol and even the liquefied natural gas projects, which had been shelved earlier.[6] This renewal of industrial policy, focused on the energy sector, became the centrepiece of the development strategy. The budget speech of 1994 stated: "[The government] selected the energy and energy-related industries for early attention since we were of the view that this area could have the greatest impact in terms of growth and foreign exchange earnings over the medium term."[7]

The policy changes and initiatives to be implemented were the reform of petroleum taxation; the further development of industries downstream of natural gas, including liquefied natural gas; the abolition of exchange controls and institutional reform; the development of tourism and non-energy industries; and the divestment of state enterprises. These are discussed in turn below.

The UNC administration, during its tenure from 1995 to 2001, saw no reason to depart from these policies and initiatives and pursued them vigorously, even though that administration harboured politicians and trade unionists who were avowedly left of centre on the ideological spectrum. The prime minister, Basdeo Panday, had himself come from a trade union background as president of the sugar industry union and had often castigated publicly the so-called parasitic oligarchy, which he claimed ruled the country for their benefit. It was significant therefore that the prime minister chose Brian Kuei Tung, a businessman and accountant, as his minister of finance and fully supported the business-friendly policies that he continued to implement. In the 1998 Budget Statement, the minister of finance stated: "Over the years, Trinidad and Tobago has repeatedly squandered its chance [*sic*] to become the 'Economic Tiger of Latin America and the Caribbean'. . . . [I]t has become abundantly clear that what this country urgently needed was the new and aggressive business acumen which the Panday administration has brought to the Government."[8]

The rhetoric of the budget speeches presented by Kuei Tung included references to "equity" and poverty alleviation, but otherwise the thrust of policy was wholly consistent with what had gone before under both the PNM and the NAR administrations.[9] Minister Kuei Tung was clear in stating: "this Government will not embark on an economic policy that will serve to undermine the macroeconomic environment. Government intends to consolidate whatever may have been achieved thus far, and fine-tune the existing policy framework where appropriate, to extract a higher level of effectiveness and efficiency."[10]

Reform of Petroleum Taxation

In the face of falling crude oil production, lower oil prices, and stagnating natural gas reserves and production, the government moved quickly to reform the petroleum tax regime so as to encourage exploration and development of both crude oil and natural gas. The sets of allowances granted for deduction against the supplemental petroleum tax were expanded and the tax itself was transformed into a sliding-scale tax with rates rising as prices increased, and a differential between land and marine operations and between pre-1988 and post-1988 operations (table 14.1).

The Second Wave: Downstream Energy Industries and Liquefied Natural Gas

Those investments in ammonia, methanol and gas transportation, which had actually started in the late 1970s with the Point Lisas strategy of resource-based industrialization, were implemented during the lost decade of the 1980s at a time of depressed commodity prices. Those projects that had not yet started were placed on hold. As the economy recovered, the new administration determined to initiate investments in some of the projects planned since the 1970s, as well as newly

Table 14.1 Evolution of Petroleum Taxation, 1980–2005

Oil Taxation	1980	1989	1992	2005
Base	Consolidation of producing fields permitted, but refining and marketing separate	Base oil (Dec.1987) and additional oil	Gross income (allowances applied separately to land and marine operations)	Gross income
Pricing	Actual arm's length or reported prices	Actual arm's length or reported prices	Actual arm's length or reported prices	Actual arm's length or reported prices
Expenses	Capitalized and amortized over the life of the well	Capitalized and amortized over the life of the well	Capitalized and amortized over the life of the well	Capitalized and amortized over the life of the well
Royalty	10%–12 ½%	10%–12 ½%	10%–12 ½%	10%–12 ½%
Corporation tax/petroleum profits tax	45% Supplemental petroleum tax, royalty, depreciation, operating costs are deductions for petroleum profits tax throughput tax abolished and replaced with supplemental refining tax	45% Supplemental petroleum tax, royalty, depreciation, operating costs are deductions for petroleum profits tax	50% Supplemental petroleum tax, royalty, depreciation, operating costs are deductions for petroleum profits tax	50% Supplemental petroleum tax, royalty, depreciation, operating costs are deductions for petroleum profits tax
Supplemental petroleum tax	Land 35%; Marine 60% Levied on gross income net of certain deductions	Land 15%; marine 55% on base oil – land 5%; marine 20% on additional oil	Sliding scale beginning at US$13/barrel (0% supplemental petroleum tax) for marine and US$14 (0%) for land rising in increments of US$1 up to US$21/barrel and increments of US$1.50	Marine 0% to 42%; land 0% to 35%; deep water 0% to 18%

(continued)

Table 14.1 (*continued*)

Oil Taxation	1980	1989	1992	2005
			thereafter up to US$49.50 with the top band attracting supplemental petroleum tax of 45% and 36% for marine and 38% and 21% for land (pre- and post-1988)	Royalty and overriding royalty are the only deductions on gross income for supplemental petroleum tax
Deductions to supplemental petroleum tax	Production allowance; exploration drilling (150%) enhanced recovery (140%) royalty	Production allowance; exploration drilling (150%) enhanced recovery (140%) royalty	50% of geological and geophysical costs; exploration allowance of 100% of the direct cost of drilling exploration wells; heavy oil – 100% of all capital expenditure incurred in the drilling of wells and in the acquisition of machinery and plant for use in marine thermal recovery schemes; investment allowance: 40% of direct intangible drilling costs, and 40% of tangible costs; enhanced recovery (100%)	
Unemployment levy	5%	5%	5%	5%

formulated projects. Given the government's fiscal constraints, investment in these projects had to come from the private sector.

The NGC and the NEC took on the task of locating and securing the interest of foreign investors in the expansion of ammonia, methanol and urea production, as well as the production of liquefied natural gas, which had been mooted since the mid-1970s. The key difference between the "first wave" of resource-based industrialization and the "second wave" was that private sector companies were the principal investors and not the Government of Trinidad and Tobago. What is also remarkable is that one local private sector conglomerate, CL Financial – parent company of the largest insurance company in the country – decided to invest in the petrochemicals sector, specifically methanol, and by the end of the 1990s, had become the largest producer of methanol in the country and one of the largest exporters of methanol in the world, with production from several world-scale plants.

The reform of petroleum taxation had helped to boost natural gas reserves and production. Natural gas reserves doubled between 1993 and 2000 on the basis of increased production from companies committed to explore for and develop gas (figure 14.1).

Amoco, the major oil company operating in the country and the dominant supplier of gas, was persuaded to co-invest in the first liquefied natural gas plant, which began operation in 1999, along with British Gas, the Spanish firm Repsol and the state-owned NGC. By the end of the first decade of the new millennium, Trinidad and Tobago had become a significant exporter of liquefied natural gas to the United States.

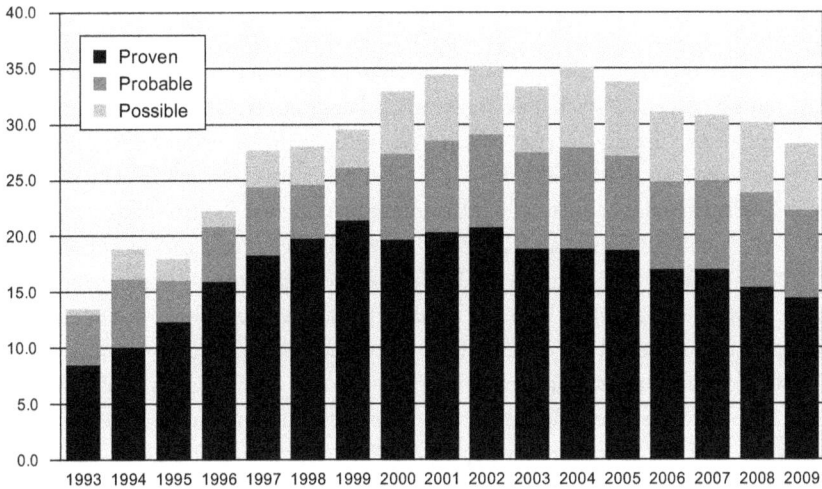

Figure 14.1 PPP Natural gas reserves, 1993–2009 (tcf)

Major petrochemical companies, such as Potash Corporation of Saskatchewan (PCS), Methanex, and new oil and gas companies like Repsol of Spain, made their appearance on the industrial landscape in this period.

More important, by the middle of the first decade of the new century, the queue of companies wishing to establish operations based on natural gas in Trinidad and Tobago had grown long and the availability of natural gas was becoming the critical constraint. Other constraints that began to emerge were the physical capacity of the Point Lisas industrial estate, which had become crowded; the availability of water; and the capacity of the port, which was open to general cargo. The liquefied natural gas trains were established in Point Fortin where Shell had once operated a refinery and had a good deep-water port. However, if additional plants were to be accommodated, new industrial estates needed to be built.

Energy-based industries need not only industrial estates from which to operate but also need vast quantities of water, electricity, port services and a reliable telecommunications system. Government was the facilitator for the provision of these infrastructure services. A desalination plant was built as a joint venture between Ionics (subsequently acquired by GE) with a local investor. Electricity generation capacity was added with the introduction of the Inncogen plant, a private-sector venture. A new airport terminal was built and the port facilities at Point Lisas were upgraded with new equipment and berthing.[11]

Abolition of Exchange Controls and Institutional Reform

The thinking underlying the Washington Consensus was allergic to any form of wage or price controls or controls over current transactions on the balance of payments by means of exchange controls. Exchange controls had been introduced in Trinidad and Tobago during World War II under the defence (finance) regulations and then strengthened with the Exchange Control Act of 1971. Up to the mid-1980s, exchange controls had been exercised by the central bank only over the services account and capital account. Control over merchandise imports was exercised through the Ministry of Trade and the negative list. During the crisis of the mid-1980s, controls by the central bank had been extended briefly to merchandise imports until the devaluations permitted relaxation of those controls.

The new administration determined to abolish exchange controls entirely, including controls over capital account transactions, an unprecedented policy move at the time even for developed market economies. The key elements of the policy when implemented over the Easter weekend in 1993 were as follows:

Table 14.2 Establishment of Energy-Based Plants at Point Lisas, 1993–2008:
The "Second Wave"

Plant	Start-Up Year	Ownership
Caribbean Methanol Company [Methanol Holdings Trinidad Limited (MHTL)]	1993	Local and foreign private joint venture: CL Financial, CLICO and Ferrostaal AG
T&T Methanol Company (MHTL)	1996	Formerly government; divested to CLICO, Ferrostaal AG, Helm AG and GE Capital in 1997
PCS Nitrogen III and IV	1996/1998	Private: formerly Arcadian
Farmland Misschem	1998	Foreign private
Methanol IV (MHTL)	1998	Local and foreign private joint venture: CL Financial, CLICO and Ferrostaal AG
Cleveland Cliffs Direct Reduced Iron	1999	Foreign private
Atlantic LNG Train 1	1999	Foreign private with local participation: BP Amoco, British Gas, Repsol/YPF, Tractebel and NGC
Titan Methanol (Methanex)	1999	Foreign private: Methanex Corporation
Atlantic LNG Train 2	2002	Foreign private: BP Amoco, British Gas, Repsol/YPF
Caribbean Nitrogen Company	2002	CL Financial with Helm AG, Ferrostaal AG, OPAG
Atlantic LNG Train 3	2003	Foreign private: BP Amoco, British Gas, Repsol/YPF
Atlas Methanol (Methanex)	2003	Foreign private joint venture between Methanex Corporation (63.1%) and BP Trinidad and Tobago LLC (36.9%)
N 2000	2004	CL Financial with Helm AG, Ferrostaal AG and others
M 5000 (MHTL)	2005	CL Financial with Helm AG, Ferrostaal AG and others
Atlantic LNG Train 4	2005	Foreign private: BP, NGC, Repsol/YPF
AUM (MHTL)	2009/2010	CL Financial with Helm AG, Ferrostaal AG and others

Source: Central Bank of Trinidad and Tobago, Balance of Payments, 2006 and 2007.

(1) further adjustment of the exchange rate to TT$5.76/US$1 in anticipation of a depreciation once controls were removed; (2) repeal of the Exchange Control Act; (3) allowing citizens to hold foreign currency accounts in local commercial banks; and (4) institutional arrangements for the management of the exchange rate so as to avoid dramatic falls in the selling price of foreign exchange, which could cause panic. The institutional arrangements were based on the facts that the majority of foreign exchange inflows accrued directly to the central bank through the government's tax take from oil companies in US dollars, and hence the central bank was a net seller of foreign exchange to the market and not a net buyer; and there were only a few commercial banks operating in the country, and so achieving the desired behaviour from those banks was relatively easy.

These elements made for a successful implementation and the system endured over the period without crises, although there are occasionally "queues" for foreign exchange in the commercial banks. Not insignificantly, residents of Trinidad and Tobago have accumulated over US$2.5 billion in foreign currency deposits at local commercial banks since the abolition of exchange controls.

Several initiatives to effect institutional reform were undertaken in the 1990s. These included promulgation in 1995 of a new Companies Act based largely on the Canadian model, replacing the old 1929 Companies Ordinance with which business had been operating, and the establishment of a revamped Companies Registry; promulgation of the Financial Institutions Act and the Securities Exchange Act establishing the Securities and Exchange Commission (SEC); establishment of an Intellectual Property Office and promulgation of a revised Patents Act; and implementation of the Tobago House of Assembly Act (1996), which provided for devolution of certain government functions to the THA.

Development of Tourism and Non-Energy Industries

During the planning years, economic diversification had meant essentially the expansion of the manufacturing sector through import substitution industrialization. At the industry level, the focus was on labour-intensive industries such as textiles and garments, assembly, and agro-processing, encouraged by various tax incentives and protected by import quotas and high tariffs.[12] Trade preferences were pursued under Commonwealth arrangements and later on through the Caribbean Basin Initiative with the United States; CARIBCAN, with Canada; and the Lomé Convention with the European Economic Community. Regional economic integration was also high on the agenda in those years culminating with the Treaty of Chaguaramas establishing the Caribbean Community in 1973, which would extend the free-trade arrangements to a common external tariff and possibly industrial programming or what later came to be termed "production integration".

In the emerging paradigm of the Washington Consensus, protection of domestic industry was frowned upon, as were preferential trading arrangements, and the example of the export-led East Asian economies suggested that development policy should place emphasis on export promotion rather than import substitution, whether national or regional.[13] It was also infra dig for governments to get involved in directly productive activities at the expense of the private sector, whether local or foreign, and worse still for governments to attempt to "pick winners" among industries. Tax incentives, especially long tax holidays, had been challenged by academic writers for being either unnecessary or ineffective. Regional integration movements or trading blocs were accepted by the Washington Consensus, but the emphasis was to be placed on free movement of capital and labour, and competition policy rather than on trade.

In this context, the development of non-energy industries was to be encouraged by institutional means and providing infrastructure, training and skills development. In respect of tourism, the Tourism and Industrial Development Company was established, combining the former Industrial Development Corporation and the former Tourism Board. Tax deductions were provided for equity investments in tourism projects. In 2002 a standing committee of cabinet on tourism was established and in 2004, a separate tourism development company was formed. A tourism master plan was commissioned in 1995. The Tourism Development Act was passed in 2000. Given the fiscal constraints in the 1990s, much of the effort in developing tourism was made by the marketing expenditure of the Tourism and Industrial Development Corporation to promote the country as a destination. The major private sector projects over the period were the hotel and resort development at Lowlands in Tobago and the construction of a hotel and conference centre on the Port of Spain waterfront. The idea of Trinidad and Tobago as the business and financial centre of the Caribbean surfaced and got some impetus with the effort to establish Port of Spain as the headquarters site of the proposed Free Trade Area of the Americas (FTAA), an initiative that was eventually stillborn.

Additional institutions were created to drive the development of the non-energy sector. These included the National Entrepreneurship Development Corporation, the Business Development Company, e Teck, Free Zones Company and the National Agricultural Marketing Development Company. Training and skills development was encouraged through a plethora of institutions such as the Trinidad and Tobago Hospitality and Tourism Institute, Youth Training and Employment Partnership Programme (YTEPP), Multi-Sector Skills Training Programme (MUST), Helping Youth Prepare for Employment (HYPE), National Energy Skills

Centre, National Skills Development Programme and in 2004 the University of Trinidad and Tobago was established.

In the 1990s, still under the more or less direct influence of the Washington institutions through World Bank loans and under fiscal constraints, successive administrations moved forward with the divestment of state enterprises and extended the process to the public utilities – water and electricity – in order to improve efficiency. An English water company (Severn Trent) was brought in to manage the Water and Sewerage Authority. Electricity generation was excised from distribution, with the Trinidad and Tobago Electricity Commission (TTEC) retaining sole responsibility for distribution, but electricity generation was placed in 1994 in the hands of a joint venture (Powergen), with a US company, Mirant, owning 39 per cent, BP owning 10 per cent and TTEC 51 per cent. In 1999, a wholly private company, Inncogen (Trinity Power) established a power genera-tion plant at Brechin Castle in central Trinidad. By 2006, the country's generation capacity had grown to 1,624 MW across combined cycle, gas turbine, diesel (To-bago) and steam-generation plants.[14]

In the subperiod from 2000 to 2008, the government sought to place greater emphasis on enabling industrial development. The Telecommunications Act of 2001 sought to provide for the entry of new providers for mobile and broadband services, interconnection, spectrum management and the regulation of tele-communications matters through a telecommunications authority. In 2003 the government prepared and published its strategy, dubbed "FastForward", for the development of the information and communication technology sector.[15] The document proposed fourteen initiatives over five years to 2008, costing US$82 million to achieve the goals of the information and communication technology strategy.

In a potentially significant departure from the strict neoliberal approach to industrial development, the government from 2003 sought to identify spe-cific industries on which it would focus its incentive and development efforts. Seven industries were identified. These were (1) yachting (leisure marine); (2) fish and fish processing; (3) merchant marine; (4) music and entertainment; (5) film; (6) food and beverage; and (7) printing and packaging. Strategic plans were developed for each of these in consultation with "stakeholder" groups. The role of government was declared to remain largely facilitative, with the ac-tual implementation of the strategic plans the responsibility of the stakeholder groups.

Much of government's development expenditure in the second subperiod, from 2003 to 2008, flowed through two institutions: the Urban Development Corporation of Trinidad and Tobago (UDECOTT) and the Housing Develop-ment Corporation. UDECOTT was formed in 1994 as a state enterprise, but its construction activities began in earnest after 2003 when it began to undertake several large-scale projects for public buildings in the capital city of Port of Spain, the city of San Fernando, as well as a variety of residential housing, stadiums and other projects across the island.

The government, arguing that housing was a "basic need" and lamenting the inadequate response of the private sector in this regard, announced in 2002 that nine thousand houses needed to be built per year to address the housing deficit, of which the government would seek to provide eight thousand per year. The private sector would deliver the rest, mainly to upper-middle and upper income groups. The Housing Development Corporation was established in 2005 as a statutory corporation replacing the National Housing Authority, and proceeded over the period after its establishment, to construct low- and middle-income housing on both green field sites as well as infill developments across the island. The housing construction effort was supplemented by adjustments in the mortgage finance programme to lower interest rates and down-payment requirements, as well as the introduction of tax benefits for first-time home owners.

Divestment of State Enterprises and Formation of Special-Purpose State Enterprises

Over the period characterized here as the neoliberal phase, there were important shifts in the policy towards state enterprises. In the early part of the period, while the country was still in the thrall of the multilateral institutions, it was de rigueur to divest state enterprises as part of the overall thrust to reduce the role and scope of government in the economy, and also as a practical means of revenue raising. A divestment secretariat was established within the Ministry of Finance to oversee the sale of nonstrategic state companies or close loss-making entities. In the 1990s the government undertook the partial divestment of the National Flour Mills and Trinidad Cement Limited.

Without doubt the most important divestment undertaken was the reorganization of Caroni (1975) Limited, the sugar manufacturing company, and with it the effective dismantling of the sugar industry in Trinidad and Tobago. The sugar industry had for a long time been a sacred cow. It was clear that it was un-economic even in social terms for several decades. But the fact that it employed several thousand persons, mostly of East Indian descent, and was concentrated in central Trinidad where a great deal of economic activity revolved around the sugar industry had given pause to successive governments who were minded to reduce or eliminate the massive subsidies the industry enjoyed. Over the years there had been several reports and commissions on the future of the sugar industry and how it might be made viable. However, the removal of preferences with the creation of the European Union was the final nail in the coffin of the sugar industry.

The reorganization of Caroni (1975) Limited, the largest landowner in the nation, began in 2003 and involved an enhanced Voluntary Separation of Employment Programme to all employees of Caroni; transfer of all lands to the state; lease back to Caroni (1975) Limited lands that were needed for the pursuit of its core agricultural business and lease of lands to cane farmers who were continuing cane production; and establishment of the Estate Management and Business Development Company Limited to manage the lands leased to them by the state for the purpose of stimulating and facilitating new business activity in the areas of light and heavy industrial manufacturing, agricultural estates, housing estates, and commercial complexes. Caroni (1975) Limited remained in the sugar processing business until 2007 on the basis of cane production by cane farmers.

Another sacred cow was the loss-making national airline, BWIA. In 2005 a task force was appointed under the chairmanship of Arthur Lok Jack to advise on the future of BWIA.[16] The task force considered seriously all options, including the closure of the airline without any replacement and the establishment of a new airline, and eventually recommended the restructuring of the airline provided that a range of issues in respect of the management of the airline and other conditions of its operation were addressed. The government accepted this approach and established a restructured BWIA under the name Caribbean Airlines Limited (CAL).

The government became increasingly concerned about the limitations of the mainstream public service in the efficient and effective implementation of its plans and policies. This had long been a concern and explains the institutional mechanisms employed in the 1970s to implement the Point Lisas strategy.[17] The public service enjoyed constitutional protections from the politicians. These protections came to be viewed, not without justification, as the source of bureaucracy, slowness in programme implementation and "maximum administrative delay". Efforts at reform had begun during the 1991–95 PNM administration and continued through successive administrations. Ministers of government found that they could not exercise effective discipline over public officers. At the same time, the compensation arrangements within the public service were geared to maximize the numbers employed rather than attract and keep the best and the brightest in the public service. Performance management was weak.

As reform efforts were stymied, the PNM government of 2002–8 developed and made extensive use of the Special Purpose State Enterprises (SPSEs) as a workaround. Unlike the state enterprises of the 1960s and 1970s, which were commercial enterprises, many of these SPSEs were not really commercial enterprises but rather performed services that might otherwise have been located within the public service.

By 2008, there were fifty-seven state enterprises, several of which – such as UDECOTT, the Housing Development Corporation and the University of Trinidad and Tobago – were responsible for the expenditure of public funds running into the hundreds of millions with procurement guidelines and governance structures that were less than ideal.[18]

Private Sector Investments in the Caribbean

The essence of the neoliberal approach to economic management is the ceding of space by the government to the private sector. It is appropriate therefore to note the developments in the local private sector during the neoliberal phase from 1993 to 2008.

Already noted is the fact that a large local conglomerate, CL Financial, became one of the major investors in the energy-based downstream industries from the 1990s. However, several other local private sector companies began to expand aggressively in the Caribbean in the late 1990s and into the new millennium. The regional expansion strategy of these companies was facilitated by the removal of exchange controls, including controls on the capital account; and a strong and growing economy in the home market of Trinidad and Tobago. Jamaica was a favoured destination market since it was perceived as a fairly large market, its financial sector had run into trouble and the government there opened the market to foreign and, especially, regional investment. However, local companies searched for acquisition targets anywhere in the region, including the Spanish-speaking territories and even extraregionally. A non-exhaustive list of acquisitions and expansions is provided in table 14.3.

In addition to the acquisitions and expansions identified, smaller Trinidad and Tobago insurance companies have established branches or agencies in several Caribbean states. Acquisitions or expansion initiatives by other Caribbean private sector companies have been fewer, notably the forays of the Jamaican companies, Grace Kennedy and AIC and the Barbados-based Goddard's group.

While these forays into the regional market have been mostly successful and have consolidated Trinidad and Tobago as the dominant market in the region, some acquisitions or expansions were not successful, notably Guardian Holdings' extraregional acquisitions in the United Kingdom, Prestige Holdings' expansion into Puerto Rico, and Republic Bank's acquisition in the Dominican Republic.

Table 14.3 Acquisitions and/or Expansion by Trinidad and Tobago Private Sector Companies

Company	Business Activity	Destination	Acquisitions/ Expansion
Guardian Holdings Limited	Life, health and pensions insurance	Jamaica, Netherlands Antilles, United Kingdom	Jamaica Mutual, West Indies Alliance, Fatum Link/Zenith/ Lloyds Syndicate
Trinidad Cement Limited	Cement	Barbados, Jamaica	Arawak Cement Carib Cement
Bermudez	Biscuits and snack foods	Jamaica	
RBTT Financial Holdings Limited	Commercial banking	Jamaica, Netherlands Antilles, Eastern Caribbean	Union Bank
Republic Bank	Commercial banking	Dominican Republic, Barbados, Guyana, Grenada	
Angostura Limited	Alcoholic beverages	Jamaica	Lascelles de Mercado
Neal and Massy Holdings	Manufacturing, distribution	Barbados	BS&T Holdings
Ansa McAl	Manufacturing, distribution	Barbados	
Prestige Holdings	Restaurants	Puerto Rico, Jamaica, Barbados	
Caribbean Communications Network Ltd	Media	Grenada, Barbados	Grenada Broadcasting Nation Corporation
CL Financial	Conglomerate	Guyana	Caribbean Resources Ltd

Note: The Barbados-based insurance company Sagicor also invested in Jamaica, the United States and the United Kingdom; though Sagicor was formerly the Barbados Mutual Insurance, since demutualization, Sagicor has had a plurality of Trinidad and Tobago ownership. First Citizens Bank, which is state-owned, acquired a subsidiary in St Lucia in the Eastern Caribbean and has also recently acquired Caribbean Money Market Brokers (CMMB), which has branches in the Organization of Eastern Caribbean States. RBTT Financial has since been acquired by the Canadian bank RBC Royal Bank.

Conclusion

This chapter has surveyed the sets of policies pursued over the years 1993 to 2008 by successive administrations, and described the domestic and international contexts within which those policies were developed.

In 2003, and in parallel with the initiatives being pursued in housing, infrastructure and public buildings, and the development of new educational institutions, the government embarked on its Vision 2020 planning exercise to develop a long-term plan to chart the course for the attainment of "developed country status" by the year 2020. This exercise is described in detail in the next chapter.

15

Vision 2020

The "Strategic Plan"

The PNM returned to government in 2002 after the second general elections within two years following the 18:18 deadlock in the 2001 elections. In 2003, the government initiated its Vision 2020 project. The objective of the project was to develop a national "strategic plan" that would see Trinidad and Tobago attain "developed country status" by the year 2020.[1] This approach to long-term perspective planning – the articulation of a set of objectives targeted to a specific end point in time, ten or more years in the future – had been pursued with success by other countries such as Singapore and Malaysia.

Planning was not to be understood in the same way as "development planning" in the 1960s and 1970s. Rather, borrowing concepts from the relatively new discipline of strategic management such as "vision statements" or "aspiration statements", and embracing the ideas of "competitiveness" and private sector–led growth, these "perspective plans" sought to broaden the consultative process and establish goals and objectives across social, cultural and economic spheres. Unlike the early development plans of the 1950s and 1960s, perspective plans were not articulated because of a belief that markets do not work.[2] Rather these plans also sought to increase the confidence of stakeholders in the trajectory of government policy and achieve a high degree of consensus in the society about the goals and objectives that needed to be achieved. A critical pillar of this approach is the soundness of macroeconomic policies, that is, avoidance of large fiscal deficits financed by money creation, inflation control and maintenance of manageable deficits on the current account of the balance of payments.

The approach to planning for Vision 2020 was unlike anything that the country had attempted before (see table 15.1). A "multisectoral (core) group" was formed under the chairmanship of Arthur Lok Jack, a leading local businessman.[3] The Multi-Sectoral Group in turn formed twenty-eight subcommittees covering various aspects of economic, social and cultural life, and chaired either by private sector or public sector leaders who drew on persons with expertise in the various areas to work on the subcommittees. In total over six hundred persons were involved in the work of the subcommittees. The secretariat of the Vision 2020 exercise was the Programme Management Office initially established with the Ministry of Planning and Development.

Table 15.1 Comparison of Vision 2020 and Previous Plans

	First, Second and Third Five-Year Plans	Vision 2020
Leadership	Plans developed mainly by government economists and some social planners.	Initial process led by a leading Trinidad and Tobago businessman, Arthur Lok Jack, and a Core Group comprising other private sector and public sector membership.
Consultation	Top down; ex-post consultation with private sector and trade unions	Inclusive, collaborative multisectoral approach involving subject matter experts and broad-based consultation with citizenry and interest groups ("stakeholders")
Theoretical framework	Incentives to foreign and local private sector to increase investment in import substitution and export promotion activities; government as provider of infrastructure and "ring-holder"	Eclectic, pragmatic, expedient are the words that can be used; government as providing the enabling environment but also as a major investor and risk-taker
Methodology	Target setting; use of traditional macroeconomic policy management tools	Aspirational; microinterventions to address specific problems diagnosed or identified at the industry or subsectoral level.

There was an extensive period of consultation throughout the country in 2003 and 2004 involving the subcommittees and various stakeholder groups and the general public. Over eighty consultations were undertaken over the period. The secretariat established a website, and there were radio and television programmes involving members of the various subcommittees with call-in segments, as well as town hall–type meetings with interest groups. Ministerial reviews were conducted to solicit the views of government ministries. Vision 2020 commercials were produced and aired on television and radio along with a logo for the Multi-Sectoral Group, which eventually became the logo for the entire Vision 2020 exercise. Experts from various international organizations were also involved in the review process.

The language of the plan document reflects more contemporary strategic planning and implementation in a business context than the development plans of yesteryear. The document itself is called a "strategic plan", not a "development plan", and it speaks in terms of "dashboards", "benchmarks", "actions", "strategic architecture", "competencies" "capabilities", and so on. The references in the document are to business school writings by authors such as Gary Hamel, Prahalad, Porter and Mintzberg, and extensive use is made of the global competitiveness index in assessing where Trinidad and Tobago was placed relative to other developed and developing countries.

The concept of "development" embraced by the Vision 2020 team was, however, multifaceted and holistic, entailing economic or material, cultural, social, and political factors or considerations. Accordingly, the development of the society was seen as involving five development priorities or "pillars":

1. Nurturing a caring society – this was seen to mean a society intolerant of disease, discrimination, economic and social marginalization, and substandard living conditions and one which promotes trust, caring, tolerance, civic pride, and integrity.
2. Enabling competitive business – this was seen to involve strong competitive businesses promoting high productivity and good incomes, founded on entrepreneurship and innovation.
3. Investing in sound infrastructure and environment – this was seen to involve well-built, well-maintained and -operated, safe public transportation systems, as well as reliable water, electricity, wastewater, telecommunications and postal systems.
4. Governing effectively – this was seen to involve the upholding of rights and the rule of law, the sanctity of contracts, dispute resolution, the electoral process, an independent judiciary and a professional civil service.

5. Developing innovative people – this was seen to involve lifelong learning, generation of new ideas, risk-taking, creativity and problem-solving.

The lexicon of the Vision 2020 Plan was therefore quite different from that of the early planning years when development thinking was dominated by economists. In this twenty-first-century effort, the experience of developing countries with traditional planning, as well as postcolonial political and social upheavals and the growth of neoliberalism, had moved development thinking towards a new paradigm that was prepared to engage a range of cultural, attitudinal, political and social factors, as well as economic ones. The influence of the "managerial" approach to development encouraged a focus on micro- rather than macroactivity, and specific industries rather than broad sectors. This made the planning process considerably more challenging both methodologically and intellectually, creating demands for new and different data sets and the search for policy instruments that could address these factors.[4]

The Vision 2020 Plan Process

The planning process followed by the Multi-Sectoral Group is illustrated schematically in figure 15.1. The composition of the leadership of the subcommittees engaged in the development of the subsectoral plans reflected a variety of experienced persons from the public sector, private sector and the university. The work of the subcommittees was initiated by terms of reference drawn up by the group. But apart from that, no further direction was given to the subcommittees who were left to develop their own approaches and methodologies in developing the subsectoral plans. The result of this was significant variability in the quality and usefulness of the subcommittee reports and resulting subsectoral plans.

Once the subcommittee reports were in hand, the Multi-Sectoral Group needed to collate these into the Draft National Strategic Plan. A smaller group from the group along with personnel from the University of the West Indies' School of Business were engaged to develop "Frameworks for Action" from the various subsectoral plans, which encompassed actions, timelines, measures, resource requirements and responsible agency in accordance with the standard approach for the development of strategic action plans. This process was also to eliminate duplicated recommendations and inconsistencies and fill any gaps identified.

The Multi-Sectoral Group as the framers of the Draft National Strategic Plan took the view that the plan document would set out the strategic direction and sets of options, but that "much work needs to be done *once the document enters*

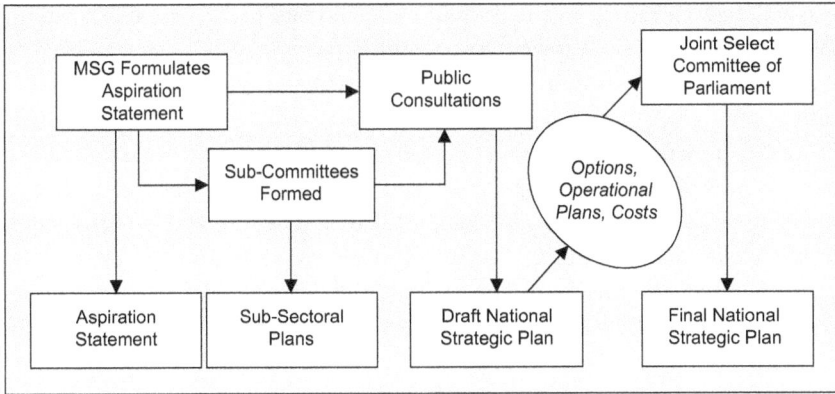

Figure 15.1 Vision 2020 plan process

the government realm. This includes making choices from among the options presented, detailing cost and operational planning and developing and forming the structures for implementation and monitoring, as well as continuous planning."[5]

The Draft National Strategic Plan proposed the formation of an independent council that would be responsible for progress tracking and measurement; ongoing stakeholder outreach; research; periodic recommendations for policies or actions; and communication and reporting. The "government realm" would see a Programme Management Office, housed within the Office of the Prime Minister, responsible for coordination across ministries and departments, programme and project planning and management, capacity building and knowledge sharing.[6] The plan also expected that Vision 2020 would continue as a "open, multi-participatory process".

In 2007, the Ministry of Planning and Development prepared the Vision 2020 Operational Plan 2007–10, which was issued along with the budget documents in that year. The operational plan identified the goals of economic and social transformation as:

- diversification away from dependence on the energy sector, with particular emphasis on agriculture (food security), tourism and financial services
- protection and preservation of the environment
- creation of a knowledge-based society through the overhaul of the education system

Government was to play an enabling role through the provision of economic and social infrastructure and implementing changes in governance in respect of decentralization and devolution to enhance participation in the policymaking process. Civil society was also important in that citizens needed to make the necessary attitudinal changes to foster self-reliance and "epistemic independence".[7]

The operational plan discussed specific initiatives and projects under the five development pillars and presented the projected expenditure associated with each initiative or project over the years 2007 to 2010 and the ministry or agency that would "champion" the initiative or project. What was achieved in the operational plan was essentially a reclassification of the public sector investment programme and expenditure under the development programme under the five Vision 2020 development pillars, and an attempt to relate these expenditures to the goals as outlined in the plan.

The operational plan noted that some projects to be delivered or started within the time frame were still being developed and some others were financed "under recurrent expenditure".

Assessment of Vision 2020

The Vision 2020 process officially ended with the change of government in 2010 continuing the unfortunate practice whereby each incoming administration jettisons the plans of the previous government and starts all over again. Unofficially, the Vision 2020 process had ended long before. It is possible, however, to make

Table 15.2 Projected Expenditure under the Five Development Pillars, 2007–2010
($ million)

	FY2007	FY2008	FY2009	FY2010
Nurturing a caring society	1,148.5	3,271.9	3,148.6	2,539.9
Enabling competitive business	21.9	18.2	12.8	5.5
Investing in sound infrastructure and environment	4,483.1	10,070.9	6,028.6	3,212.8
Governing effectively	2.0	2.8	0.4	0.1
Developing innovative people	1,155.4	5,661.9	3,101.5	892.9

Source: Government of Trinidad and Tobago, *Vision 2020 Operational Plan 2007–2010.*

some assessment of the process. The first positive that should be noted is that the consultation process was comprehensive. It lived up to the Vision 2020 motto: "Ideas without boundaries . . . we are listening". This occurred notwithstanding the initial scepticism of both the members of the subcommittees and the public itself, and the lack of participation by the party in opposition. Apart from the round of public consultation undertaken by the Wooding Commission on constitutional reform in the 1970s, there has probably not been as extensive a consultation process since that also made good use of the mass media.

However, even as the Vision 2020 teams were engaged in developing the plan, the government of the day was pursuing in parallel several major initiatives. These were massive infrastructural development works under the rubric of UDECOTT, the establishment of the University of Trinidad and Tobago, the FastForward Plan for the development of the information and communication technology sector, and the drive to build up to eight thousand houses per year across the country. In addition, certain key persons involved in the implementation of policy initiatives elected not to participate. Calder Hart, chairman of UDECOTT, was slated to be a member of the Multi-Sectoral Group, but did not participate. Ken Julien, president of the University of Trinidad and Tobago, and Noel Garcia, head of the Housing Development Corporation, key agencies in the implementation of government policy, also were not part of the Vision 2020 exercise.

The planning methodology was incomplete. It would have been appropriate for the subcommittees to identify or suggest investments to support the initiatives proposed. Then the Programme Management Office should have developed and prioritized those strategic investments and, together with the Ministry of Finance, phased those investment projects into the annual budget exercise and the capital expenditure programme. The programming model as developed and further elaborated would have allowed for the input of the projected investments to determine what rate of growth of income and output these would yield, as well as the impact on other variables of interest such as unemployment and inflation. The strategic investments identified by the Vision 2020 plan would not have been coterminous with the ongoing capital expenditure programme of the various ministries, but would have been a few specific initiatives directed to achieve specific strategic goals as prioritized by the Multi-Sectoral Group/planning council and the government.

There are several reasons why this did not happen. First, the subcommittees were plagued by the inadequacy of data. Over the decades since the abandonment of planning, the Central Statistical Office has steadily declined in terms of the quantity and quality of its statistical output, so much so that there are now serious questions about the integrity and reliability of certain data produced.[8] Second, subcommittees developed and worked with their own approaches and methodologies without input from the Multi-Sectoral Group beyond their initial terms of reference. This led to the uneven quality of reports, so that it was difficult in some instances to develop the frameworks for action from them. Third, it is clear that the politicians wanted to retain control over investments. Fourth, the general elections of 2007 returned the PNM to power but with significant changes in the composition of the cabinet, with new ministers responsible for finance and for planning.

The Trinidad and Tobago Vision 2020 Plan has been praised, and attempts have been made to emulate it – for example: Jamaica's Vision 2030 Plan. However, following the publication of the draft plan in 2007, the plan was not presented to a joint select committee of parliament to obtain bipartisan support at the parliamentary level. The transformation of the Multi-Sectoral Group into a national planning council to oversee the implementation and monitoring and to roll the plan forward did not happen, the Vision 2020 secretariat gradually fell away, and the plan has collapsed back into the annual budgeting and capital expenditure programme. The public service was never quite comfortable with the intimate involvement of private sector and university persons in the planning process, and worked to recapture control. Having regained control, the stasis characteristic of the public service took over and the process inevitably stalled. "Vision 2020" became more of a slogan than a plan in implementation as the various infrastructure, housing and social sector projects undertaken by special purpose state enterprises such as UDECOTT, the Housing Development Corporation, e TECK and the University of Trinidad and Tobago were all billed as "Vision 2020". Far from being an exercise in charting the long-term future of the country, Vision 2020 ended as an exercise in futility.

16

A Golden Age

Growth and Macroeconomic Performance, 1993–2008

Lloyd Best, in his historiography of the Caribbean plantation economy, described periods of economic decline as "Gall and Wormwood" and periods of growth and expansion as a "Golden Age". In the Golden Age, export staple prices are high, import prices are moderate and hence the terms of trade are favourable, and profit margins in the staple sector are strong. In the plantation economy, the terms of trade are exogenously determined, and the rents generated are appropriated by the merchants and planters and are not reinvested or recycled in the local economy to grow the "residentiary" sector, which is defined by Lloyd Best as domestic production for domestic consumption.

Between 1993 and 2008, Trinidad and Tobago experienced fifteen years of uninterrupted growth in real GDP, comparable to and indeed exceeding the postwar boom, and also surpassing the petrodollar boom between 1973 and 1982 in respect of the duration and the consistency of growth (figure 16.1). This chapter examines that growth performance, discusses the policy instruments that were used to produce that performance and assesses whether or to what extent growth was accompanied by development and transformation.

The reasons for this exceptional growth performance are not difficult to discern. Two subperiods can be identified within the fifteen-year span. In the first subperiod from 1993 to 2002, oil prices averaged US$20.70/barrel and oil

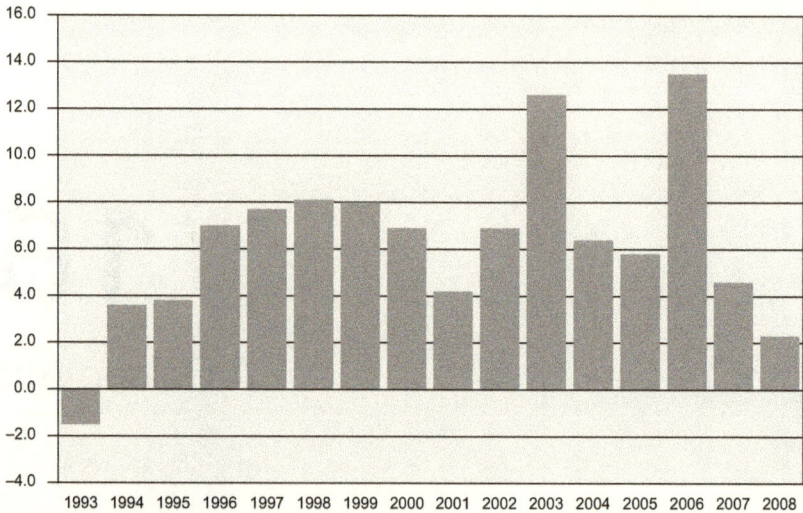

Figure 16.1 Real GDP growth rates, 1993–2008 (%)

production averaged 124.6 thousand barrels per day. Oil revenue as a proportion of total government revenue was 26 per cent. In the second subperiod from 2003 to 2008, oil prices averaged US$61/barrel (three times higher than the first subperiod) and oil production averaged 130,000 barrels per day. Oil revenue as a proportion of total revenue averaged 47 per cent, reaching as high as 54 per cent in 2008.

The surge in oil prices and revenues removed the fiscal constraint. Expenditure, recurrent and capital, rose strongly but substantial surpluses still emerged owing to the sustained rise in revenues.

The increase in oil revenues and energy exports as a whole also removed the foreign exchange constraint. Foreign exchange reserves, which were negative in 1992, rose from US$206 million in 1993 to over US$10 billion at the end of 2008. In addition to the official foreign reserves, exchange control liberalization permitted residents to hold foreign currency deposits in local banks. These deposits soared from US$152.5 million in 1993 to US$2,560 million in 2008. Over the same period the country's public sector external debt declined more or less steadily.

Per capita national income rose over the post 1993 period from US$3,002 to US$5,885 in 2002. However, it was not until 2003 at US$7,100 that per capita national income again attained the level reached in 1982 some twenty years earlier at the height of the previous boom. By 2008, per capita GDP had reached about US$16,000, twice as high as the level attained in 2003, just five years earlier.

Unemployment fell over the period, indicating an improvement in welfare, while inflation moderated, remaining around 5 per cent before beginning to rise sharply in 2005 as a result of increases in food prices driven by increases in global commodity prices. Indices of poverty and inequality also improved over the period. The percentage of the population below the poverty line fell from 24 per cent in 1997 to 17 per cent in 2005, while the Gini coefficient improved from about 0.42 in 1992 to 0.39 in 2005.

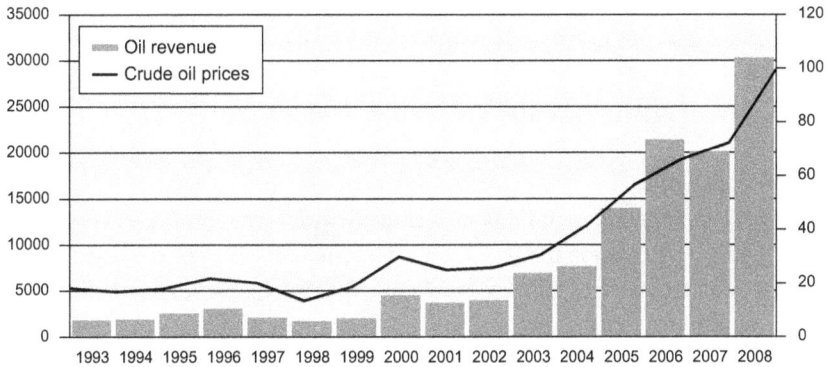

Figure 16.2 Oil prices (US$/bbl) and oil revenue ($M), 1993–2008

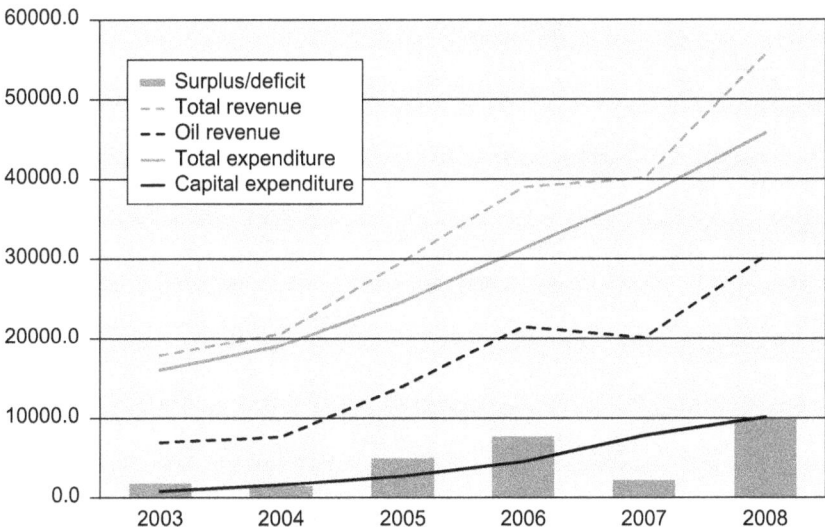

Figure 16.3 Fiscal operations ($M), 2003–2008

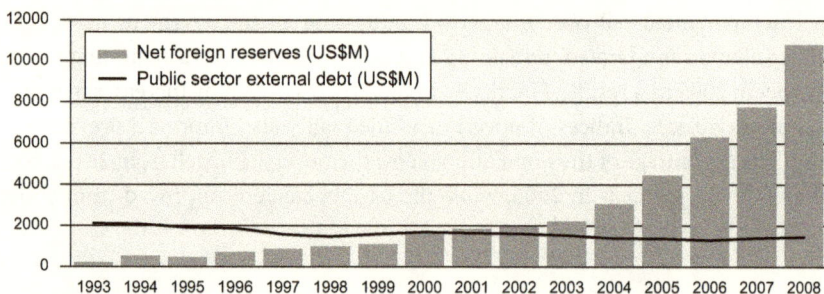

Figure 16.4 Net foreign reserves and public sector external debt (US$M), 1993–2008

Policy Instruments and Their Effectiveness

The influence of Washington Consensus thinking, working in part through the IMF and World Bank conditionalities to which the country was subject in the early 1990s, is reflected in the sets of policy instruments selected and used to first effect stabilization and adjustment, and also to promote growth and employment.

The abolition of exchange controls and the adjustment of the exchange rate in 1993 set the stage for the improvement in the balance of payments and the stimulation of the non-oil economy. Following the major devaluation in 1993, the nominal exchange rate was allowed to depreciate over the period to 2008. However, most of the depreciation occurred in the period up to 2000. Thereafter,

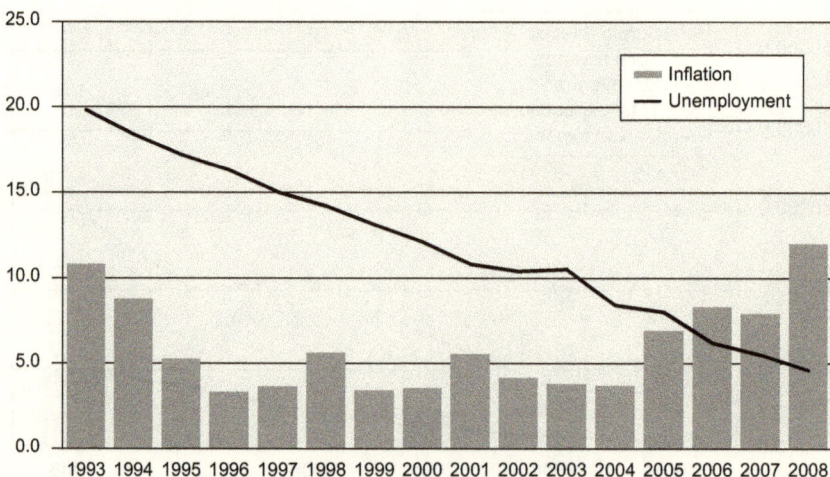

Figure 16.5 Unemployment and inflation rates (%), 1993–2008

higher inflation in the domestic economy relative to the United States as the major trading partner led to appreciation of the real exchange rate in several of the years between 2001 and 2008 (figure 16.6).[1]

Exports of manufactured goods responded to the depreciation of the exchange rate and in the context of moderate oil prices, the share of manufactured goods in total merchandise exports reached a high of 20 per cent in 1998 and averaged 16 per cent of total exports from 1993 to 2000. As oil prices and exports rose after 1999, the share of manufactured exports declined, averaging only 8 per cent over the period 2001 to 2008. In dollar terms, exports of manufactured goods increased from US$240 million in 1993 to US$922 million in 2008, an average annual growth rate of 9.4 per cent. Similarly, the investments in petrochemicals saw a surge in exports of chemicals averaging 23 per cent over the period 1993 to 2000, with a peak share of total merchandise exports of 29 per cent in 1994. The average share fell to 19 per cent over the period 2001 to 2008 as oil exports surged. In dollar terms, exports of chemicals rose from US$277 million in 1993 to US$3.4 billion in 2008, an average annual rate of growth of 18.2 per cent.

Tax reform, a key element of the Washington Consensus policy set, was implemented over the period of the neoliberal phase. The introduction of the value added tax from January 1990 during the NAR administration was the first major

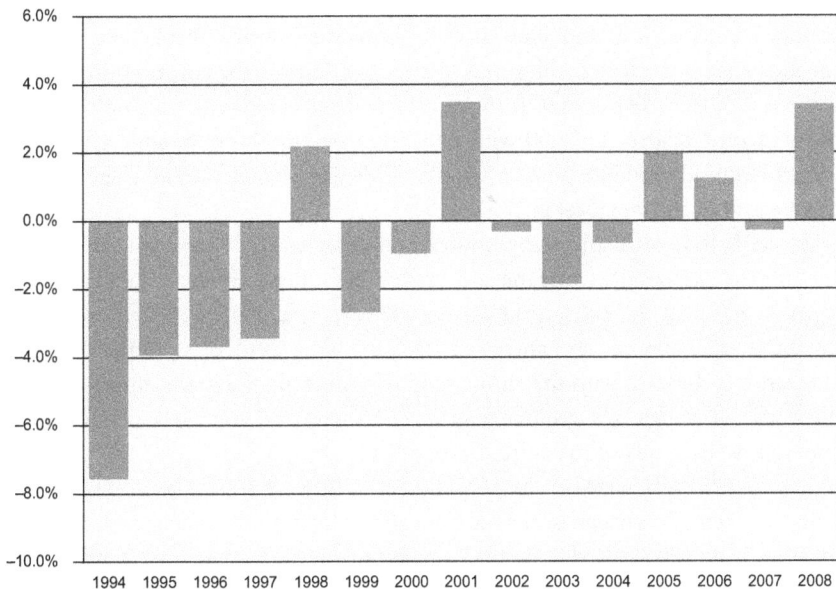

Figure 16.6 Change in real exchange rate, 1994–2008

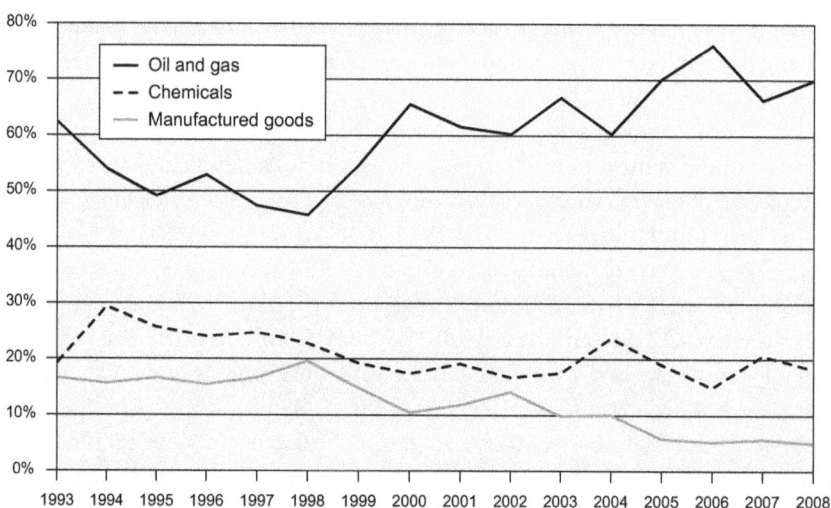

Figure 16.7 Shares of merchandise exports, 1993–2008

step in the shift from income taxation to expenditure taxation. In 1995, under the PNM administration, the corporation tax for non-energy companies was reduced from 45 per cent to 38 per cent and with the 15 per cent tax credit, lowered to 23 per cent for approved small companies and other approved companies. In 1997, under the UNC administration, the personal allowance was increased. The plethora of deductions and allowances for individuals were consolidated, though the mortgage interest deduction was spared. In addition, the corporation tax rate was reduced from 38 per cent to 35 per cent. In 1998 persons earning only emolument income of over $50,000 with deduction by employers at source were no longer required to file income tax returns. This was extended to all wage earners irrespective of income level in 2001.

In 2003, individual income tax rates were reduced to 25 per cent and 30 per cent for the two bands, while the corporation tax rate was reduced to 30 per cent from 35 per cent. In 2006, a flat 25 per cent tax rate was implemented for individuals and (non-energy) corporations along with an increase in the personal allowance to $60,000 with the elimination of almost all other allowances and deductions. These changes cumulatively gave Trinidad and Tobago one of the most competitive income tax structures in the world.

Increases in real wages in the period up to 2002 were moderate, averaging less than 2 per cent. This began to change from 2003, although the sharp acceleration of inflation from 2005 served to mute increases in real wages somewhat (figure 16.8). Moderate increases in real wages, plus the increasingly favourable tax regime for corporate profits, led to a steady improvement in the share of profits (proxied by

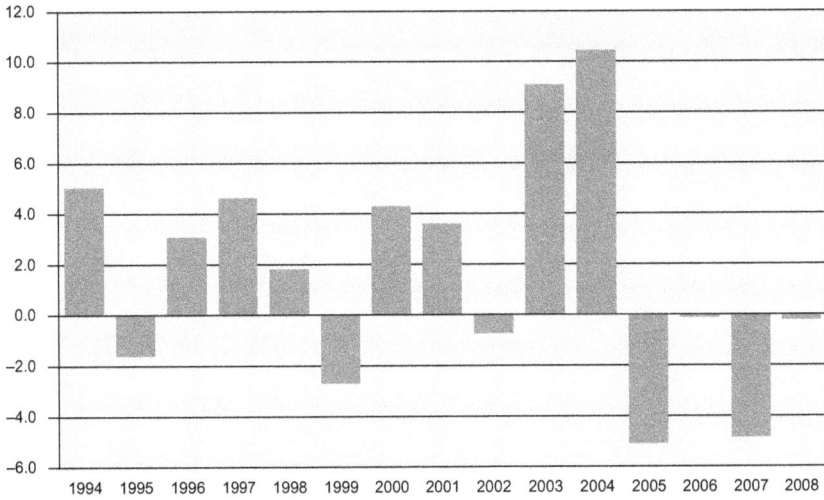

Figure 16.8 Change in real wage (%), 1994–2008

the operating surplus) in GDP over the period to 2005, rising from less than 30 per cent in 1993 to 54 per cent in 2005 (figure 16.9).

The reform of the petroleum taxation regime in 1992, including revisions to the production-sharing contracts, had impelled significant increases in natural gas production and utilization downstream in the earlier years of the period.

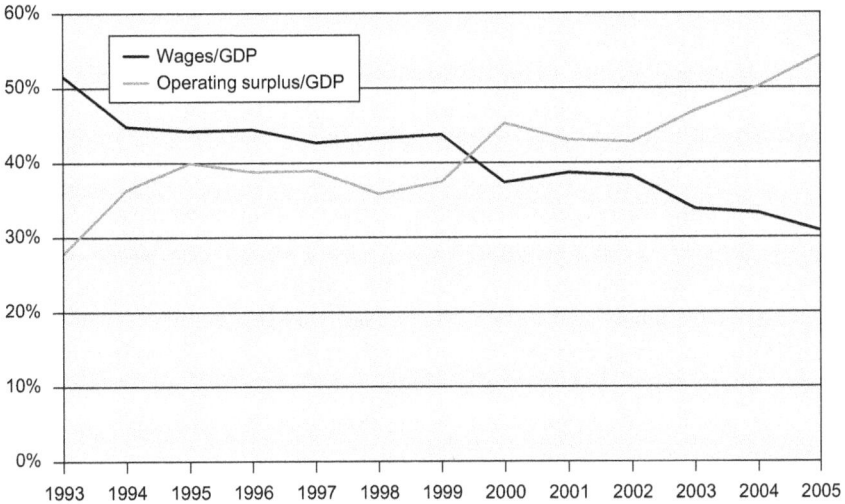

Figure 16.9 Relative income shares, 1993–2005

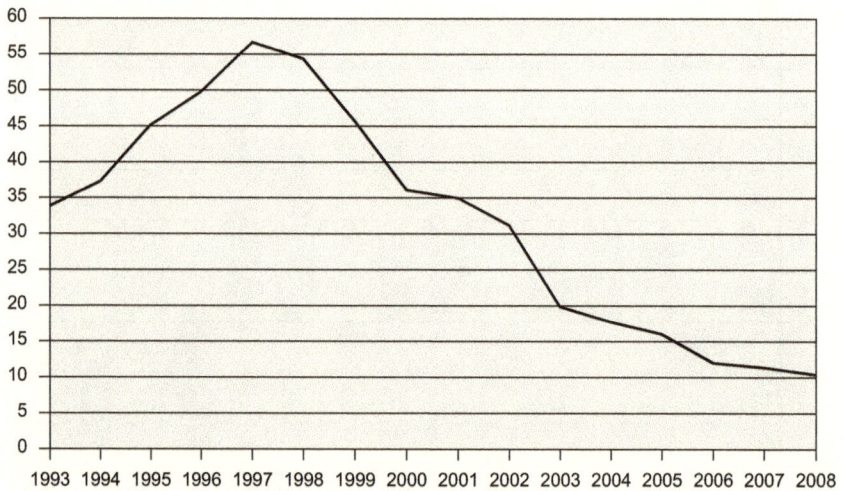

Figure 16.10 Natural gas: R/P ratio (years), 1993–2008

However, exploration and development of gas reserves did not keep pace with commitments for the utilization of gas for liquefied natural gas exports and petrochemicals production, and as a result the key reserves-to-production ratio for natural gas began to fall precipitously after 1997 and particularly after 2002 (figure 16.10). Further adjustments were made to the taxation regime in July 2005 (table 14.1), but global developments in the oil and gas industry, reflected in the weak response to the competitive bid rounds, have conspired to keep exploration and development activity low.

Consistent with the tenets of the Washington Consensus and neoliberal economic policy, monetary policy remained tight during the course of the 1990s, but began to be relaxed from 2002. Real interest rates were positive, and significantly so up to 2002. However, from 2005, real interest rates turned negative as inflation accelerated while interest rates remained relatively low in the context of reductions in the reserve requirement and a move towards open market operations. Lending rates were high during the 1990s with bank prime averaging over 15 per cent and residential mortgage rates averaging over 16 per cent in the period up to 2002. Both bank prime and residential mortgage rates averaged less than 11 per cent in the ensuing period up to 2008.

Investment improved significantly from the close of the lost decade when the rate of investment was only about 15 per cent of GDP to 22 per cent in the period 1993 to 1997 and further to 24 per cent in the period from 1998 to 2002. It is significant that the majority of the investment in this period up to 2002 was undertaken by the private sector as government's fiscal circumstances were still constrained.

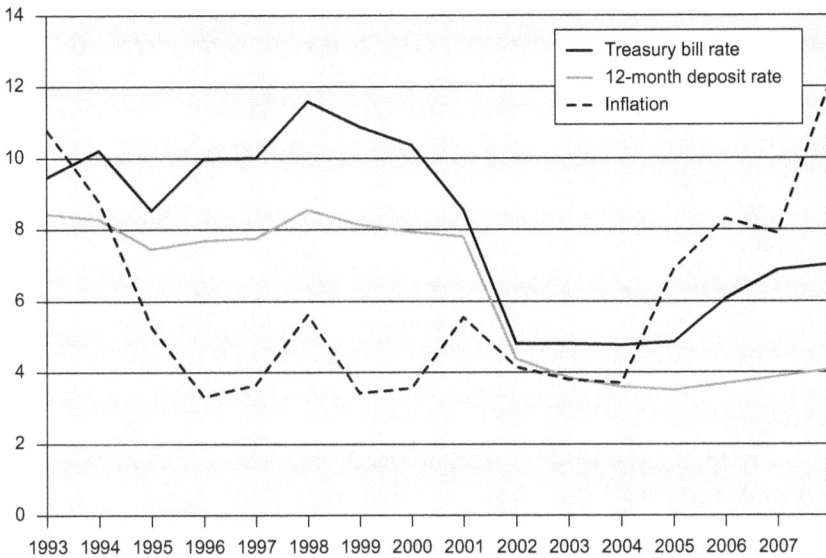

Figure 16.11 Interest rates, 1993–2008

Also of significance was that over 40 per cent of gross capital formation came from foreign direct investment, the highest levels seen since the late 1950s.

However, in the period from 2002 to 2008, government stepped up its invest-ment activity, mainly in housing, infrastructure and building construction, while private sector investment, particularly investment in energy, was comparatively lower. Foreign direct investment declined to 35 per cent of gross capital formation.

Table 16.1 Investment Performance, 1993–2008

	1993–1997	1998–2002	2002–2008
Gross capital formation/ gross domestic product	22%	24%	17%
Foreign direct investment/ gross capital formation	44%	41%	35%
Government capital ex-penditure/gross capital formation	9%	8%	21%

Note: Some care is needed here as not all government capital expenditure is properly really capital formation. However, government's role in investing activities is certainly understated since invest-ments by state enterprises and other government agencies are not accounted for here.

Overall, the investment rate was lower in the period from 2002 to 2008, with implications for the growth performance of the economy over the medium term.

Transformation in the Neoliberal Phase

An examination of the changes in the structure of output (GDP) over the period 1993 to 2008 to assess the extent to which growth was attended by structural transformation is made difficult by data deficiencies, specifically constant price series at the industry level. Table 16.2 shows the structure of GDP at current prices for selected years from 1992 to 2008 where the strong price increases in the petroleum sector, especially after 2002, overshadowed the performance of the other sectors.

Figure 16.12 identifies those industries in the non-energy sector whose rates of growth at constant (2000) prices exceeded the rate of the growth of the non-energy sector as a whole (5.5 per cent) over the period 2000 to 2008. These industries also grew strongly in the earlier period 1993 to 2000. We have included the distribution sector since that sector enjoyed strong growth over much of the entire period beginning in 1993, but was somewhat weaker between 2000 and 2004 before accelerating again from 2004 to 2008. In particular, the restaurant subsector grew at 27 per cent per annum in current prices between 2000 and 2006.

Table 16.2 Structure of GDP (Current Prices) Selected Years, 1992–2008

Sector	1992	1997	2002	2008
Agriculture	2.5%	2.2%	1.3%	0.4%
Petroleum	23.6%	25.5%	27.8%	48.0%
Construction	8.4%	7.8%	6.7%	8.6%
Government	11.8%	9.2%	7.8%	6.2%
Finance, insurance, real estate	13.7%	14.0%	14.2%	9.5%
Manufacturing	9.2%	7.9%	7.8%	4.7%
Distribution, incl. restaurants	13.4%	16.6%	16.8%	12.9%
Transport storage communications	9.6%	9.0%	10.7%	4.6%
Other services	7.7%	7.8%	7.0%	5.1%
Total GDP	100%	100%	100%	100%

Source: Central Statistical Office, *National Income of Trinidad and Tobago.*

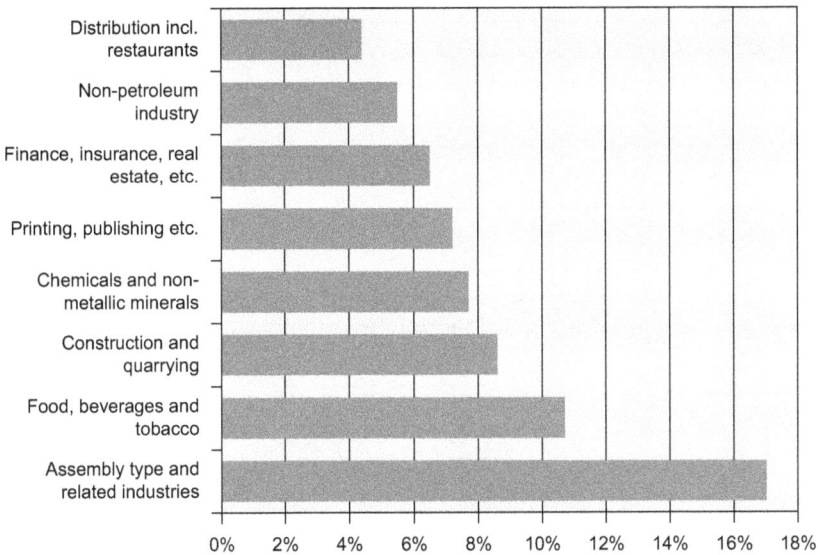

Figure 16.12 Industry growth rates (%), 2000–2008 constant prices

Using the relative industry growth rates at current prices as well as the available sectoral constant prices data for the subperiod from 2000 to 2008, certain observations on the extent of structural transformation can be made. First, the agriculture sector, both domestic and export agriculture, continued its secular decline with the share in GDP falling below 1 per cent in 2008. The sugar industry was effectively dismantled in 2007 when subsidies were withdrawn and the lands under sugar began to be reallocated. Second, petrochemicals has become one of the largest industries in the economy, accounting for 8 per cent of GDP at current prices in 2008. Third, there have been significant shifts within the manufacturing sector, so that while overall the share of manufacturing has declined to 5 per cent in current prices (8 per cent in constant 2000 prices), textiles and garments, which had been given much emphasis in the planning years, accounted for less than 1 per cent of GDP, but food, beverages and tobacco performed strongly over the period. Fourth, the other significant sectors in terms of shares of GDP were finance, insurance and real estate and distribution, including restaurants. Fifth, two sectors that might have expected to become more significant given the emphasis of policy over the years were hotels and guest houses (tourism), and the telecommunications industry – both industries growing more slowly than non-oil GDP as a whole between 1993 and 2008. Tourist arrivals grew at only 4.1 per cent per annum between 1995 and 2008, from around 255,000 to 430,513, with a peak of 463,191 arrivals in 2005.

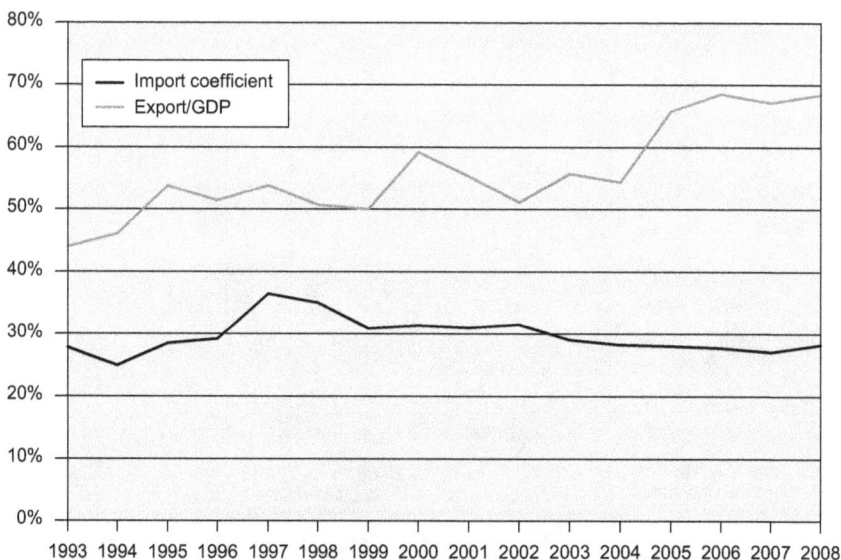

Figure 16.13 Import and export coefficients, 1993–2008

Evidence of transformation can be sought by examination of the export and import coefficients.[2] Over the period, the exports-GDP ratio trended upward, lifted by the increased production and exports of petroleum, natural gas and petrochemicals, reaching 68 per cent in 2008. While this might be seen by structuralists as evidence of continued "export dependence", the changing composition of merchandise exports noted earlier (figure 16.7) suggests some diversification of merchandise exports. The slow decline of the import coefficient since the late 1990s might perhaps be even more suggestive of structural change, but for the fact that the investment rate declined since the late 1990s and the change in the composition of investment, with greater emphasis on housing and infrastructure and proportionately less private capital investment, may account for the observed decline. Nonetheless the import coefficient from 1993 to 2008 is significantly lower than that observed in the pre- and post-independence period, and would almost certainly have been regarded by structuralists, such as Demas, as indicative of some degree of transformation.

The growth of productivity, especially in relation to the growth of wages, is also important in making an assessment of the transformation achieved over the neoliberal phase. Data deficiencies also pose problems here, since the only productivity measures available relate to the goods-producing industries, and the official data series uses an index of gross output rather than value added or GDP as the output measure. Table 16.3 shows the average annual change in

Table 16.3 Average Annual Change in Productivity and Earnings, 2000–2008
(Selected Industries)

	Index	Real GDP	Earnings
Food processing	9.9%	9.6%	3.1%
Textiles, garments	11.0%	0.7%	−1.4%
Printing, publishing and paper converters	12.5%	5.7%	2.9%
Wood and related products	10.8%	−3.1%	7.3%
Chemicals	2.8%	3.1%	7.3%
Assembly type and related products	13.5%	13.9%	9.2%
Miscellaneous manufacturing	−0.8%	0.8%	2.2%
Sugar	−7.0%	5.7%	−6.2%
Petrochemicals	7.5%	7.7%	11.6%
Oil and gas exploration and production	6.8%	12.6%	3.9%
All manufacturing	13.2%	9.5%	8.3%

Source: Central Statistical Office, *Index of Domestic Production and National Income Accounts.*

productivity (output/hours worked) for the period 2000 to 2008, showing the index measure as well as the constant prices measure for selected manufacturing and petroleum industries. Overall, productivity increased significantly (9.5 per cent per annum) over the eight-year period, and in excess of the increase in earnings. The food processing and assembly and related industries stand out in terms of productivity growth relative to earnings growth, while other industries, notably chemicals and petrochemicals, experienced productivity growth lower than the increase in earnings over the period.

Policy Shift

The beginning of a shift in the configuration of development policy can be discerned in the period after 2002 (table 16.4). While the thrust of policy remained essentially neoliberal, the removal of the fiscal and foreign exchange constraints permitted the government to reassert a role as investor. In contrast with the period of resource-based industrialization from 1974 to 1982, the government, frustrated by the slow pace of implementation within the public service, formed and utilized several state enterprises and statutory corporations to undertake major

Table 16.4 Comparison of Policy: 1993–2002 and 2003–2008

	1993–2002	2003–2008
Strategic thrust	Export of output of gas-based industries	Infrastructure, housing, selected industries
Role of government	Facilitator, enabler; provision of infrastructure and social overhead capital	Major investor, mainly through state enterprises in infrastructure
Role of private sector	Engine of growth through investment	Junior partner in fostering growth
Policy objectives	Labour absorption savings and investment growth balanced relative to foreign exchange and fiscal constraints	Rapid investment growth; "big push"; income growth from government spending and multiplier effect
Policy instruments	Petroleum taxation; production sharing contracts; tax reform	Reduction in tax rates; easy monetary policy;

investments in the areas of housing, highway expansion, tertiary education and the construction of public buildings.

In addition, the stance of macroeconomic policy was relaxed on several fronts. The authorities allowed interest rates to fall as reserve requirements were reduced, resulting in the emergence of negative real interest rates. Higher domestic inflation and the maintenance of the nominal exchange rate permitted real exchange rate appreciation with medium-term consequences for the evolution of the non-energy exporting industries. Higher revenues allowed expenditure on transfers and subsidies to escalate, much as had occurred in the 1970s, and the suppression of real wages could create the context for increased trade union militancy and demands for higher wages in the public sector as occurred in the early 1980s.[3]

Conclusion

The neoliberal phase from 1993 to 2008 was probably the country's most successful period of growth and development. The sets of policies pursued up to 2002 were appropriate and consistent, and yielded good rates of growth, increased employment, moderate inflation and some degree of structural transformation. What cannot be ignored is that the international economic environment,

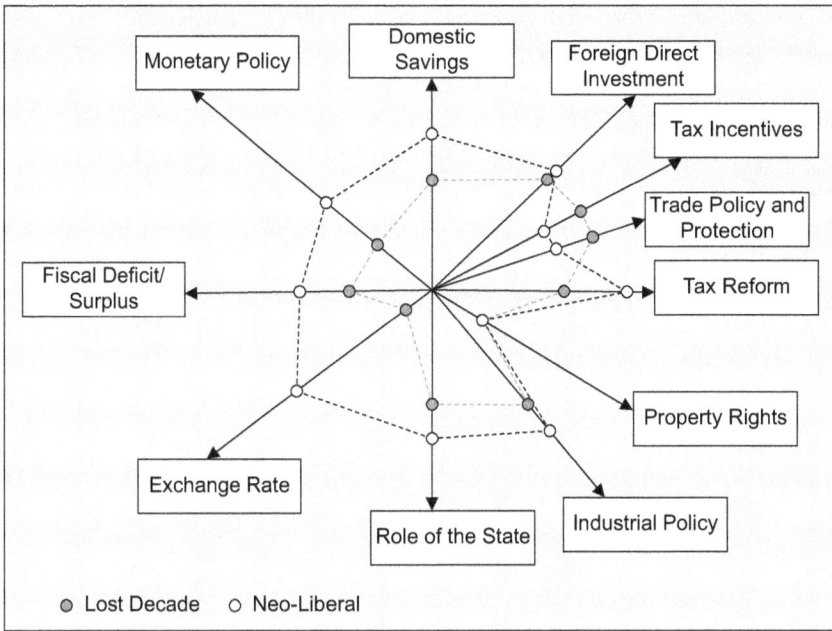

Figure 16.14 Policy map: neoliberal strategy

especially the prices of oil, gas and petrochemicals, was propitious and reserves of natural gas increased substantially, propelling increased exports and incomes. A shift in policy after 2002 can be detected, and this led to the implementation of somewhat less appropriate sets of policies engendering negative real interest rates and a lower investment rate focused on social infrastructure and public buildings. However, the higher oil prices and government revenues accruing since 2002 also contributed to the higher foreign exchange reserves and lower external debt, making for a manageable macroeconomic situation up to the time of the global recession in 2008.

The neoliberal phase was, however, marked by adverse social developments. Serious crimes, including murder and kidnapping for ransom, escalated notwithstanding the falling unemployment rate and increases in transfers. There were also several corruption scandals amounting to millions of dollars in respect of the construction of the new airport terminal in the 1990s and the projects undertaken by UDECOTT in the first decade of the new century. These issues are considered more closely in the part 6.

The policy map in figure 16.14 shows how policy changed from the earlier period of the lost decade. It should be noted that the role of the state is indicated as more expansive than in the previous period, and this is particularly true in the period after 2002 as the fiscal constraints were loosened and the shift from strict neoliberal orthodoxy began to be evident. Monetary policy and fiscal policy are more expansive than under strict Washington Consensus prescriptions, and there is a retreat from the depreciation of the 1990s to a preference for a more stable nominal exchange rate. However, we think that the shift is not yet so significant as to constitute a change of the stance of policy from what might be characterized as neoliberal, in part because it is not clear what the elements of that new paradigm might be. The Vision 2020 exercise hinted at the possible embrace of a more "managerial" approach to development and transformation, but that exercise as already noted was effectively aborted.

Part 6

Evaluation

17

Development Strategy and Policy over Five Decades

T his chapter begins the evaluation of the success of policy in promoting economic growth and development in Trinidad and Tobago over the last fifty years. The first section reviews with a bird's eye the changes in policy over the entire period and attempts to draw some conclusions therefrom. The second section reviews, with a similar bird's eye, the changes in institutions that have been made to formulate and implement those policies. The third section undertakes a comparison of the outcomes in Trinidad and Tobago with those of selected countries.

Policy Changes

The previous sections of the study have surveyed development strategy and policy in Trinidad and Tobago spanning import substituting industrialization over the "planning years" (1958 to 1973), the repudiation of planning and the shift to resource-based industrialization (1974 to 1983), the "imperatives of adjustment" (1984 to 1992), the so-called lost decade, and the post-1992 shift to neoliberal policies based to some extent on the policy prescriptions of the so-called Washington Consensus.

In table 17.1 we have sought to summarize the changes in policy that were made over the span of five decades across the various dimensions of policy. Reviewing development strategy and policy over the long sweep of history from the colonial period to the present and tested against development theory and thinking at the relevant time allows certain observations to be made and certain conclusions to be drawn.

First, at the heart of the Lewis model is an incomes policy. The model assumed that wages in the modern sector would be suppressed during capital accumulation owing to the pool of workers in the subsistence sector and that wages in the modern sector would not begin to rise until labour absorption from the subsistence sector was complete. In small island economies where the distance, geographically and otherwise, between town and country is small and the demonstration effect on wages is strong, capital accumulation along the lines of the Lewis model required some incomes policy that would keep wages in check, while at the same time encouraging the reinvestment of profits by the capitalist class. The correlate of an incomes policy along those lines is that the functional distribution of income would be tilted in favour of profits and against wages.

Trade unions had been at the forefront of the anticolonial struggle and the pre-independence political leaders – Cipriani, Cola-Rienzi, Butler – all had their bases of support in trade unions. Trade union militancy carried over into the post-independence period. Policymakers in Trinidad and Tobago made one attempt at incomes policy in implementing the Industrial Stabilization Act in 1965. The response of the trade unions to that measure was robust and sustained and led to the replacement of the Industrial Stabilization Act with the Industrial Relations Act in 1972. After 1972, no government attempted to raise the idea of an incomes policy. Wage setting, even in the face of high unemployment, became a contest between union and employer, with "ability to pay" being the most important criterion for wage settlements, workers' rights powerfully protected by the Industrial Court, and trade union solidarity ensuring that a local dispute could become a national cause célèbre for the trade union movement as a whole. In the absence of an incomes or wages policy, the adjustment of real wages fell on other instruments of policy, including exchange rate adjustment.

Second, the policymakers stayed with import substitution industrialization developed in the colonial period after it was clear that the strategy was not having the desired impact in terms of labour absorption. I have argued elsewhere that Caribbean governments, including Trinidad and Tobago, did not follow Lewis's development strategy, which argued the case for export promotion so that businesses could take advantage of scale economies and increasing returns to be externally competitive. Rather, post-independence governments followed the

Table 17.1 Key Policy Changes, 1950–2008

	1950–1957	1958–1962	1963–1967	1968–1972	1973–1977	1978–1982	1983–1987	1988–1992	1993–1997	1998–2002	2003–2008
	Colonial Policy	Import Substituting Industrialization			Abandonment of Planning/ Resource-Based Industries		Imperatives of Adjustment		Neoliberalism		Vision 2020
Energy Policy				Petroleum Act	Petroleum Taxes Act; Production Sharing	Shift from Tax Reference prices; National Oil Company		Reform of Petroleum Taxes Act			Amendment to petroleum taxation
Industrial Policy	Import substitution (Manufacturing)					Government investment in gas-based industries			Encouragement of investment in gas-based industries via gas pricing		
Fiscal Policy	Tax incentives for pioneer industries		Revision (increase) of income taxation	Unemployment levy	Special funds established			Value added tax introduced	Reduction in individual and corporate income tax		Special funds reintroduced; Heritage and Stabilization Fund
Commercial Policy			Negative List (import licensing) introduced		Localization of financial services	New state enterprises formed		Divestment of state enterprises			Creation of new state enterprises
Trade Policy			Accession to CARIFTA		Treaty of Chaguaramas CARICOM			Negative List dismantled		Revised CARICOM treaty	
Monetary and Exchange Policy			Sterling devaluation		Shift to US dollar peg		Exchange controls; devaluation		Floating of TT dollar		
Incomes Policy			Industrial Stabilization Act	Industrial Relations Act							

strategy promoted by the local colonial administrations, which called for import substitution (import replacement) rather than exports of manufactured goods, which might threaten industry in the mother country.[1] Import licensing (negative list) as well as accession to the CARICOM common external tariff reinforced the strategy of import replacement until these were dismantled during the neoliberal phase.

Third, in the absence of any real affinity between the political directorate and the business elite (foreign and local), drawn as they were from different class positions and different ethnicities, the government quickly lost faith in the ability of the private sector to drive growth and development, and assumed the mantle of "prime mover" for itself. This meant that fiscal policy became very "active". Rising unemployment was addressed by absorbing more persons into the public sector and by unemployment relief programmes, which added to recurrent expenditures. It also meant government investment through acquisition or start-up of directly productive businesses that might otherwise have been in the domain of the private sector. The financing of fiscal deficits became challenging. There was resort to increased taxation with high marginal rates of individual and corporate taxes, until the fiscal situation was rescued by the oil price shocks. High taxation was a further disincentive to capital accumulation and growth.

The foreign private sector was vilified and attacked during and after the black power uprising of 1970. The government, encouraged by popular sentiment, embarked on a policy of localization targeted as we have discussed earlier at financial services and also created a national oil company, a unit trust corporation as a mobilizer of savings of the "small man". The effect of this was a lower rate of foreign direct investment, which did not recover until the neoliberal phase in the 1990s.

Even in the neoliberal phase, beginning in 1992, the government did not fully embrace the private sector and once the financing constraint was eased after 2002, government reverted to staking out a larger role for government in the economy, albeit in housing, public buildings and infrastructure rather than in directly productive activities as before. Notably, it was in this phase when taxation of companies and individuals was significantly reduced and government was constrained by moderate oil prices that locally owned private sector companies began to expand and invest in industries, which were normally the habitat of foreign multinationals, and to invest extensively in the Caribbean region.

Fourth, the maximization of the rents from the country's oil and natural gas assets depended on acquiring and building the requisite skills, knowledge and negotiating capabilities within the ministry responsible for petroleum and mines, later called the Ministry of Energy. Developments in the international petroleum market, with the decisive shift in power from the multinationals to the producing countries, assisted Trinidad and Tobago in formulating petroleum taxation policies that were consistent with emerging thinking in producing countries and the maximization of rents. The disposition of these rents was, however, not dealt with separately from the general revenues and expenditures of government, which as noted earlier in this section tended to be directed to ameliorating the effects of unemployment through short-term expenditures. It was not until 2003 that a Heritage and Stabilization Fund was introduced (replacing the Revenue Stabilization Fund), recognizing belatedly the critical necessity of saving a portion of oil and gas reserves monetized through extraction for future generations but still conflating this objective with the quite different objective of revenue stabilization.

Fifth, development theories, whether in the neoclassical version of the Solow model, or the managerial theories, have emphasized the impact that increases in productivity have on growth and development. However, formulating and implementing policies to promote productivity growth are notoriously difficult. At base, productivity improvements arise from a better-educated and -trained workforce, and from the adoption and effective use of technologies including, in the last twenty years, information and communications technologies. Policy can induce improvements in productivity by fostering competitiveness and concomitantly by limiting the size and growth of the public sector where it is difficult to measure productivity. Given the long period of high effective protection of industry, as well as the dominant size and role of the public sector, we can conclude that policies to drive increases in productivity are not likely to have been effective.

Institutional Changes for Policy Formulation and Implementation

Table 17.2 attempts to describe how the institutional framework for planning, policy formulation and implementation has evolved over the fifty years from the first five-year plan. The first observation is the "patchiness" of the institutions involved in policy formulation over the period. Institutions were created and then fell into desuetude, only to be revived before lapsing again. Essentially, there has been little institutional continuity in respect of policy formulation and planning over the period.[2]

The importance attached to long-term planning can be gauged by the status of the government minister charged with this responsibility. In the early planning years, this responsibility rested with the prime minister. Later on, the

Table 17.2 Institutional Changes, 1958–2008

	1958–1962	1963–1967	1968–1972	1973–1977	1978–1982	1983–1987	1988–1992	1993–1997	1998–2002	2003–2008
	Import Substituting Industrialization			Abandonment of Planning/Resource-Based Industries		Imperatives of Adjustment		Neoliberalism		Vision 2020
Policy Formulation										
Coordination	Economic Planning Department	Ministry of Planning and Development		Coordinating Task Force	National Advisory Council	Demas Task Force				Vision 2020 Multisectoral Core Group
Consultation		National Economic Advisory Council					National Economic Advisory Council/JCC			
Oversight		National Planning Commission					National Planning Commission			
Implementation										
Manufacturing Industry			Industrial Development Corporation						Tourism and Industrial Development Corporation	
Tourism				Tourist Board						Tourism Development Company
Energy		Ministry of Petroleum and Mines					Ministry of Energy, National Energy Corporation and National Gas Company			
Agriculture		Ministry of Agriculture; Agricultural Development Bank						National Agricultural Marketing Development Company		
Tobago			Ministry Responsible for Tobago Affairs					Tobago House of Assembly		
Trade and Integration					Ministry Responsible for Trade, Commerce and Industry					
Infrastructure							Special Purpose State Enterprises (National Infrastructure Development Company, UDECOTT, e TECK, Housing Development Corporation)			

responsibility rested with junior ministers, some of whom were not even members of the cabinet. During the NAR administration (1986–1991) the prime minister chaired a revived National Planning Commission, which, however, never really functioned effectively in the teeth of adjustment and stabilization efforts at the time. During the neoliberal phase, no institutions for coordination, consultation and oversight at an economy-wide level were created until the Vision 2020 exercise in 2003. That task force recommended the establishment of a national planning commission but that recommendation, along with all the other recommendations, was stillborn. In effect, since 1992, the Ministry of Planning has coordinated the Public Sector Investment Programme within the context of the annual budget exercise.

In respect of implementation, there has been greater institutional continuity in respect of certain economic ministries, such as agriculture. It was only in the 1990s that the National Agricultural Marketing Development Company (NAMDEVCO) was established. Because of Eric Williams's well-known antipathy towards tourism, the Tourist Board existed but never achieved real significance. In the 1990s, it was combined with the Industrial Development Corporation to create the Tourism and Industrial Development Corporation and later on, tourism development was put back on its own under the Tourism Development Company. The Industrial Development Corporation, which had played a prominent role during the import substitution phase, gradually lost its prominence, and its role in the promotion of industry was ceded to the Coordinating Task Force and the NEC, as well as agencies promoting small business such as the Business Development Company and the National Enterprise Development Company. The role of the Industrial Development Corporation in the development of industrial estates was also ceded to the NEC since the new industrial estates were intended not for light manufacturing industries but for energy-related businesses.

In the 2000s, several agencies were created that focused on infrastructure development. These included UDECOTT, e TECK, the Housing Development Corporation, which replaced the former National Housing Authority, the Estate Management and Business Development Company and the National Infrastructure Development Company.

Comparison with Selected Countries

One useful way of elucidating the effectiveness or otherwise of the policies pursued to achieve development in Trinidad and Tobago is to compare its performance across various dimensions of development with those of selected countries.

Cross-country comparisons can be useful if constructed carefully and correctly, but can also be misleading. In the first chapter, we identified three characteristics of Trinidad and Tobago – size, ethnic composition, oil and gas resources – which should factor into any comparisons that are made. We sought comparator countries of a similar size in terms of population and land area. We also needed to have comparator countries that were ethnically diverse, and that might have oil and gas resources so that we could "control" for these factors in comparing development outcomes over several decades.

For the purpose at hand, Singapore, Barbados and Norway have been selected for comparison with Trinidad and Tobago. Singapore and Barbados are, like Trinidad and Tobago, small countries both in terms of geographical size and population. Norway has a much larger land area than the other comparator countries, but its population is also small. Indeed, while Norway had twice the population of Singapore in 1960, Singapore – with a much faster rate of population growth – had by 2008 overtaken Norway. None of the countries are isolated. Air and sea transportation links have always been excellent. Norway and Singapore were directly affected by the military conflict during World War II, while Trinidad and Tobago was indirectly affected, but apart from that, none of the countries have experienced war or civil strife for any prolonged period since 1960, the year from which the comparisons are started.

Singapore, like Trinidad and Tobago, is a multi-ethnic society, although the Chinese segment is preponderant, estimated at about 72 per cent, with significant Malay (23 per cent) and Indian (9 per cent) minorities. Barbados (mostly persons of African descent) and Norway (mostly persons of Caucasian descent)

Table 17.3 Population and Land Area of Comparator Countries

	1960	1970	1980	1990	2000	2008	Average Annual Growth Rate 1960–2008	Land Area (sq km)
Trinidad & Tobago	843,005	970,867	1,081,764	1,218,783	1,295,100	1,333,388	0.9%	5,130
Singapore	1,646,000	2,075,000	2,414,000	3,047,000	4,027,900	4,839,400	2.3%	670
Norway	3,580,998	3,877,000	4,091,000	4,241,500	4,491,000	4,768,212	0.6%	304,280
Barbados	230,662	238,751	248,981	259,668	251,656	255,203	0.2%	430

Source: World Bank, *World Development Indicators.*

are ethnically homogeneous societies, even though Barbados has a small percentage of whites (Caucasian) as well as a small percentage of East Indians and other
minorities. Like Trinidad and Tobago, Norway possesses and has had to manage hydrocarbon resources. Norway produces about three million barrels of oil
per day (bpd), making it one of the top ten producers of oil in the world, while
Trinidad and Tobago, at peak, produced about 0.25 million bpd. Norway also has
significant natural gas reserves, ranking seventeenth in the world compared to
Trinidad and Tobago, which is ranked thirty-fourth in the world. By contrast,
Singapore and Barbados are natural resource–poor, relying mainly on services for
economic activity. Other possible comparator countries were Cyprus and Ireland,
which were used in the World Bank study.[3] Both Cyprus and Ireland, however,
have enjoyed a special relationship with and within the European Union, respectively, and between Ireland and the United Kingdom, which has no comparison in
the economic relations of Trinidad and Tobago.

Using these three countries for comparison also removes from the field considerations relating to governance and the rule of law. All countries have democratic
societies with regular general elections, active judicial systems and law-making
through parliamentary processes. For example, in 2008, Singapore scores a perfect ten in the World Bank's index of "Strength of Legal Rights", while Trinidad
and Tobago scores eight and Norway, seven. However, the question of corruption
needs to be considered separately since corruption can be a major factor in resource misallocation and the timely implementation of projects.

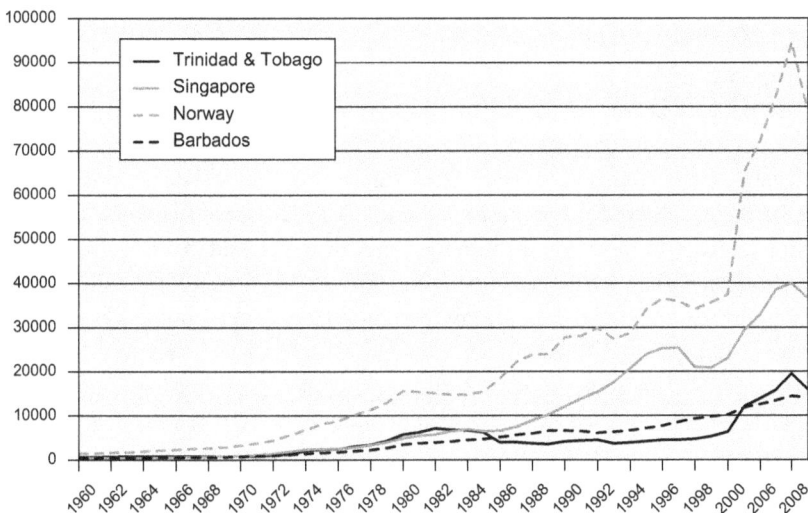

Figure 17.1 GDP per capita US$

The indicators or dimensions used for comparison are: GDP per capita (US dollars); inflation, as a proxy for macroeconomic stability; unemployment; life expectancy, infant and maternal mortality; poverty and income distribution; literacy and school enrolment (tertiary); and corruption. Clearly, these are not the only indicators of development that can be used for comparison. Indeed the World Bank dataset contains hundreds of variables appropriate to analysing various aspects of development, including gender issues; infrastructure development; health, mortality and morbidity; the status of the environment; and so on. In the twenty-first century indicators such as Internet and broadband usage, mobile telephone and computer penetration are increasingly used. The seven variables identified are, however, both basic and comprehensive in terms of what most analysts would regard as development, encompassing economic, social and human dimensions of development.

GDP Per Capita

In respect of GDP per capita in US dollars, Trinidad and Tobago in 1960 (US$ 635) enjoyed a level that was 44 per cent of that of Norway (US$1442), and 61 per cent and 67 per cent higher than those of Singapore (US$395) and Barbados (US$379), respectively. By 1970, Singapore had overtaken Trinidad and Tobago, although the strong growth spurt in the latter half of the 1970s pushed Trinidad and Tobago ahead on Singapore for a few years between 1978 and 1983. Barbados went ahead of Trinidad and Tobago in 1986 and remained ahead until 2005. By 2008, Trinidad and Tobago's GDP per capita was only 21 per cent of Norway's, and 49 per cent of Singapore's.

Arguably, a better measure than GDP per capita in US dollars is to measure GDP per capita using Purchasing Power Parity (PPP) exchange rates, and using constant dollars, here a base year of 2005 (table 17.4). These data are not available for Barbados, except for one observation in 2005, and are available for the other countries from 1980. While the underperformance of Trinidad and Tobago in delivering growth in per capita income is not as stark in PPP terms, the conclusion of underperformance relative to the comparator countries is unambiguous. The gap between Trinidad and Tobago and Norway and Singapore widened over the period between 1980 and 2008. In 2005 Barbados, in PPP terms, enjoyed a level of per capita income roughly equivalent to that of oil- and gas-rich Trinidad and Tobago.

Figure 17.2 graphically presents the data on GDP per capita in PPP constant dollars. Here the lost decade for Trinidad and Tobago from 1982 to 1992 is clearly evident. Over this period, Norway and Singapore continued to improve the average standard of living of their citizens.

Table 17.4 GDP Per Capita, PPP (constant 2005 international $)

	1980	1985	1990	1995	2000	2005	2008
Trinidad and Tobago	15,254.4	12,524.6	10,791.1	11,143.3	13,870.0	20,013.9	24,032.1
Singapore	14,453.5	17,368.7	23,429.0	30,942.7	36,792.8	45,374.3	48,001.8
Norway	25,972.5	30,143.5	32,117.4	37,517.9	43,642.1	47,305.5	49,070.0
Barbados						19,188.6	

Source: World Bank, *World Development Indicators*.

Inflation

Macroeconomic stability is an important condition that should obtain if develop-ment is to proceed more or less steadily, given the particular set of policies pur-sued. Where macroeconomic stabilization and adjustment dominate the policy agenda, longer-term planning and projects are sidelined in order to "fight fires" and bring the economy back under control. We use inflation performance as a proxy for macroeconomic stability on the argument that the higher the rate of inflation, the shorter the investment horizon for businesses and governments, the greater the degree of macroeconomic uncertainty and the higher the rate of dis-count on investment projects. Apart from the rate of inflation, the variability of inflation also adds to uncertainty and instability.

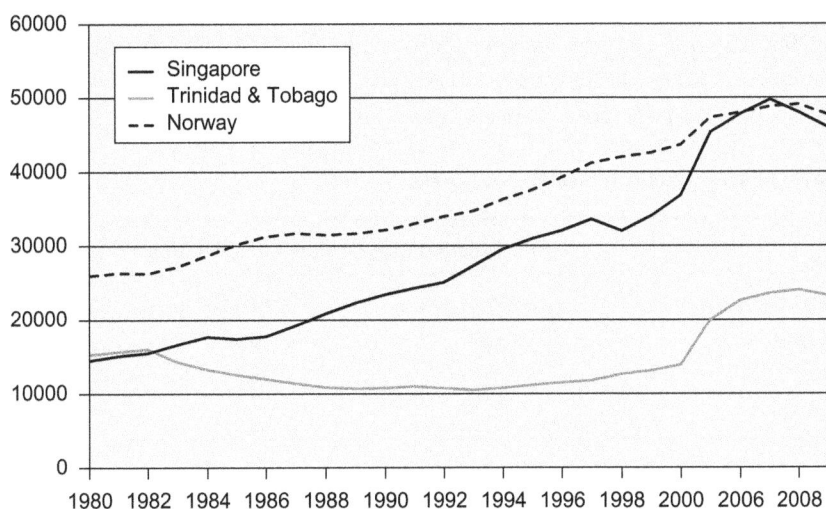

Figure 17.2 GDP per capita PPP, 2005 US$

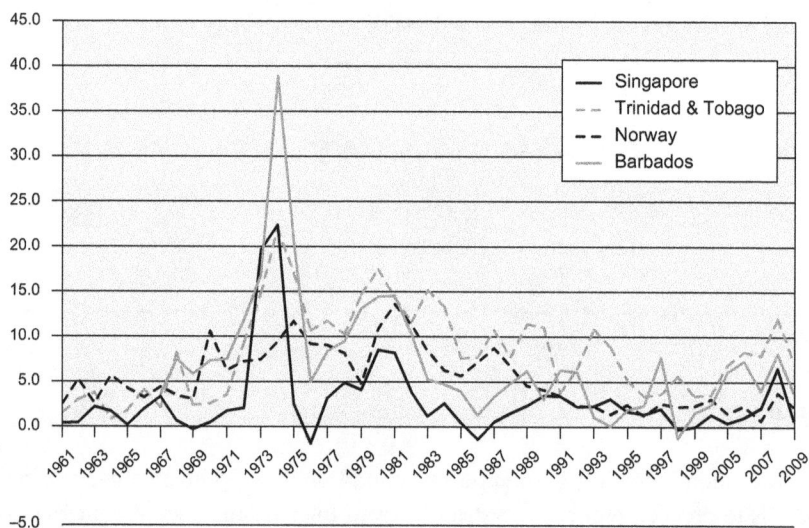

Figure 17.3 Comparative inflation performance, 1961–2009 (%)

Figure 17.3 shows the inflation rates for the comparator countries over the period 1961 to 2009 (Barbados from 1967). Apart from the period of the oil price shock, when inflation in Barbados and Singapore spiked, the inflation rate in Trinidad and Tobago dominates the inflation rates of the comparator countries from the 1970s onward.

Table 17.5 indicates that over the period, annual inflation in Trinidad and Tobago averaged 7.9 per cent, the highest of the comparator countries, followed by Barbados and Norway. Moreover, inflation in Trinidad and Tobago was more variable than those of Singapore and Norway, and is more variable than that of Barbados if the post-oil shock observations for Barbados are excluded.

Table 17.5 Variability of Inflation, 1961–2009

	Average Inflation (%)	**Standard Deviation**
Trinidad and Tobago	7.9	4.90
Singapore	2.7	4.34
Norway	5.0	3.31
Barbados*	6.8	6.88

Source: World Bank, *World Development Indicators.*
*Data for Barbados are from 1967; if the inflation rates for Barbados and Singapore following the oil price shocks are excluded, the standard deviation for Barbados falls to about 4.0 and to about 2.0 for Singapore.

Unemployment

Figure 17.4 presents the comparative data on unemployment in the four comparator countries from 1980 to 2008. The disparity between unemployment in Trinidad and Tobago and Barbados on the one hand and Norway and Singapore on the
other is striking. The latter two countries have been able to maintain unemployment rates below 5 per cent for most of the period, whereas Trinidad and Tobago
and Barbados had suffered high unemployment rates exceeding 10 per cent and
occasionally above 20 per cent. Since 2000 unemployment rates have fallen below
10 per cent in Trinidad and Tobago and Barbados, but are yet to reach the levels
enjoyed by Singapore and Norway.

High levels of unemployment speak not only to the economic costs associated
with low productivity and capacity utilization, but also to the social costs of associated poverty, crime and inadequate household amenities.

Life Expectancy, Infant and Maternal Mortality

Life expectancy has been used for a long time as a general indicator of the health
status and living conditions of a population, as it summarizes the impact of the
prevalence of diseases as well as the quality of health care in respect of chronic
diseases such as diabetes and hypertension. Infant and maternal mortality indices

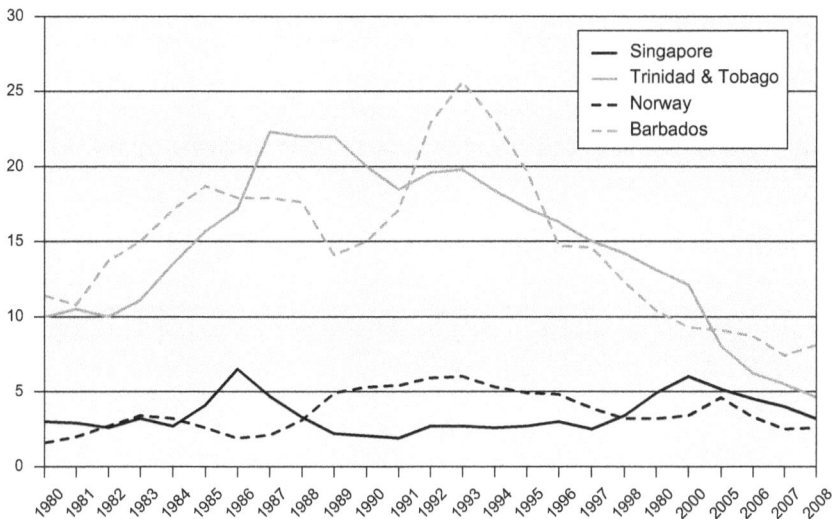

Figure 17.4 Comparative unemployment rates (%)

Table 17.6 Life Expectancy at Birth, Total (Years)

	1960	1965	1970	1975	1980	1985	1990	1995	2000	2005	2008
Trinidad & Tobago	63.5	65.4	65.6	66.4	67.4	68.3	69.0	69.0	68.4	68.6	69.3
Singapore	63.7	65.7	67.7	69.9	71.5	72.9	74.3	76.4	78.1	80.0	80.7
Norway	73.5	73.7	74.1	74.8	75.7	75.9	76.5	77.7	78.6	80.2	80.7
Barbados	64.5	66.8	68.5	70.3	72.0	73.3	74.4	74.8	75.2	76.3	77.0

Source: World Bank, *World Development Indicators.*

speak even more directly to the quality of health care delivery for a section of the population that is perhaps the most vulnerable.

Table 17.6 presents the comparative data from 1960 to 2008, and the results are striking. In 1960, life expectancy in Trinidad and Tobago was the same as in Singapore and in Barbados, while Norway had already attained a level of 73.5 years. By 2008, Trinidad and Tobago had improved life expectancy to only 69.3 years, whereas Singapore had reached 80.7 years and Barbados 77 years.

The data on infant and maternal mortality are no less striking. While infant mortality has been halved in Trinidad and Tobago since 1960 from 60.4/1,000 live births to about 31/1,000, this indicator remains at a level higher than that of Singapore in 1965. Barbados has brought infant mortality down to less than 10/1,000 and Singapore has long attained the standard of more developed countries of less than 3/1,000 live births (table 17.7).

Maternal mortality similarly is extremely high in Trinidad and Tobago (55/100,000 live births) and, strangely perhaps, in Barbados as well, where it is actually higher than in Trinidad and Tobago. These countries compare unfavourably with Norway and Singapore in this regard where maternal mortality per 100,000 live births is less than 10 in both countries (table 17.8).

Table 17.7 Mortality Rate, Infant (per 1,000 Live Births)

	1960	1965	1970	1975	1980	1985	1990	1995	2000	2005	2008	2009
Trinidad & Tobago	60.4	53	46.4	40.6	35.5	31	30.4	29.8	30.3	31.1	31.1	31.1
Singapore	36	27	21.9	14.6	11.5	8.8	6.2	3.9	3	2.2	2.3	2.3
Norway	18.4	16.1	12.9	10.4	8.2	8.1	7.3	4.5	3.8	3.2	2.9	2.8
Barbados					22.9	17.2	14.8	13.7	12.9	11	10.1	9.8

Source: World Bank, *World Development Indicators.*

Table 17.8 Maternal Mortality Ratio (Modelled Estimate, per 100,000 Live Births)

	1990	1995	2000	2005	2008
Trinidad and Tobago	86	90	59	55	55
Singapore	6	6	15	10	9
Norway	9	4	8	9	7
Barbados	120	42	50	62	64

Source: World Bank, *World Development Indicators.*

Poverty and Income Distribution

Cross-country comparisons of poverty are difficult, as most studies rely on local delineation of the poverty line for particular countries. The (absolute) poverty line is based on caloric intake for adults of 2,400 calories and 720 for children under twelve, but how caloric intake is met varies among countries since diets vary and not all consumption is effected through purchases in a market. Most countries or international organizations study poverty and inequality occasionally through special household expenditure surveys and for different research purposes so that there are no consistent data by period. However, poverty and inequality evolve slowly so that not much is lost by these data drawbacks in a comparative assessment such as this.

Table 17.9 presents the available data on poverty and inequality for the comparator countries. There are no poverty data for Norway and Singapore, and we can assume that whatever poverty does exist in those countries is miniscule. Poverty in Trinidad and Tobago has declined, but the latest data indicate 17 per cent of households are below the poverty line. The most recent data for Barbados (1997) indicate that 14 per cent of households were below the poverty line at that time.

In respect of income inequality, as measured by the Gini coefficient, Norway has one of the most equal distributions of income in the world. Income inequality in Singapore, Barbados, and Trinidad and Tobago is greater, with inequality in Singapore being higher than the other comparator countries.

Literacy and School Enrolment

In all comparator countries, literacy is virtually complete – in excess of 95 per cent – although how this variable is measured differs across countries.

Table 17.9 Comparative Poverty and Inequality

		1970	1980	1990	2000	2005
Trinidad and Tobago	% below poverty line	25		21		17
	GINI	0.51	0.45	0.43		0.39
Barbados	% below poverty line				13.9	
	GINI				0.39	
Singapore	% below poverty line				–	–
	GINI				0.42	
Norway	% below poverty line				–	–
	GINI				0.25	

Sources: Thomas McDonald and Eleanor Wint, "Inequality and Poverty in the Eastern Caribbean" (paper presented at the ECCB Seventh Annual Development conference, 21–22 November 2002, Basseterre, St Kitts); and World Bank, *World Development Indicators.*
Note: Data are for the survey years closest to the decade year indicated in the table.

So that although Trinidad and Tobago has long advertised literacy of over 95 per cent, reflecting (compulsory) attendance at the primary school level, "functional illiteracy" is known to be high.

In all comparator countries progression to secondary schooling is almost complete, running at 99 per cent for Barbados and Norway but 90 per cent for Trinidad and Tobago. Tertiary school enrolment data for Trinidad and Tobago and Norway are shown in Table 17.10. In both countries, female enrolment at the tertiary level has overtaken male enrolment in Norway by a wide margin. However, in Trinidad

Table 17.10 Comparative Tertiary School Enrolment (Selected Years), 1975 to 2005

		1975	1980	1985	1990	1995[*]	2000	2005
Trinidad & Tobago	School enrolment, tertiary, female (% gross)	2.2	3.6	3.4	5.1	6.1	6.9	13.0
	School enrolment, tertiary, male (% gross)	3.4	5.3	5.5	7.6	8.6	4.6	10.2
Norway	School enrolment, tertiary, female (% gross)	15.7	24.2	30.5	42.3	60.5	82.5	95.3
	School enrolment, tertiary, male (% gross)	26.5	26.7	29.0	34.9	48.4	56.5	62.3

Souce: World Bank, *World Development Indicators.*
[*]Data for Trinidad and Tobago for 1995 are 1993 data.

and Tobago, tertiary school enrolment is still well below that of Norway for both males and females. In 2005, Trinidad and Tobago still had not attained the levels of tertiary school enrolment achieved by Norway in 1975.

Corruption

Corruption has a significant impact on a country's development in diverting resources from production into consumption and diverting resources overseas. Corruption is also demotivating for citizens who are aware that others in a position to do so benefit disproportionately from the country's resources, and citizens themselves may be then inclined to engage in petty corrupt practices in order to enhance their own standard of living. Corruption then becomes endemic and difficult to root out.

Trinidad and Tobago has long had a reputation for corruption ranging from petty graft ("bobol") to major scandals involving multimillion-dollar incidents, including acquisition of aircraft by the national airline, construction of the Piarco airport terminal and construction of public buildings in Port of Spain. Several of these incidents have been the subject of commissions of enquiry, and a few have reached the law courts.

There are no objective measures of corruption; the indicator relied on is the corruption perception index, which is developed from survey data administered in countries around the world and then ranked on a scale of one to ten, with higher numbers indicating lower perceived extent of corruption. Trinidad and Tobago fares poorly in the corruption rankings. Singapore is ranked first in the world, and Norway and Barbados are ranked in the top twenty countries worldwide. Trinidad and Tobago is ranked seventy-third in the world and its index has worsened over the period of 2004 to 2010, while Barbados has continued to improve (table 17.11).

Table 17.11 Corruption Perception

	Global Rank	2004	2006	2008	2010
Trinidad and Tobago	73	4.2	3.2	3.6	3.6
Singapore	1	9.4	9.2	9.2	9.3
Norway	10	8.8	8.8	7.9	8.6
Barbados	17		6.7	7.0	7.8

Source: World Bank, *World Development Indicators.*

Conclusion

Trinidad and Tobago has underperformed in respect of its growth and development over the last fifty years. When compared with other countries that were
more or less similarly placed around 1960, it is clear that Trinidad and Tobago
has not achieved in key areas of health care delivery, education access, and income and wealth. Its substantial resources of oil and gas have, like so many other
resource-based economies, failed to deliver on the promise of those resources. Per
capita income is today substantially below that of a country like Singapore, which
started off less well off than Trinidad and Tobago and has no natural resources at
all. Per capita income is around the same level as neighboring Barbados, which
also has no natural resources to speak of and relies heavily on tourism. Economic
progress in Trinidad and Tobago has been attended by greater variability and,
hence, uncertainty for investors and consumers alike.[4]

In respect of the development policies pursued, we have noted that these were
not adapted quickly to changing circumstances and that the government urged
upon itself a large role in the economy, not out of any ideological disposition,
but out of a mistrust of and poor relationships with both the local and foreign
private sectors. Policy unwittingly helped to foster the dependence of large sections of the population – the urban, Afro-Trinidadian segment as well as the rural
Indo-Trinidadian segment – on the government for jobs and income. Policy also
fostered a rentier-type economy, consuming sometimes lavishly out of the rents
accruing from the oil and gas resources.

Possible reasons for these outcomes are explored in the next chapter.

18

The Underachieving Society

W
e now seek to address the key question, which is why, despite its obvious resource advantages, Trinidad and Tobago has underperformed in delivering development to its citizens? We identify four possible factors that might account for this underperformance. These are deficiencies and mistakes in policy; the problem of implementation; the impact of ethnicity; and the "culture" factor. It must be emphasized that these factors are not separate, distinct and mutually exclusive, but are interrelated and mutually interactive, and in attempting to answer why the country has underperformed, all are probably relevant.

Deficiencies and Mistakes in Policy

The review of policy over the half-century since 1958 in the previous chapter suggests areas in which development policies themselves may have been deficient. One is necessarily guarded in making judgments such as these since hindsight is always twenty-twenty. However, the fact that other countries faced with the same environment and circumstances made different choices that redounded to the benefit of their citizens lends weight to the judgment that the policies chosen were less than optimal.

The first observation in this regard relates to the strategy of import substitution industrialization (ISI). This strategy was developed as import replacement behind tariffs and quantitative restrictions and was inspired and advocated by the then local colonial administration. ISI as a development strategy has fundamental limitations compared with the strategy of export promotion industrialization (EPI). We have already noted that Arthur Lewis, in whose name the strategy is usually invoked, did not recommend ISI but advocated EPI.[1] Balassa summarized the ways in which ISI limits development compared to export promotion when he observed that

> exports of manufactured goods can play an important role in industrial development by increasing foreign exchange earnings and enabling firms to use large-scale production methods. Instead of production on a small scale exclusively for domestic markets, the expansion of export markets makes possible specialization according to comparative advantage, reduction in product variety in individual firms, and participation in the international division of the production process by the production of parts and components for assembly abroad. . . . Familiarity with foreign markets and competition abroad will provide incentives for technological change and product improvement.[2]

Lewis understood these limitations quite well and also appreciated the difficulties of a strategy of export promotion. This is why he advocated inviting foreign investors into the region and our learning the "tricks of the trade". The idea of "wooing and fawning" on foreign capital was repugnant to the sensibilities of the politicians engaged in the anticolonial struggle. The strategy of import replacement offered the line of least resistance.

The argument for import replacement was that once in train, protection could be reduced over time and the manufacturers could then seek to penetrate export markets from a secure domestic base. However, without the discipline of competition and world prices, manufacturers were content to remain behind protective tariffs and quotas for as long as possible, even though domestic markets were too small for economical production and as a result consumers suffered high prices and products of substandard quality. A classic case in point was the motor vehicle assembly industry in Trinidad.

The second area of policy where there were deficiencies was incomes policy. The models of development with surplus labour suggest that if the wage rate in the modern sector is set higher than the subsistence wage (plus a premium), the result will be a lower rate of capital accumulation and unemployment. The models abstract from the presence of trade unions and from the existence of an offshore "enclave" sector, both of which may influence the dynamics of wage rate determination in the "modern" sector. They also abstract from government in its role of employer of labour.

Having failed to defang the trade unions with the Industrial Stabilization Act, the government simply gave up on an incomes (wages) policy, leaving wage determination to the contest of wills between employer and union, and to the perspectives of an industrial court whose grasp of the importance of wider development objectives and concerns was limited. In addition, the government itself compromised any semblance of incomes policy by instituting a minimum wage and by itself becoming a sponge for the unemployed by facilitating low-level, low-productivity employment in the civil service, the local government bodies and statutory corporations, and later on in state enterprises.

The expansion of government employment had two perverse effects in terms of development policy. First, very high proportions of government expenditure were directed to wages and salaries as well as transfers to state enterprises and households, which were ultimately paid out as wages and salaries. This meant that correspondingly less of government expenditure was available to be directed to capital expenditure on social overhead capital and infrastructure that could promote external economies and increase productivity. The lower rate of public sector investment would have implications for growth and development over time.

Second, government employment, which was in effect "lifetime" employment, fostered a culture of dependency on government that congealed over time into a sense of entitlement. It is not uncommon for the argument to be made that public sector wages are deserved on distributional grounds related to the country's oil wealth, whereby the government becomes a mechanism for redistributing the country's hydrocarbon resources to the rest of the country to be consumed and which requires no concomitant productive work to be earned.

A third area of policy that was deficient was the conduct of macroeconomic policy. The compromising of the government budgetary operations by expanding public sector employment has already been noted. The implications of this as well as the government's adoption of the role of "prime mover" in the economy meant that the budget needed to be large. At times of buoyant oil revenues, an expansive budget is not really a problem. It is when, over the course of the commodity cycle that oil revenues decline sharply, the problem of the financing of the budget is exposed. Active government with the posture of a welfare state is difficult to countervail with monetary policy. The consequence is that inflation is higher than it should be, and adjustment has to be effected using drastic measures such as devaluations.

An additional observation in this area relates to the lack of data and the lack of appreciation for data in the formulation of policy. In the immediate post-independence period, the Central Statistical Office was well resourced, had high status, and attracted high-quality professionals. With the demise of planning in the 1970s, attention to data collection and analysis declined, such that the

Central Statistical Office today is a shadow of its former self. Lags in the production of data are long, the quality of critical data series, including the population census itself, is suspect and the range of data produced has shrunk rather than expanded over the years. Good policy formulation demands good data, and good data makes for better policy formulation. Trinidad and Tobago has been deficient in this important regard.

A fourth area of deficiency in policy relates to the perverse incentives created by government employment and more generally private sector dependence on government expenditure. As Norman Girvan has observed: "[A]s long as it is easier and less risky to make quick returns from importing, trading, fast food, restaurants, taxi driving, auto parts, insurance, finance, property and real estate development, and fêtes; and public sector employment whether Unemployment Relief Programme (URP), Community-Based Environmental Protection and Enhancement Programme (CEPEP) or parastatals compared to agriculture, export manufacturing and new export services, then the former will flourish and the latter will not, and there will be little diversification!"[3]

There is little technology transfer, innovation or research and development occurring in any industry in Trinidad and Tobago, and the creative industries and professional services generally lack meaningful support.

The Problem of Implementation

A striking feature of the five-year development plans and of successive budgets is the extent to which public sector projects are not implemented at all or take very long to implement, even allowing for the fact that projects are often "announced" in budget speeches, although they are then only at a conceptual stage. One factor in poor implementation is the bureaucracy within the public service prior to the award of a contract by the Central Tenders Board, which makes for delay in project execution, and which has prompted calls over many years for the reform of public procurement procedures.

However, there is also considerable delay *after* contracts for projects are awarded. Examples of delay, cost overruns and incomplete projects abound, both small and large. One egregious example of incompletion was the Caroni Racing Complex for horse racing, which was halted by the George Chambers administration after significant sums had already been expended.

The Uff Commission of Enquiry into the Construction Sector and UDECOTT identified delays and overruns in a range of public sector projects undertaken in the period from 2000 to 2008. Some of these projects are summarized in table 18.1.

Table 18.1 Delays and Overruns in Selected Public Sector Construction Projects

Project	Sponsor	Start Date	Original Completion Date	Actual Completion Date	Original or Adjusted Contract Cost ($M)	Final Cost	Cost Overrun (%)
Scarborough Hospital	NIPDEC	January 2003	2005	Ongoing (2011)	135.9	550.3#	304%
Customs and Excise Building	UDECOTT	May 2004	March 2006	Ongoing (2011)	99.5*	113	13%
Belmont Police Station	NIPDEC	Sept. 2005	July 2006	January 2008	11.8	15.8	25%
Chancery Lane	UDECOTT	2005	n/a	2009	413	732	70%
International Waterfront Project	UDECOTT	2005	n/a	n/a	1,663.6	n/a	0%
National Academy for the Performing Arts (North)	UDECOTT	2006	January 2009	October 2009	458	n/a	0%
Prime Minister's Residence & Diplomatic Centre	UDECOTT	2006	n/a	n/a	>200	Unknown	Unknown
Government Campus Plaza†	UDECOTT	2004/ 2005	2006/2007	Ongoing (2011)	1,393.2	1,527.3	11%

Source: Report of the Commission of Enquiry into the Construction Sector Trinidad and Tobago (Uff Commission), March 2010.

#The original contract sum was expended and the project stopped for three years; a new contract was let to a different contractor for $415 million with a scheduled completion of April 2010; the project was still incomplete in August 2011.

*Value added tax exclusive.

†Government Campus Plaza includes the Customs and Excise Building (package 1) and involved several different contractors across several packages. At the time of writing, the tower buildings comprising the plaza are not occupied, but the car park is operational.

While delays and cost overruns waste resources, the quality of workmanship is also a perennial problem on construction projects that results in rework or higher cost of maintenance and repair later on.

It is not only construction projects that suffer from poor implementation. Over the years, the government has undertaken a host of "reforms", change management exercises, strategic planning exercises, commissions of enquiry and other interventions whose outputs have remained "on the shelf". Legislation sometimes takes quite long to get on the statute books and then when enacted and proclaimed, these laws are not enforced. Computerization projects that are intended to improve efficiency in several areas of government are often stillborn.[4]

The mainstream public service is not organized for entrepreneurship. Indeed the culture of the public service is based on conformity to established practice and rules. Moreover, public service compensation rules can provide no "carrots" to public servants for exercising initiative and "out of the box" thinking, and at the same time, public service regulations make it very difficult to use "sticks" for weak performance or lack of initiative. The result is the default option for maintenance of the status quo.

Yet another problem of the mainstream public service is its lack of effective consultation and articulation with the private sector and nongovernmental organizations (NGOs). Public servants are rarely recruited from the private sector and have a suspicion of, if not antipathy towards, the private sector. Notwithstanding the ritual "consultation", which occurs at the time of the annual budget exercise, the private sector is not embraced and included in the development of plans and programmes within the public sector. Ministers who come to government from the private sector are confronted with the complexity of regulation, the ponderous decision-making of cabinet government, and the "bubble" inhabited by senior public servants. The lack of dialogue and intercourse between public and private sectors slows implementation and concertation and cooperation efforts. During the planning years, the private sector was marginalized by the planners. During the period of resource-based industrialization, the Ken Julien Task Force, which was developing a sectoral plan, had limited interaction with or need for the input of the local private sector. The Vision 2020 exercise led by businessman Arthur Lok Jack was outflanked by a set of government-sponsored projects undertaken by special purpose state enterprises.

The special purpose state enterprises are yet another attempt to circumvent the lack of implementation capacity within the mainstream public service, together with the desire of government to drive economic activity. Another mechanism used was the "government to government" arrangements where the executing agency is sponsored by another government so as to provide some greater assurance of probity and performance of the contracts. In addition, international agencies such as the World Bank, the UNDP and the Inter-American Development Bank have expended considerable time and resources in attempting to improve project planning and execution capability within the mainstream public service. In recent times, the government has also resorted to hiring public officers on contract outside the terms and conditions of the mainstream public service in an attempt to attract better-qualified and -motivated talent to the tasks of project planning and execution. Liberal use has been made of a variety of committees, task forces, and commissions to address and make recommendations on specific problem issues.

Ethnicity and Development Policy

It was noted in chapter 17 that of the comparator countries, Norway and Barbados are largely homogeneous, and while Singapore is ethnically heterogeneous, the Chinese segment of the population is dominant. This is not so in Trinidad and Tobago where no ethnic group constitutes a majority of the population, but because of the composition of the political parties and their bases, political administrations tend to be dominated by one or another ethnic group.

In many countries, ethnic or tribal conflict, which occasionally degenerates into open warfare, has had a deleterious effect on economic development by destroying lives and productive capacity, engendering instability and uncertainty, lowering savings and investment, encouraging capital flight and emigration, and diverting state resources into arms and ammunition. While this has never occurred in Trinidad and Tobago, it is not to say that ethnicity has had no impact on development policy. In the context of a rentier economy such as Trinidad and Tobago, the competition for the rents accruing to the society through the government from the country's hydrocarbon resources has an ethnic dimension, which leads to suboptimal allocation of state resources. The impacts are mainly in terms of distribution and arise from the implementation of policy in the context of an historical pattern of occupational and regional distribution of the population along ethnic lines.[5]

It is relatively easy to identify situations where the implementation of policy has consequences for the distribution of resources among the various ethnic groups and more particularly the two larger groups of Afro- and Indo-Trinidadians, and the people of Tobago. The Unemployment Relief Programme, which started in the late 1960s, was intended to address open, urban unemployment and as a consequence, was skewed towards the low-income Afro-Trinidadian segment of the population. The subsidy provided to the unviable sugar industry over several decades until the industry was dismantled in 2007 benefited mainly the rural Indo-Trinidadian segment of the population working in that industry. The tax incentives for the manufacturing industry benefited mainly the "French Creole" owners of these businesses. Government expenditure on the construction and frequent resurfacing of highways benefited mainly the Indo-Trinidadian owners and workers of the few firms involved in this activity. The decision to locate industrial activity for the gas-based sector in Point Lisas near the town of Couva would have benefited mainly Indo-Trinidadian businesses in that region, while the location of manufacturing plants in the East-West Corridor would have benefited the Afro-Trinidadian segment, which constitutes the majority in that region. The centralization of government services in the capital city of Port of Spain has imposed high costs on those citizens, especially those in the island of Tobago, in accessing these services.

On the other hand, it is difficult to find instances of specific, overt discrimination against one or another ethnic group in the *formulation* of policy. There have been numerous instances that have been litigated in the courts where individual persons have claimed infringement of their constitutional rights on the basis of denial of promotion or, in the case of the Maha Sabha, which represents most of the Hindu community, the denial of a radio station licence and the concomitant award of a license to a known supporter of the ruling party. An Equal Opportunity Commission (EOC) has been established to address grievances that are allegedly born out of ethnic, gender or other forms of discrimination; a sensible and long overdue response to disentangling perception of discrimination from the reality in particular cases, without resort to expensive litigation in the courts.[6]

Since the distributional consequences of policy initiatives are well appreciated by technocrats and politicians, policymaking may be retarded and delayed while issues around the communication of the policy and the mitigation of obvious impacts are contemplated or investigated. In some instances this may mean trying to ensure that the distribution of development projects is such that no group or segment feels aggrieved.

"We Like It So": The Culture Factor

An important argument that should not be discounted too easily is that the people of a country may actually *not* aspire to the standard of living of the richer and more developed countries. They may *choose* to work less hard, be less innovative and productive, and consume more because they value leisure, conviviality and pleasure more than they value work, and the income and wealth it produces. In other words some societies may display a combination of values, attitudes and behaviours that do not emphasize wealth accumulation and prosperity in purely economic or material terms. Alternatively, while they may well aspire to greater wealth and economic prosperity, the values, attitudes and behaviours

they embrace may lead to their making choices of strategy and policy that ultimately do not conduce to growth and development.

The people of Trinidad and Tobago have been stereotyped as having a "carnival mentality" and enjoying parties and "liming". Work is as much or more about
socializing and sustaining relationships as it is about producing or contributing.[7]
In addition, Trinidad and Tobago has a large number of public holidays. There are
fourteen official public holidays and the two Carnival days constitute de facto public holidays, making a total of sixteen public holidays. These attitudes towards work
and productivity often mean that systems and processes do not work well. Since
citizens do not expect or trust that systems will work well, resort is had early in any
transaction to the identification of a contact within the system who can expedite
accomplishment of the transaction. This further compromises the efficiency of the
system and discriminates in favour of those persons who are well connected.

Another aspect of the culture of Trinidadians and Tobagonians is ambivalence
towards things local and things foreign. V.S. Naipaul, Trinidad and Tobago–born
Nobel Laureate in Literature, has pejoratively described the country's people as
"mimic men". Frantz Fanon wrote of the "black skins, white masks" of the post-
colonial elite.[8]

On the face, local cultural practices and products are celebrated, vaunted even.
Trinidadians and Tobagonians are proud, and justifiably so, of the steel pan musical instrument that was invented here, of the Carnival celebrations that are always
described as the "biggest in the world", of the gift to the world of calypso and soca
music, of the success of the country's athletes at premier events such as the Olym-
pics, the English Premier League, of the fact that this country is the smallest ever
to qualify for the Soccer World Cup (2006), of the contribution to West Indies
cricket, and of the phenomenal success of their women at international beauty
pageants. For a country of only 1.3 million in an English-speaking Caribbean of
only five million, we punch above our weight in the international arena. This is
true not only in respect of sports, music and beauty contests. Trinidadians and
West Indians more generally have indeed excelled on the international stage in
politics, international relations and international law, playing critical roles in introducing the Law of the Sea and the exclusive economic zone, in the efforts at the
United Nations and Commonwealth Secretariat to bring an end to apartheid in
South Africa, and earlier through the efforts of Jamaican Marcus Garvey, Trinidadian Stokely Carmichael (Kwame Ture) and George Padmore to the pan-African
movement, in the development of black consciousness and the success of the civil
rights movement in the United States.

At the same time, the country's elite hanker after metropolitan tastes and lifestyles, including foreign travel to metropolitan capitals, and measure their personal
achievements against those of people living in those countries. Having grown up

with British institutions and practices in law and jurisprudence, medicine, party politics and parliament, these institutions and practices have become the yard-stick against which local institutions and practices are routinely measured. This is not to say that no institutional innovations have been made. Trinidad and Tobago moved to republicanism in 1976, while Jamaica, Barbados and other Caribbean territories have remained constitutional monarchies. Yet Trinidad and Tobago, despite being the seat of the Caribbean Court of Justice (to which Barbados and Guyana have acceded), retains the United Kingdom Privy Council as the final court of appeal.

Not surprisingly, the intellectual fountains from which the country's leaders and technocrats drink are located in the metropolitan schools, media and acad-emies. It was Lloyd Best who famously "called out" the intellectual elites of the region when he opined on

> the cultural anarchy created by an economy where men – among them the most capable – are forced, by the needs of living, to show excellence in purveying met-ropolitan propaganda – political and academic; where other men, standing always on the wings of power, have no choice but to preoccupy themselves with public relations; where the working people are confined to technological mimicry and the assembly of parts, where the population seeks dignity in a scramble for consumer durables; and where the political leadership survives by submissiveness to imperial power.[9]

Best castigated the "plantation mind" of the region's intellectual elite. For him, Arthur Lewis "was epistemologically an Englishman . . . brought up by Ricardian and Smithian theories . . . he had to be an Englishman". Lewis's model was not suitable for the Caribbean since the Caribbean is constituted from the outside by foreign investors, comprised of transplanted populations brought as slaves and indentured workers, with no households, no production for domestic consump-tion, and no families.[10]

With such a mentality, the political and technocratic elites, which sought to promote development, could hardly be expected to fully come to terms with the Caribbean reality and formulate and implement appropriate policies to foster growth and development.[11]

The third cultural characteristic of Trinidad and Tobago, and perhaps Caribbean society as a whole, is the precedence of relationship over rules. The significance of personal relationships (which may have an ethnic dimension) was identified by the Uff Commission of Enquiry speaking on the apparent attempt to influence the placing of a contract in these terms: "[R]ather than indicating corruption, we think this is more a reflection on local culture in a society where no one is anony-mous and business at any level is made more complicated by the undoubted exis-tence on many levels of personal relationships involving predispositions to favour one person over another. Such a culture cannot be changed but the consequences in terms of potential corruption must be guarded against."[12]

Societies that aspire to and achieve development are disciplined in terms of both the setting of rules and in ensuring conformity and obedience to the rules. It is not that there are no rules governing all spheres of life in Trinidad and Tobago, but perhaps because of the size of the society where social networks are numerically small, it is the enforcement of the rules that suffers.

The Uff Commission of Enquiry noted as follows: "We have observed in the context of contractual issues as well as regulatory matters that there exists a culture of non-enforcement which appears to operate on a mutual basis. Contractors seem reluctant to issue proceedings for payments overdue or to enforce claims and employers in turn refrain from enforcing time obligations which are routinely not complied with."[13]

It is not only construction contracts and regulations relating to building construction that are not properly enforced. Lack of enforcement of rules is pervasive. The use of the roadway by drivers in Trinidad and Tobago causes great alarm to visitors. Yet the routine flouting of the rules of the road, leading to a high accident rate, has brought only weak and sporadic enforcement of the traffic laws. Customs regulations are avoided, promoting corruption and reducing government revenues. Rules regarding the acquisition of permissions for land use from the Town and Country Planning Department or for environmental safeguards are often ignored, and the relevant government departments do not apply sanctions. The rules promulgated by the Integrity Commission relating to the compulsory submission of declarations of assets are flouted by "persons in public life" who are part of the country's governing elite.

In a society where rule enforcement is observed more in the breach, whenever there is an attempt to actually enforce the rules, the sanction may then appear to be exemplary and inequitable.

While part of mutual non-enforcement of rules may be attributed to the precedence of relationship over rules, another part may be attributed to the tendency to avoid confrontation since confrontation may escalate dramatically and turn quickly into conflict. One can therefore observe a tendency to threats, bluffing and blustering, with apparently open, vigorous challenge or opposition to some issue, but compromise and accommodation behind the scenes.

What Is to Be Done?

Historically, Trinidad and Tobago's economy cycles from boom to bust depending on what happens to the price of oil. The carefree, undisciplined lifestyle of most of the population is occasionally perturbed by a paroxysm of social unrest. Downturns are accompanied by ritual incantations by government officials of the need for "diversification" to reduce the country's dependence on oil and the energy-based industries, the formation of new committees, task forces and boards, and considerable hand-wringing and angst about the "sustainability" of government fiscal operations. Seemingly bold new initiatives and projects are announced, and all the while everyone is waiting and secretly hoping for a quick turnaround in the price of oil, ammonia, methanol and natural gas so that rents will again begin to accrue, government spending programmes can restart and the fête can resume. Trinidad and Tobago will not achieve its potential for development unless and until this cycle is broken.

Perhaps the first order of business is to ensure that the theoretical foundations of development policy for the new millennium are correctly laid.[14] Although the specific business activities that might be promoted in the twenty-first century will be different from those promoted in the 1950s and 1960s, the underlying principles articulated by development theory remain valid. There are four key principles – external economies, economies of scale, incomes policy and sound macroeconomic policy.

External economies involve the building out of social overhead capital at state expense to improve productivity in the private sector. This means airports and seaports; highways and freeways; bridges and public transportation; parks and nature reserves for recreation; business parks and industrial estates to promote agglomeration effects; and schools, universities and essential public buildings. A critical piece of twenty-first-century social overhead capital in the telecommunications network must include a high-speed Internet backbone and gateway that permits connectivity by every household and business in the country at minimal cost. The actual sequencing of these investments and how the projects are implemented (state investments, public-private partnerships, or "build-operate-transfer") are matters of specific policy at particular junctures in the country's history depending on the resources and capabilities available to the government.

The importance of economies of scale arises from the fact that business activity must be capable of addressing large markets so as to achieve lower unit costs of production. Manufacturing plants need to be world-scale, and other businesses need to be able to scale up quickly. They must have the "DNA of an elephant". Like the tourism industries, other sectors must learn to address the global market in order to achieve economies of scale. In today's world, the Caribbean regional market is merely a starting point, the de facto home market for Caribbean businesses. Yet while the deepening and widening of Caribbean integration, including labour mobility, tax harmonization, joint investment promotion and coordination of financial regulation is recognized by analysts and commentators as being critical to Caribbean competitiveness, little progress has been achieved in terms of meaningful economic integration. Trinidad and Tobago–based businesses have acquired a significant presence in certain sectors in other Caribbean territories, albeit with some resistance and not a little resentment. There is undoubtedly scope for capital and human resources from Trinidad and Tobago to be deployed in the development of infrastructure, agriculture and resource extraction in territories such as Guyana, Suriname and Haiti, and these projects can be defined and implemented on a bilateral basis to the benefit of the countries involved.

In respect of incomes policy the experience of developing countries that have broken through is clear. Redistribution and a more equal distribution of income must come at a later stage of development. During the development process, even as workers earn a decent wage conforming to the norms of the society and which encourages consumption and saving, profits must increase faster so as to promote accelerated investment. There is no point in "redistributing poverty" as many developing countries sought to do in the 1950s and 1960s. At the same time, there is a need to encourage the reinvestment of profits in the domestic economy in the right kinds of business activities, but short of punitive taxation and without the use of unavailing tax incentives.

Macroeconomic policy, which promotes stability, investor certainty and sound public finances with serviceable debt levels, is an essential hygiene factor in securing growth and development. Macroeconomic stability does not in and of itself promote growth and development. Macroeconomic instability and crises are, however, a serious drag on growth and development as it results in lower investment rates, waste of resources and contraction of income and wealth, especially for the most vulnerable groups in the society. It makes sense to establish certain benchmark indicators covering the following variables: foreign exchange reserves; current account deficit; exchange rate variation; fiscal deficit and surplus; inflation rate; and external debt-service ratio. The public and the business community should be clear that macroeconomic policy will be managed conservatively within the specified parameters so that investment decisions can be made with minimal uncertainty arising from macroeconomic conditions.

The second order of business is to get serious and seriously disciplined about development. There needs to be a collective epiphany that growth and development will not just happen and, more particularly, will not happen only when oil and natural gas prices are propitious. Development and transformation require hard work from a disciplined and focused people. For some businesses, it may mean the realization that entertainment and recreation are a serious business with defined processes and service delivery standards that ensure the delivery of a consistent product that satisfies the customer, whether that customer is "playing mas" at Carnival, patronizing a reggae or calypso concert, or taking a nature tour in the Northern Range.[15] In other areas, it must mean that the culture of entitlement and dependency is disrupted, enterprise and initiative are rewarded, and laws and regulations are consistently and seriously enforced. However, a society that does not care for its children, its elderly and those of its members who are physically or mentally challenged will inevitably crumble from within. Social policy and programmes delivered efficiently by government agencies and government-supported NGOs are critical to development in the wider sense of the promotion of human respect and freedoms.

The third order of business is to establish a permanent professional development agency, that is, one that is not dissolved with every change of government or repopulated with supporters or hacks of whichever is the current ruling party. This agency must be staffed with the best available minds with an understanding of economics, sociology, engineering and science. The agency must be able to draw staff who have had experience working in the private sector and who may also have worked or studied abroad so that they possess an appreciation of what is possible and what it takes to succeed in a globalized world. The agency will incorporate or draw on the work of an independent statistical institute that will engage in constant data gathering, surveys and publication of data and statistics. The agency will craft key areas of policy in respect of energy, land use, and competitiveness and productivity, and take these areas of policy outside of the hurly-burly of partisan politics and policy changes by successive administrations.

The fourth order of business is to tackle the problem of implementation or execution. Larry Bossidy and Ram Charan, in their book on "execution", noted: "Execution is a systematic process of rigorously discussing hows and whats, questioning, tenaciously following through, and ensuring accountability. It includes making assumptions about the business environment, assessing the organization's capabilities, linking strategy to operations and the people who are going to implement the strategy, synchronizing those people and their various disciplines, and linking rewards to outcomes."[16]

While Bossidy and Charan are writing in the context of private sector businesses, the definition applies equally and mutatis mutandis to public sector projects and initiatives. Implementation needs to be addressed in respect of identifying, developing and prioritizing a programme of projects; procurement policies and practices; project management and supervision; and postimplementation evaluation and maintenance.

The identification, development and prioritizing of development projects needs to take place at both local government and central government levels. Local government project identification will allow the needs of local communities to be addressed including maintenance of roadways and sidewalks; development and maintenance of parks and places of recreation; garbage disposal; water distribution; and the regulation of community life in areas such as shopping, parking facilities, places of entertainment, and so on. Central government project identification would focus on projects that are national in scope and that carry the greatest impact in respect of the generation of external economies. These would include national transportation networks, electrification, water production and distribution, communications networks, museums and other major cultural facilities, industrial estates, and the development of new towns and housing estates. Projects at both levels must be subject to project evaluation and ranking, and the techniques and methods for so doing must be part of the equipment of the professionals developing the public sector investment programme.

Procurement policies define how and by whom projects are to be delivered. Traditionally, the overriding concern of public sector procurement has been transparency, and projects were usually tendered through the Central Tenders Board. This procedure proved to be a major bottleneck to project implementation and also did not address pre-award assurance of value for money, for example the prevention of bid-rigging, nor did it address post-award accountability for the on time, within budget delivery of the project. With the use of special purpose state enterprises, which had their own tender committees as well as government-to-government arrangements that avoided tendering altogether, governments sought to accelerate procurement while maintaining some degree of transparency and accountability, but opened up the procurement process to various forms of corrupt practices. There is clearly need for regulation of procurement for public sector projects. The proposals being considered in 2012 by the parliament of Trinidad and Tobago focus on the establishment of mandatory guidelines for decentralized tendering, a regulator who will review the award of contracts for conformity with the guidelines and penalties for breaches of the guidelines, and the formation of a national procurement advisory council, which will bring private sector stakeholders in the award of government contracts into the picture. These cannot be legislated too soon.

Project management and supervision is perhaps the most critical step in ensuring effective implementation of properly conceived, designed and costed projects. It is here that transparency, accountability and value for money are actually assured through attention to detail and the vigilant management of the processes and procedures for the execution of projects by contractors. It is here that the "mutual non-enforcement of rules" must be avoided.

Continuous improvement in standards of design, construction and workmanship can be achieved by evaluation and review of projects after implementation so that problems and issues with implementation can be identified and corrected and perhaps incorporated into the implementation processes for future projects. In addition, public infrastructure is notoriously not maintained. This shortens the life of public buildings and other works and increases the lifetime cost of the project. The overweening concern for the expenditure of "taxpayers' money" is somehow not translated into an equivalent concern for the maintenance and preservation of the assets that taxpayers' money has acquired.

The fifth and final order of business is to exorcise "race" and "ethnicity" from the discourse in government and policy. "Race" or "ethnicity" cannot be ignored as if it were a "pink elephant in the room". Equally, it should not be placed, spoken or unspoken, at the centre of every debate or decision. In a multi-ethnic society where for historical reasons, ethnic competition is rife, that competition needs to be directed into various institutional channels where fact can be separated from fiction, prejudice separated from process, and fairness assured as best as humanly possible. Some progress has been made in this regard. The establishment of an EOC is one such institutional channel into which allegations of unfairness arising from age, ethnicity, gender or other forms of discrimination can be assessed, mediated or adjudicated, provided that this institution, too, is not derailed or suborned by political agendas. Parliamentary oversight over the award and execution of contracts through the office of a regulator is another such institutional channel. These channels must work and work effectively if "race" and "ethnicity" are to be exorcised and the society is able to minimize a major hurdle to effective policy implementation.

Notes

Preface and Acknowledgements

1. Reginald Dumas, *In the Service of the Public* (Kingston: Canoe Press, 1995); Wendell Mottley, *Trinidad and Tobago Industrial Policy 1959–2008* (Kingston: Ian Randle, 2008); Lloyd Best (with Eric St Cyr), *Transforming the Plantation Economy: Economic Policy and Management Choices* (Port of Spain: Lloyd Best Institute, 2012). See also Selwyn Ryan, *Eric Williams: The Myth and the Man* (Kingston: University of the West Indies Press, 2009); and Doddridge H.N. Alleyne, *Export/Import Trends and Economic Development in Trinidad 1919–1939* (Kingston: Canoe Press, 2010).

Chapter 1

1. See William G. Demas, *The Economics of Development in Small Countries with Special Reference to the Caribbean* (Montreal: McGill-Queen's University Press for the Centre for Developing-Area Studies, 1965); Lloyd Best, "Size and Survival", in *Readings in the Political Economy of the Caribbean,* ed. Norman Girvan and Owen Jefferson (Kingston: New World Group, 1971).
2. Eric Williams, *History of the People of Trinidad and Tobago* (Port of Spain: PNM Publishing, 1962), 69. See also Bridget Brereton, *A History of Modern Trinidad: 1783–1962* (Portsmouth, NH: Heinemann, 1981). The fact is that there were only fifty years or so between the Cedula of Population in 1783 that brought French planters and slaves to Trinidad in numbers and the end of slavery – a period disrupted by English conquest (1797), the end of the slave trade (1807), and the institution of British Crown Colony government.
3. G.W. Roberts, "Movements in Population and Labour Force", in *The Economy of the West Indies*, ed. George Cumper (Kingston: Institute of Social and Economic Research, 1960).
4. For a comprehensive history of Tobago, see Susan Craig-James, *The Changing Society of Tobago 1838–1938*, 2 vols. (Arima: Cornerstone Press, 2008).
5. One unique festival in south Trinidad sees Catholic and Hindu devotees venerating the same "saint".

6. Lloyd Braithwaite, *Social Stratification in Trinidad* (St Augustine, Trinidad: Institute of Social and Economic Research, 1953); M.G. Smith, *The Plural Society in the British West Indies* (Los Angeles: University of California Press, 1965) and *Pluralism, Politics and Ideology in the Creole Caribbean* (New York: Research Institute for the Study of Man, 1991). The "plural society"/social stratification debate is reprised and discussed for contemporary Trinidad in Selwyn Ryan, ed., *Social and Occupational Stratification in Contemporary Trinidad and Tobago* (St Augustine, Trinidad: Institute of Social and Economic Research,1991).

7. See Selwyn Ryan, *The Jhandi and the Cross: The Clash of Cultures in Post-Creole Trinidad and Tobago* (Kingston: Sir Arthur Lewis Institute of Social and Economic Studies, 1999). The term "Afro-creole" was used by Smith, *Pluralism*.

8. See the excellent judgment of Justice Peter Jamadar, H.C.A. No. Cv. S. 2065/2004.

9. Lou Ann Barclay, "The Syrian/Lebanese Community in Trinidad and Tobago: A Preliminary Study of a Commercial Ethnic Minority", in *Entrepreneurship in the Caribbean*, ed. Selwyn Ryan and Taimoon Stewart (St Augustine, Trinidad: Institute of Social and Economic Research, 1994). Perhaps the defining event here was the acquisition of the French creole McEnearney-Alstons group by Anthony Sabga, one of the most successful Syrian-Lebanese businessmen in Trinidad and Tobago and establishing what is now "Ansa-McAl", one of the region's largest conglomerates.

10. See Selwyn Ryan and Lou Ann Barclay, *Sharks and Sardines: Blacks in Business in Trinidad and Tobago* (St Augustine, Trinidad: Institute of Social and Economic Research,1992).

11. See Brereton, *History of Modern Trinidad.*

12. In fact, the National Alliance for Reconstruction (NAR), which unseated the PNM by a landslide in 1986, was a coalition of parties comprising the United Labour Front (mainly Indo-Trinidadian support base), the Organisation for National Reconstruction with support drawn from the mixed population and the middle classes, and the Democratic Action Congress representing Tobago. It would not be until 1995 that Trinidad and Tobago would have its first prime minister of East Indian descent in Basdeo Panday. Its second prime minister of East Indian descent, Kamla Persad-Bissessar, was elected in 2010 and is also the country's first female prime minister.

13. Smith, *Pluralism*, 46 (my emphasis).

14. These difficult questions are discussed in Ryan, *Jhandi and the Cross*. In my master's thesis, on which part of this work is based, I posited that in Trinidad and Tobago, the constituent groups embraced a transcendent or core set of values that are universal and that purely ethnic considerations do not influence policy formulation or seek to promote one group over the other. But see Smith, *Pluralism*, 68–69, who argued otherwise. A fascinating case in point in the context of Trinidad and Tobago relates to the closure of the sugar industry.

15. Krishna Persad, *The Petroleum Geology and Prospects of Trinidad and Tobago* (Port of Spain: Ministry of Energy and Energy Industries, 2008), a publication celebrating a century of commercial oil production in Trinidad and Tobago.

16. See chapter 2.

17. Terry Lynn Karl, *The Paradox of Plenty; Oil Booms and Petro-States* (Los Angeles: University of California Press, 1997), xvi. Karl discusses the case of Venezuela in depth.
18. Ibid., 7.
19. Demas, *Economics of Development.*

Chapter 2

1. This is developed further in the section on policy mapping at the end of chapter 3.
2. A good deal of ink has been used in the discussion of the measurement of "output" and "income" in the context of developing countries, including accounting for unpaid labour, the size and nature of the "informal economy", and the size and nature of the "underground economy". These issues, important as they indeed are, are not addressed beyond this footnote in this work.
3. Perhaps the earliest formulation of this is Weber's "Protestant ethic" as the driver of capitalism. Other authors over the years have explored the significance of cultural factors in economic growth and development. See David Landes, *The Wealth and Poverty of Nations* (New York: Norton, 1999), and the discussion on culture below.
4. See Albert O. Hirschman, *The Strategy of Economic Development* (New Haven: Yale University Press, 1958).
5. An interesting contrast to the mainstream literature is the notion that colonialism and imperialism were responsible for underdevelopment. See Walter Rodney, *How Europe Underdeveloped Africa* (London: Bogle-L'Ouverture, 1973); and C.Y. Thomas,*The Poor and the Powerless* (New York: Monthly Review, 1988).
6. Demas, *Economics of Development*, 20.
7. Amartya Sen, *Development as Freedom* (New York: Anchor Books, 1999), 3.
8. Ibid., 53
9. Rodney, *How Europe Underdeveloped Africa*, ch.1.
10. Herve Carrier, SJ, *The Social Doctrine of the Church Revisited* (Vatican City: Pontifical Council for Justice and Peace, 1990), 20; also *Compendium of the Social Doctrine of the Church* (Vatican City: Pontifical Council for Justice and Peace, 2004).
11. Kari Levitt, *Reclaiming Development*(Kingston: Ian Randle, 2005), xxiv.
12. Partha Dasgupta, "Measuring Sustainable Development: Theory and Application", *Asian Development Review* 24, no. 1 (2007).
13. Lloyd Best famously insisted on this point. He rejected the notions of "developed" and "underdeveloped" countries, a perspective that is better appreciated when the process view is taken as well as the "cultural relativism", which underlay Best's argument.
14. Jaime Ros has remarked on the disjuncture between "growth theory" and "development economics" and has made a heroic and commendable effort to bridge the two. See Jaime Ros, *Development Theory and the Economics of Growth* (Ann Arbor: University of Michigan Press, 2001).

15. Roy Harrod, "An Essay on Dynamic Theory", *Economic Journal* (March 1939); E. Domar, "Capital Expansion, Rate of Growth and Employment", *Econometrica* (April 1946).

16. Harrod's analysis considered the "warranted" rate of growth, where the values of the savings rate and the capital-output ratio are such as to ensure sustained steady growth; and the "natural" rate of growth, where the rate of increase in the effective supply of labour and the rate of technical progress determine the maximum rate of growth that the system can achieve. See R.G.D Allen, *Macro-Economic Theory* (London: Macmillan, 1967).

17. For an exposition that systematically relaxes key assumptions within the one-sector model, see Robert M. Solow, *Growth Theory: An Exposition* (Oxford: Clarendon Press, 1970).

18. See R. Stern, *The Balance of Payments* (Chicago: Aldine, 1973), ch. 11.

19. H.G. Johnson, "Money in a Growth Model", in *Growth Economics,* ed. A. Sen (Harmondsworth: Penguin, 1970), ch. 12.

20. The term "high development theorists" is that of Paul Krugman, "The Fall and Rise of Development Economics", in *Development, Geography and Economic Theory* (Cambridge, MA: MIT Press, 1997). This group should arguably include Rostow and his model of the "Stages of Economic Growth".

21. W.A. Lewis, "Economic Development with Unlimited Supplies of Labour", *Manchester School* (May 1954), reprinted in A.N. Agarwala and S.P. Singh, *The Economics of Underdevelopment* (London: Oxford University Press 1958); see also Lewis's *Theory of Economic Growth* (London: Allen and Unwin, 1955); *Development Planning: The Essentials of Economic Policy* (London: Allen and Unwin, 1966); *Growth and Fluctuations, 1870–1913* (London: Allen and Unwin, 1978).

22. Lewis, "Economic Development", 428.

23. Ibid., 416.

24. Allyn Young, "Increasing Returns and Economic Progress", *Economic Journal* 38 (December 1928).

25. Ibid., 533.

26. Paul Krugman, *Fall and Rise*, and Ros, *Development Theory,* for expositions of a model of increasing returns that outline the case for a "big push".

27. Hirschman, *Strategy of Economic Development*, 83–84.

28. Paul Romer, "Increasing Returns and Long Run Growth", *Journal of Political Economy* 94 (1986); Murphy et al., "Industrialization and the Big Push", *Journal of Political Economy* 97 (1989); and Krugman, *Development, Geography.*

29. Ros, *Development Theory,* 135–36, and Krugman, *Fall and Rise.*

30. Ros, *Development Theory,* 212–13.

31. Jeffrey D. Sachs and Andrew M. Warner, *Natural Resource Abundance and Economic Growth,* Center for International Development and Harvard Institute for International Development (Cambridge, MA: Harvard University, 1997).

32. Richard Auty, "How Natural Resources Affect Economic Development", *Development Policy Review,*18 (2000): 347–64.

33. Ibid., 347.
34. Karl, *Paradox of Plenty.*
35. Norman Girvan, "The Development of Dependency Economics in the Caribbean and Latin America", *Social and Economic Studies* 22, no. 1 (March 1973). See also Norman Girvan, "Caribbean Dependency Thought Revisited", *Canadian Journal of International Studies* 27, no. 3 (2006).
36. H. Myint, "The Classical Theory of International Trade and the Underdeveloped Countries", *Economic Journal* 68 (1958); Hans Singer, "The Distribution of Gains Between Investing and Borrowing Countries", *American Economic Review* (May 1950).
37. Demas, *Economics of Development*, and Lloyd Best, "Size and Survival", in *Readings in the Political Economy of the Caribbean*, ed. Norman Girvan and Owen Jefferson (Kingston: New World Group, 1971).
38. Consider this opaque statement by Best and Levitt quoting Myrdal, "theory is no more than a correlated set of questions regarding the social reality under study". Best and Levitt characterized their methodological approach as *"histoire raisonée"* or reasoned history.
39. On the other hand, some Caribbean economists sought to use and extend open economy formulations of Keynesian macroeconomic and growth theory to the Caribbean context. See C. Kennedy, "Keynesian Theory in an Open Economy", *Social and Economic Studies* 15, no. 1 (March 1966); A.A. Francis, "A Model of National Economic Growth under Perfect Enclavism", *Social and Economic Studies* 18, no. 4 (December 1969); C.J. Bruce, "The Open Petroleum Economy: A Comparison of Keynesian and Alternative Formulations", *Social and Economic Studies* 21, no. 2 (June 1972). These formulations were no doubt inspired by Dudley Seers, "Mechanism of the Open Petroleum Economy", *Social and Economic Studies* 13, no. 2 (June 1964).
40. Girvan, "Development of Dependency Economics".
41. Alister McIntyre, "Lloyd Best: Reminiscences of the Early Days", in *Independent Thought and Caribbean Freedom: Essays in Honour of Lloyd Best*, ed. Selwyn Ryan (St Augustine, Trinidad: Sir Arthur Lewis Institute of Social and Economic Studies, 2003), 392–93.
42. Terrence W. Farrell, "Structural Adjustment and Transformation in the Caribbean: Management Strategies Based on the Lessons of Experience", in *Peace Development and Security in the Caribbean*, ed. A. Bryan, J.E. Greene and T.M. Shaw (London: Macmillan, 1990); Delisle Worrell and Compton Bourne, eds., *Economic Adjustment Policies for Small Nations: Theory and Experience in the English-Speaking Caribbean* (New York: Praeger, 1989).
43. J.J. Polak, *The Two Monetary Approaches to the Balance of Payments: Keynesian and Johnsonian* (Washington, DC: IMF Working Papers, August 2001).
44. These now go under the rubric of "neo-liberalism". Williamson though has argued that the Washington Consensus is not to be identified with neo-liberalism, which he thinks encapsulates monetarism, supply-side economics, the minimal state and capital account liberalization. See John Williamson, *Did the Washington Consensus Fail?* (Washington, DC: Center for Strategic and International Studies, 2002).

45. Landes, *Wealth and Poverty*, 516.
46. Ibid., 217.
47. Lewis, *Theory of Economic Growth*, ch. 3. Lewis's historical work includes *Growth and Fluctuations, 1870–1913*.
48. See Michael Porter, *The Competitive Advantage of Nations* (London: Palgrave Macmillan, 1998); and William Lewis, *The Power of Productivity* (Chicago: University of Chicago Press, 2004).

Chapter 3

1. Jan Tinbergen, *Economic Policy: Principles and Design* (Amsterdam: North Holland, 1956).
2. Econometricians are familiar with the concepts of "structural models" and "reduced-form models" of economic processes.
3. Tinbergen, *Economic Policy*, 3.
4. Karl, *Paradox of Plenty*, 58.
5. Alister McIntyre, "Some Issues of Trade Policy in the West Indies", in *Readings in the Political Economy of the Caribbean*, ed. Norman Girvan and Owen Jefferson (Kingston: New World, 1971), 166.
6. Havelock Brewster, "Economic Dependence: A Quantitative Interpretation", *Social and Economic Studies* 22, no. 1 (March 1973): 91.
7. Ibid., 94. Brewster's characterization might seem harsh, but it has considerable merit. See chapter 18.
8. In the 1970s and 1980s, Keynesian thinking gave way to the Monetarist and Rational Expectations schools embodied in the Reagan-Thatcher policies and the "Washington Consensus", which repudiated the notion of active government and advocated the shrinking of the role of government, free markets and deregulation. The economic crisis of 2008–9 has now witnessed a resurgence of Keynesian thinking, re-regulation and scepticism that markets will always deliver the right results.
9. See George Cumper, ed.,*The Economy of the West Indies* (Kingston: Institute of Social and Economic Research, UWI 1960).
10. Demas, *Economics of Development*.
11. Here we have analysts such as Girvan, "Development of Dependency Economics". For a critique of this article see G.E. Cumper, "Dependence, Development and the Sociology of Economic Thought", *Social and Economic Studies* 23, no. 3 (1974).
12. C.Y.Thomas, *Dependence and Transformation* (New York: Monthly Review Press, 1974). Thomas defines "structural dependence" as "the extent to which the economic structure of these economies depends on foreign trade, payments, capital, technology and decision-making to generate domestic economic processes" (30).
13. Lloyd Best and Kari Levitt, "Outline of a General Theory of Caribbean Economy", in *Essays on the Theory of Plantation Economy: An Institutional and Historical Approach to Caribbean Economic Development* (Kingston: University of the West Indies Press, 2009).

14. Studies on employment practices in Trinidad and Tobago show that firms owned by certain ethnic groups tend to employ persons disproportionately from the same group. Employment in government services and state enterprises will have favoured Afro-Trinidadians disproportionately over the years. See Selwyn Ryan, "Race and Occupational Stratification in Trinidad and Tobago", in Ryan, *Social and Occupational Stratification*.
15. This is the theory of "indicative planning". See V. Lutz, *Central Planning for the Market Economy* (London: Longmans, Green, 1968), and the references therein.
16. Susan Rose-Ackerman, *Corruption and Government: Causes, Consequences and Reform* (New York: Cambridge University Press, 1999), 3.
17. Ibid., 30.

Chapter 4

1. John Stuart Mill, *Principles of Political Economy* (1848), book 3, ch. 25, para. 5, 182, in *The Collected Works of John Stuart Mill*, vol.3 (Indianapolis: Online Library of Liberty, 2009). See also Lloyd Best, "A Model of Pure Plantation Economy", *Social and Economic Studies* 17, no. 3 (1968).
2. The significance of the creole elite has been missed by several commentators who focused exclusively on the Colonial Office in London as the source of thought and policy. See for example, C.Y. Thomas, *The Poor and the Powerless: Economic Policy and Change in the Caribbean* (New York: Monthly Review, 1988), ch. 4.
3. For a seminal discussion, see Lloyd Best, "Independent Thought and Caribbean Freedom", in *Readings in the Political Economy of the Caribbean,* ed. N. Girvan and O. Jefferson (Kingston: New World 1971). Some West Indian intellectuals made excursions into alternative intellectual traditions such as "African Socialism" and before long returned to the mainstream. A Marxist school did develop in the region and influenced the "Grenada Revolution" in 1979–83. Many of these "Marxists" now sit comfortably within parliaments in the region.
4. Of the former British colonies, only Guyana and Trinidad and Tobago moved away from a constitutional monarchy to republican status. And to date, only Guyana, Barbados and Belize have removed the Privy Council as the final court of appeal and embraced the Caribbean Court of Justice.
5. For a discussion of postwar trade policy and imperial preference see McIntyre, "Some Issues".
6. The Trinidad and Tobago petroleum industry and the role of the multinational corporations are discussed in Trevor Farrell, "The Multinational Corporations, the Petroleum Industry and Economic Underdevelopment in Trinidad and Tobago" (PhD diss., Cornell University, 1974).
7. See Selwyn Ryan, *Race and Nationalism in Trinidad and Tobago* (Toronto: University of Toronto Press, 1972), 30–33; and Kelvin Singh, *Race and Class Struggles in a Colonial State, Trinidad and Tobago 1917–1945* (Kingston: University of the West Indies Press, 1994).

8. See Brereton, *History of Modern Trinidad*.

9. Gordon K. Lewis, *The Growth of the Modern West Indies* (New York: Monthly Review, 1968), 206–7. Cipriani and, after him, Butler were emblematic of the colonial elite, characterized by an ambivalence in their relationship with the "mother country".

10. It is instructive to note that Rienzi was of East Indian descent, Butler was of African descent and Gomes was of Portuguese descent. However ethnic considerations and loyalties seemed to have trumped class affiliation in the formation of political parties later on.

11. E.E. Williams, minister of finance, budget speech, 1958, *Hansard*, Legislative Council Debates, vol. 8, 1957–58, 547–716.

12. Great Britain Colonial Office, West Indies Royal Commission (Moyne) Report, HMSO, 1945, Cmnd. 6607.

13. Ibid., 428.

14. See E.R. Wicker, "Colonial Development and Welfare 1929–1957", *Social and Economic Studies* 12, no. 4 (1963).

15. Williams, budget speech, 1958.

16. Terrence W. Farrell, "Arthur Lewis and the Case for Caribbean Industrialization", *Social and Economic Studies* 29, no. 4 (December 1980).

17. See A.R. Prest, "Public Finance", in *The Economy of the West Indies*, ed. George Cumper (Kingston: Institute of Social and Economic Research, 1960).

18. Prest (ibid.) questioned the impact of accelerated depreciation allowances in a situation of labour surplus, though conceding that foreign firms would have more than likely chosen technology they considered appropriate without regard to local labour surpluses.

19. See A. McIntyre and B. Watson, *Studies in Foreign Investment in the Commonwealth Caribbean*, no. 1, *Trinidad and Tobago* (Kingston: Institute of Social and Economic Research, 1971)

20. Eric Williams brought in Arthur Lewis who was an advocate of export promotion industrialization rather than the limited import substitution policy advocated by the Shaw Committee. Williams also felt that implementation needed to be faster and more effective. See Terrence Farrell, "Arthur Lewis and the Case for Caribbean Industrialization", *Social and Economic Studies* 29, no. 4 (December 1980), and chapter 5.

21. In British Guiana (Guyana) there was open violence between the two major ethnic groups in 1961.

Chapter 5

1. J.K. Galbraith, *The Affluent Society* (Boston: Houghton Mifflin, 1958).

2. See Ryan, *Eric Williams*, and his earlier work *Race and Nationalism*.

3. Ivor Oxaal, *Black Intellectuals Come to Power* (Cambridge, MA: Schenkman, 1968), 123.

4. Ryan, *Race and Nationalism*, 71–73 and 87–88.

5. Oxaal, *Black Intellectuals*, 124–28.
6. People's National Movement, "The People's Charter: Statement of Fundamental Principles", in *Major Party Documents* (Port of Spain: PNM Publishing, 1966), 19–40.
7. See in particular, Eric Williams, "My Relations with the Caribbean Commission 1949–1955" (speech at Woodford Square, June 1955), reprinted in *Eric E. Williams Speaks*, ed. Selwyn Cudjoe (Wellesley, MA: Calaloux, 1993), 111–65.
8. Lewis, *Growth of the Modern West Indies*, 219.
9. In that regard, Eric Williams, Grantley Adams and Norman Manley who led the independence movements in Trinidad and Tobago, Barbados, and Jamaica, respectively, proved to be far wiser than Forbes Burnham in Guyana who took that country down the road of "cooperative socialism" with ultimately disastrous consequences.
10. Government of Trinidad and Tobago, *Third Five-Year Plan 1969-1973* (Port of Spain: Government Printery, 1969), 3; hereafter referred to as *Third Plan*. The notion of "equality" and "equity", which are different concepts, continue to resonate in the politics of Trinidad and Tobago to today, probably because of the society's ethnic composition, which prompts constant comparison of who is getting what.
11. Arthur Lewis, of course, saw the surplus labour as a possible advantage, not really as a problem; the real problem was finding the ways and means to combine local labour with capital and skills to produce goods and services for export.
12. Farrell, "Arthur Lewis".
13. See Great Britain Royal Commission, Moyne Commission Report (HMSO, 1945, Cmnd. 6607), "Economic Position and Outlook".
14. W. Arthur Lewis, "The Industrialization of the British West Indies", *Caribbean Economic Review* 2 (May 1950).
15. This is the critical difference between Lewis and the other strategies. The others emphasized import substitution; more specifically, import replacement. Lewis argued for export promoting industrialization. See Farrell, "Arthur Lewis".
16. Lewis, "Industrialization", 24–27.
17. See chapter 4.
18. In Jamaica and Barbados, earnings of foreign exchange from tourism probably had the same effect of giving less urgency to the expansion of manufactured exports along the lines proposed by Lewis. In contrast, Singapore transitioned during the 1960s from import substitution to export promotion.
19. Government of Trinidad and Tobago, *Draft Second Five-Year Plan, 1964-1968* (Port of Spain: Government Printery, 1964), 147; hereafter referred to as *Second Plan*.
20. *Third Plan*, 31

Chapter 6

1. United Nations, *Planning for Economic Development* (New York: United Nations,1964), 1; Report of a Group of Experts (A/55 33/Rev.1)
2. Demas, *Economics of Development*, 121.

3. E.E. Williams, "The Purpose of Planning", in *The Crisis in Planning*, ed. Dudley Seers and Mike Faber (London: Chatto and Windus, 1972), 39.
4. See A. Waterston, *Development Planning: Lessons of Experience* (Baltimore: Johns Hopkins, 1965), ch. 8; and W.A. Lewis, *Development Planning* (London: Allen and Unwin, 1966), article 3.
5. E.E. Williams, "Economic Problems of Trinidad and Tobago", TECA Public Affairs pamphlet, no. 1 (1955), 16.
6. Eric Williams, minister of finance, budget speech, 1961, Legislative Council, 3–4.
7. Government White Paper, quoted in *Second Plan*, 1964, 10–11.
8. *Second Plan*, 1964, 10–11.
9. T&T Federation of Chambers of Industry and Commerce (Inc.), "Preliminary Comments on the Draft Trinidad and Tobago Third Five-Year Development Plan, 1969–1973" (mimeo, 1969), 1.
10. Government of Trinidad and Tobago, *Five-Year Development Programme, 1958–1962*; *Projects for 1959, 1960, 1961 and 1962*; Government of Trinidad and Tobago, *Projects for 1963*; Government of Trinidad and Tobago, *Draft Second Five-Year Plan 1964–1968*; *Projects for 1964*.
11. See articles in the special issue of *Social and Economic Studies* 23, no. 2 (1974), "Issues of Public Policy and Public Administration in the Caribbean".
12. *Third Plan*, 1969, 143.

Chapter 7

1. A.N.R Robinson, minister of finance, budget speech, 1967, 8.
2. Federation of Chambers of Commerce, Preliminary Comments on the Draft Third Five-Year Development Plan (mimeo, 1969), 11.
3. *Report of the Tripartite Committee to Review the Fiscal Policy of Trinidad and Tobago* (Port of Spain: Government Printery, 1969), 4.
4. E.E. Williams, minister of finance, budget speech, 1968, 64ff.
5. Law of Trinidad and Tobago, Central Bank Act, chapter 79:02, section 3 (3). For a more extensive and detailed discussion of the central bank and monetary policy, see Terrence W. Farrell, *Central Banking in a Developing Economy: A Study of Trinidad and Tobago, 1964–1989* (Kingston: Institute of Social and Economic Research, 1990).
6. William Demas has argued that "Economic Planning in the Caribbean can never be fully effective until such time as a solution is found for (the problem of implementing a wages policy)", *Economics of Development*, 145–46.
7. Eric Williams, "Reflections on the Industrial Stabilization Bill", People's National Movement, series of articles in the *Nation*, April–May 1965, section 2, 8.
8. See Havelock Brewster, *Wage Policy Issues in an Underdeveloped Economy; Trinidad and Tobago* (Kingston: Institute of Social and Economic Research, 1969), ch. 3.
9. Tripartite Committee on Incomes Policy, interim report (mimeo, October 1968), 5–6.

10. See chapter 3 on market and nonmarket policy instruments.

11. *Second Plan*, 17.

12. Apart from the utilities, the only ventures in which the government had ownership prior to 1968 were BWIA (the national airline), ostensibly "to ensure that the Commonwealth Caribbean had some control over the air services available to the region to support the tourist industry", and Angostura Limited, to prevent the takeover of this export industry. See Government of Trinidad and Tobago, *White Paper on Public Participation in Industrial and Commercial Activities* (Port of Spain: Government Printery, 1972), 4.

13. *Second Plan*", 84–85, 217, 223–225. Some estimates were also made of petroleum output. The third plan, wisely, avoided this "target-setting", except for certain "basic materials" industries. See *Third Plan*, 248.

14. *Second Plan*, 84. It should be noted that this implicitly assumes that social and private valuations of costs and benefits are equal or more nearly so.

15. *Third Plan*, 18.

16. *Third Plan*, 63.

17. See Government of Trinidad and Tobago, *White Paper*, 1972, 7.

18. Federation of Chambers of Industry and Commerce, Preliminary Comments on the Draft Third Five-Year Development Plan, 1969–1973 (mimeo, 1969), 5–12 and letter to the prime minister, May 11, 1970.

Chapter 8

1. The data in this section are from Frank Rampersad, *Growth and Structural Change in the Economy of Trinidad and Tobago, 1951–1961* (Kingston: Institute of Social and Economic Research, 1965).

2. Ibid., 11.

3. Government of Trinidad and Tobago, *Five-Year Development Programme, 1958–1962* (Port of Spain: Government Printery, 1958), 3–4. (*First Plan*).

4. One set of estimates gives unemployment rates in Trinidad as 1946, 7 per cent; 1955, 6.4 per cent; 1956, 6.3 per cent; 1957, 7.0 per cent; 1960, 10.6 per cent. See *Second Plan*, 149–51.

5. *Second Plan*, 36.

6. Rampersad, *Growth and Structural Change*, 21, table 6. Total sector output on Rampersad's classification also includes mining and quarrying which accounted for just 5 per cent of sector output in 1958 and the same percentage in 1961.

7. Ibid., 31.

8. *Second Plan*, 36–37

9. Data are from Rampersad, *Growth and Structural Change*, 13, 26.

10. Ibid.

11. See *Third Plan*, 1964, 399.

12. See *Second Plan*, 1964, 8, as well as chapter 7 and the discussion below.

13. Ibid., 9. Elsewhere in the plan (pp. vi and 3) the commitment to economic development by private enterprise, foreign and local, is reiterated.
14. *Second Plan*, 72.
15. Ibid., 65.
16. Ibid., ch. 12.
17. The shift in the language used on development issues reflects the emergence of the influence of the scholarship of development economists and writers from the developing countries and the beginnings of the articulation of theories of "economic imperialism" and "dependency" to explain underdevelopment rather than the traditional theories of development based on climate, rapid population growth and social factors.
18. The premise of the thrust in domestic agriculture was that the resources required – land, management, capital and credit – were sufficient and in elastic supply. This, particularly as regards arable land, was moot.
19. *Second Plan*, ch. 15.
20. Ibid., ch. 16. See also chapter 10.
21. *Third Plan*, 1969, 4.
22. Ibid., 5–9.
23. Ibid., 33.
24. Ibid., 35.
25. For a discussion of the conflict between "peasant" and plantation, see George Beckford, *Persistent Poverty*.
26. *Third Plan*, 1969, ch. 23.
27. Ibid., ch. 14.
28. Ibid., 171.
29. Government of Trinidad and Tobago, *White Paper*, 1972, 4.
30. Ibid., 5.
31. For a detailed analysis of the performance of the manufacturing sector over the period, see Terrence W. Farrell, "The Structure, Organisation and Performance of Manufacturing Industry in Trinidad and Tobago" (PhD diss., University of Toronto, 1979). Essentially while the sector grew strongly behind protective barriers, its labour absorption and export performance were not as strong, and several industries could not survive the dismantling of the structure of protection later on.
32. The operating surplus is defined as GDP less wages and salaries less capital consumption less net indirect taxes. However, the income of sole proprietors and unincorporated enterprises, as well as farmers, includes a mix of wages and profits that cannot be easily disaggregated. As a consequence, the operating surplus measure almost certainly overstates profits.
33. See E. Ahiram Distribution of Income in Trinidad and Tobago and Comparison with Distribution of Income in Jamaica, *Social and Economic Studies* 15, no. 2 (1966) and Ralph Henry, "A Note on Income Distribution and Poverty in Trinidad and Tobago", *CSO Research Papers* 8 (October 1975). Winston Dookeran, "The Distribution of Income in Trinidad and Tobago, 1957–1976", in *Review of Income and Wealth* 27 (June

1981), discusses the explanations for the changes in income distribution over the period up to 1975–76.

Chapter 9

1. E.E. Williams, minister of finance, budget speech, 1981, in Government of Trinidad and Tobago, *Budget Speeches 1958–1981*, 2:904.
2. Arguably, the use of petroleum and natural gas to develop industries downstream had been mooted even in the 1960s, as was the idea of a national participation in the industry that came later with the acquisition of BP's operations and the formation of Trinidad-Tesoro Oil Company (1969). See Ken Julien, "The Emergence of the National Energy Sector" (nineteenth Eric Williams Memorial Lecture, Central Bank of Trinidad and Tobago, 2005).
3. Budget speech, 1973, in Government of Trinidad and Tobago, *Budget Speeches 1958– 1981*, 2:622.
4. E.E. Williams, minister of finance, budget speech, 1976 (December 1975), in *Budget Speeches 1957–1981*, 2:691.
5. E.E. Williams, minister of finance, budget speech, 1977 (December 1976), in *Budget Speeches 1957–1981*, 2:728.
6. Ibid.
7. Budget speech, 1976, in *Budget Speeches 1957–1981*, 2:694.
8. Government of Trinidad and Tobago, *Accounting for the Petrodollar, 1977, Accounting for the Petrodollar, 1980* and *Accounting for the Petrodollar, 1984* (Port of Spain: Government Printery).
9. See Deryck Brown, *History of Money and Banking in Trinidad and Tobago from 1789 to 1989* (Port of Spain: Central Bank of Trinidad and Tobago, 1989).

Chapter 10

1. See Trevor Boopsingh, *Oil, Gas and Development: A View from the South* (San Juan, Trinidad: Longman, 1990), ch. 6 and 12.
2. See chapter 14.

Chapter 11

1. Alvin Hilaire, "Economic Reaction to a Sectoral Boom: Trinidad and Tobago" (PhD diss., Columbia University, 1989).

2. The global competitiveness of these industries was challenged on account of the perception that these industries enjoyed subsidized gas prices. Export of iron and steel to the United States was challenged by US producers on this score.

Chapter 12

1. In China, Deng Xiaoping also embarked on a process of reforms in that communist state, which were to lead to opening up of markets. China's inclination towards market reforms left the socialist leaning developing countries without a model to follow or a source of aid.
2. See chapter 3.
3. World Bank, *The East Asian Miracle: Economic Growth and Public Policy* (New York: Oxford University Press, 1993).
4. Ibid., and Paul Krugman, "The Myth of Asia's Miracle", *Foreign Affairs*, no.6 (November–December 1994), 73.
5. The PNM did also lose the Federal elections of 1958.
6. For an account of the insurrection and events preceding and following, see Selwyn Ryan, *The Muslimeen Grab for Power* (Port of Spain: Inprint, 1991); and Raoul Pantin, *Days of Wrath* (New York: iUniverse, 2007). The government that won the elections in May 2010 has now appropriately instituted a commission of inquiry into the 1990 attempted coup, an initiative that had been steadfastly avoided by successive Manning (PNM) and Panday (UNC) administrations.
7. Government of Trinidad and Tobago, *The Imperatives of Adjustment: Draft Development Plan 1983–1986*, vols. 1 and 2, August 1983 ("Demas Task Force Report").
8. This, despite the presence of C.J. Bruce and Eric St Cyr on the task force. Bruce was a theoretician in the Keynesian tradition and did little empirical work, while St Cyr, a capable empirical economist, was inclining to embrace the New World theories of plantation economy, which lacked rigour at the time and where the empirical work from plantation economy theorizing had not progressed beyond initial attempts to reformulate the construction of the national income accounts by Kari Levitt.
9. Prime Minister Robinson and his wife, Patricia Robinson, had both been involved in the preparation of the second and third five-year plans, the former as minister of finance and the latter as a senior economist. Patricia Robinson was also a member of the Demas Task Force appointed under the Chambers Administration.
10. Government of Trinidad and Tobago, *Restructuring for Economic Independence: Draft Medium Term Planning Framework 1989–1995* (Port of Spain: Government Printery, 1988).
11. *Draft Medium Term Planning Framework 1989–1995*, 83.
12. See Raymond Vernon, ed., *The Technology Factor in International Trade* (New York: NBER and Columbia University Press, 1970); Christopher Freeman, *The Economics of Industrial Innovation* (Harmondsworth: Penguin, 1974); Frances Stewart, *Technology and Underdevelopment* (Boulder, CO: Westview, 1977); and "Essays on Science and

Technology Policy in the Caribbean", special issue of *Social and Economic Studies* 28, no. 1 (March 1979).
13. *Draft Medium Term Planning Framework 1989–1995,* 243.

Chapter 13

1. Quoted in Farrell, *Central Banking,* 86.
2. Ibid., 88.
3. This takes into account only central government debt, not the debt of the rest of the public sector.
4. Farrell, *Central Banking,* 104–6.
5. Details of the restructuring agreements are contained in P. Soverall-O'Brien and A. Hilaire, "External Debt Rescheduling in Trinidad and Tobago, 1988–1992", *Central Bank Quarterly Economic Bulletin* 18, no. 1 (1993).
6. Selby Wilson, minister of finance, budget speech, December 1990.
7. The Central Bank had earlier implemented a marginal reserve requirement, which was later consolidated. See Farrell, *Central Banking.*
8. Ibid., ch. 9.
9. The calculation of the real exchange rate used here adjusts the nominal TT$/US$ exchange rate index by the index of the United States and Trinidad and Tobago annual inflation rates. Higher domestic inflation relative to that of the United States (the country's main trading partner) results in an effective appreciation of the exchange rate.
10. World Bank, *Poverty and Unemployment in an Oil-Based Economy* Report No. 14382-TR (October 1995), citing data from a study by R. Teekens.
11. Ibid., 3.
12. See chapter 3.

Chapter 14

1. West Indian Commission, *Time for Action* (Black Rock, Barbados: West Indian Commission, 1992).
2. For an assessment of the regional economic integration movement see Norman Girvan, "Caribbean Community: The Elusive Quest for Economic Integration", in *Growth and Development Strategies in the Caribbean, ed.* Frank Alleyne, Denny Lewis-Bynoe and Xiomara Archibald (Bridgetown, Barbados: Caribbean Development Bank, 2010).
3. In 2010, a UNC-led coalition (People's Partnership) won the general election and succeeded the PNM in government.
4. It is interesting and important to note though that, despite the hostility of the American government to Cuba, Trinidad and Tobago has always maintained a relationship with Cuba and has supported its reintegration into the American hemispheric system

through the Organization of American States. In recent times, Trinidad and Tobago has sourced medical doctors from Cuba to assist in the delivery of health services.

5. Wendell Mottley, minister of finance, budget speech, 1992, 12. This budget speech was delivered barely two months after the new administration had been elected to office.

6. Wendell Mottley, *Trinidad and Tobago Industrial Policy 1959–2008* (Kingston: Ian Randle, 2008), ch. 3. According to Mottley, another factor that influenced the adoption of the role of facilitator and privatization was the failure of the Trintomar gas development project, which brought into question the capacity of state enterprises to successfully pursue large complex projects.

7. Wendell Mottley, minister of finance, budget speech, 1994, 20.

8. Brian Kuei Tung, minister of finance, budget speech, 1998, 8.

9. What did distinguish the budget presentations by Minister Kuei Tung was the rather poor quality of the content and the delivery, comparing rather unfavourably with those of ministers Mottley (PNM) and Wilson (NAR) before him.

10. Brian Kuei Tung, minister of finance, budget speech, 1996, 6. In Trinidad and Tobago, voting at general elections has followed ethnic lines for the most part, and elections are not fought on the basis of differences in economic and social policies of the parties or on ideological differences, but on narrow questions of incompetence in office, corruption and personality.

11. What is noteworthy is that several of these projects became entangled in allegations of corruption and/or cost overruns. These issues are discussed in part 6.

12. See part 2.

13. We have argued elsewhere that Lewis in fact saw export promotion as the key strategy. Unfortunately Caribbean countries remained stuck in the import substitution model or as in the case of Trinidad and Tobago, shifted the emphasis to resource-based industries. See Farrell, *Arthur Lewis*.

14. Garth Chatoor, *Issues and Challenges in the Power Sector in Trinidad and Tobago*, Presentation to RBTT Investor Forum, December 2006.

15. Government of Trinidad and Tobago, Ministry of Public Administration and Information, *FastForward: Trinidad and Tobago, Accelerating into the Digital Future*, 2003.

16. The author was a member of this task force.

17. See chapter 10.

18. One of the findings of the Uff Commission of Enquiry into UDECOTT was that company had no obligation to report to the line minister under which it fell (Ministry of Planning).

Chapter 15

1. Government of Trinidad and Tobago, Office of the Prime Minister, Draft National Strategic Plan, 2005.

2. See chapter 6 and the quotation from William Demas.

3. The author was a member of the Multi-Sectoral Group and chairman of the macroeconomics and finance subcommittee.

4. I would think that the traditional development economists, such as Arthur Lewis, and the structuralist/institutionalist school would argue that these sociocultural and attitudinal factors were always recognized and understood, but there were no data to be had in those days, and those factors were (somehow) mediated through the traditional economic variables – savings propensity, import propensity, productivity, capital efficiency, and so on. There is no one who, on reading Lewis's major works, would suggest that he did not have an excellent appreciation of social and cultural factors in economic development.

5. Draft National Strategic Plan (2005), 1.

6. While the Programme Management Office was housed within the Ministry of Planning and Development, it sat uneasily alongside the other departments within the ministry. In addition, it was felt that the process of arbitrating competing demands for resources would require the Programme Management Office to have the clout of the prime minister. In the event, the Ministry of Finance held the view that it was and should continue to be the final arbiter of competing demands for budgetary resources.

7. Government of Trinidad and Tobago, introduction, *Vision 2020 Operational Plan, 2007–2010*, xvii–xix. The use of the term "epistemic independence" reflects, no doubt, the influence of Lloyd Best.

8. See Terrence Farrell, "Voops, Vaps and Vi-ki-Vi: Economic and Social Management in Trinidad and Tobago" (paper presented to the Central Statistical Office, January 2007). A new statistics act has been on the drawing board now since 2006, but it is yet to see the light of day.

Chapter 16

1. The measure used here probably exaggerates the extent of the appreciation as the change in the domestic retail price index is used. A better measure might be the "core inflation" estimate done by the central bank, but there is no long time series of these estimates going back to 1993.

2. The export coefficient is the ratio of exports of goods and nonfactor services to GDP, while the import coefficient is the ratio of imports of goods and nonfactor services to GDP plus imports

3. By way of postscript, there has indeed been a substantial increase in trade union militancy and industrial action in the period 2011 to 2012, notwithstanding that the new administration embraced the labour movement as a partner in the government.

Chapter 17

1. Farrell, *Arthur Lewis*. It is instructive that Singapore segued quickly from import substitution to export promotion and then later on changed the strategy from labour-intensive manufacturing to focus on technology and services.

2. This is in contrast to Singapore, which established its Economic Development Board in 1961 and is still operating, and has spun off specialized agencies and subsidiaries to

address particular aspects of development identified by the Board. It is also in contrast to India, which created its planning commission in 1950 and has recently produced India's eleventh five-year plan for the period 2007 to 2012. The newly elected (2010) government in Trinidad and Tobago has now set up an economic development board and an innovation council, continuing the previous practice of creating new institutions that ultimately do not function.

3. World Bank, *A Time to Choose: Caribbean Development in the Twenty-First Century*, Report No. 31725-LAC (Washington, DC: World Bank, 2005).

4. The World Bank has drawn similar conclusions for the Caribbean as a whole in a recent comprehensive study, World Bank, *Time to Choose*.

Chapter 18

1. Farrell, *Arthur Lewis*.

2. Bela Balassa, *The Structure of Protection in Developing Countries* (Baltimore: Johns Hopkins Press for the World Bank, 1971), 96.

3. Norman Girvan (in private communication with the author). I am grateful to him for making this point.

4. The project to computerize drivers' and motor vehicle licenses is again underway after over fifteen years of various stages of proposal and implementation and still not completed as of March 2012. The Board of Inland Revenue has now implemented a project that has computerized tax returns, including value added tax, but is yet to implement online filing, which has been standard in developed countries for several years now.

5. Alvin Hilaire has suggested in private communication that ethnic loyalties may provide substantial margins for governments to pursue inappropriate policies since they will not be readily sanctioned for so doing at the polls.

6. It is not clear, however, whether the EOC appreciates the difference between "equality", which seems to be its agenda, and "equity", which ought to be its agenda.

7. My own observations are that work in Trinidad and Tobago is accompanied by talk and exchange of information, which has nothing to do with the tasks at hand, and interaction that in other countries is limited to defined breaks. It is also difficult to tell on a Trinidad and Tobago work site precisely who is in charge.

8. This ambivalence is not peculiar to Trinidad and Tobago or the Caribbean, but is evident in most if not all postcolonial societies. Rex Nettleford discusses the Jamaican case in *Mirror Mirror: Identity, Race and Protest in Jamaica* (Kingston: LMH Publishing, 2001). The Caribbean, however, experienced the longest period of colonial rule and the deep wounds of slavery and indentureship, which arguably makes our ambivalence all the more deep-seated and striking to the observer.

9. Lloyd Best, "Independent Thought and Caribbean Freedom", reprinted in Ryan, *Independent Thought*.

10. Lloyd Best, "Reflections on the Reflections", in Ryan, *Independent Thought*. One might be tempted to think that Best was writing in 1971, some forty years ago, and that

things may (should) have changed since then. Yet today the University of the West Indies offers a "summer" school to its students, and ever larger numbers of students take external degrees offered mainly by English universities, without having to pursue studies in Caribbean history, sociology or economics.

11. This is now most painfully evident in the lack of progress of the Caribbean Community and the Caribbean Single Market and Economy where the technical foundations laid by William Demas, Alister McIntyre, Roderick Rainford and latterly Edwin Carrington have not been built on by successive heads of government, most of whom, ironically, were trained at the University of the West Indies.

12. Uff Commission, para. 32.7.

13. Ibid., para. 62.

14. I am often amused by those who use the word "theoretical" in a pejorative sense to mean "impractical" or "irrelevant" and that one should just "get on with it". I can do no better than to quote John Maynard Keynes's famous dictum: "The ideas of economists and political philosophers, both when they are right and when they are wrong, are more powerful than is commonly understood. Indeed the world is ruled by little else. Practical men, who believe themselves to be quite exempt from any intellectual influence, are usually the slaves of some defunct economist." John Maynard Keynes, *The General Theory of Employment Interest and Money* (London: Macmillan, 1936), 383. This can perhaps now be extended to include the influence of the fads and fashions of "gurus" from business schools.

15. It is instructive that several bandleaders in recent years have evolved into professional entertainment businesses that produce one or more bands at Carnival time. They use websites, DVDs and other promotional material, and have developed sophisticated systems for delivery of costumes and managing the bands on Carnival days.

16. Larry Bossidy and Ram Charan, *Execution: The Discipline of Getting Things Done* (New York: Crown Business, 2002), 22.

Selected Bibliography

Agarwala, A.N., and S.P Singh, eds. *The Economics of Underdevelopment*. London: Oxford University Press, 1958.

Ahiram, E. "Distribution of Income in Trinidad and Tobago and Comparison with Distribution of Income in Jamaica". *Social and Economic Studies* 15, no. 2 (1966).

Allen, R.G.D. *Macro-Economic Theory*. London: Macmillan, 1967.

Alleyne, Doddridge H.N. *Export/Import Trends and Economic Development in Trinidad 1919–1939*. Kingston: Canoe Press, 2010.

Barclay, Lou Ann. "The Syrian/Lebanese Community in Trinidad and Tobago: A Preliminary Study of a Commercial Ethnic Minority". In *Entrepreneurship in the Caribbean*, ed. Selwyn Ryan and Taimoon Stewart. St Augustine, Trinidad: Institute of Social and Economic Research, 1994.

Best, Lloyd. "Economic Structure in the West Indies". In *The Economy of the West Indies*, ed. George Cumper. Kingston: Institute of Social and Economic Research, 1960.

———. "Independent Thought and Caribbean Freedom". In *Readings in the Political Economy of the Caribbean,* ed. Norman Girvan and Owen Jefferson. Kingston: New World 1971.

———. "A Model of Pure Plantation Economy". *Social and Economic Studies* 17, no. 3 (1968).

———. "Size and Survival". In *Readings in the Political Economy of the Caribbean,* ed. Norman Girvan and Owen Jefferson. Kingston: New World, 1971.

Best, Lloyd, and Kari Levitt. "Outline of a General Theory of Caribbean Economy". In *Essays on the Theory of Plantation Economy: An Institutional and Historical Approach to Caribbean Economic Development*. Kingston: University of the West Indies Press, 2009.

Best, Lloyd (with Eric St Cyr). *Transforming the Plantation Economy: Economic Policy and Management Choices*. Tunapuna, Trinidad: Lloyd Best Institute of the West Indies, 2012.

Boopsingh, Trevor. *Oil, Gas and Development: A View from the South*. San Juan, Trinidad: Longman, 1990.

Bossidy, Larry, and Ram Charan. *Execution: The Discipline of Getting Things Done*. New York: Crown Business, 2002.

Braithwaite, Lloyd. *Social Stratification in Trinidad*. St Augustine, Trinidad: Institute of Social and Economic Research, 1953.

Brereton, Bridget. *A History of Modern Trinidad: 1783–1962*. Portsmouth, NH: Heinemann, 1981.

Brewster, Havelock. "Economic Dependence: A Quantitative Interpretation". *Social and Economic Studies* 22, no. 1 (March 1973).

———. *Wage Policy Issues in an Underdeveloped Economy: Trinidad and Tobago.* Kingston: Institute of Social and Economic Research, 1969.

Carrier, Herve, SJ. *The Social Doctrine of the Church Revisited.* Vatican City: Pontifical Council for Justice and Peace, 1990.

Chamber of Commerce (Trinidad and Tobago). Preliminary Comments on the Draft Third Five-Year Development Plan. Mimeo [Federation of Chambers of Commerce], 1969.

Craig-James, Susan. *The Changing Society of Tobago 1838–1938.* 2 vols. Arima, Trinidad: Cornerstone Press, 2008.

Cudjoe, Selwyn, ed. *Eric E. Williams Speaks.* Wellesley, MA: Calaloux, 1993.

Cumper, George. "Dependence, Development and the Sociology of Economic Thought". *Social and Economic Studies* 23, no. 3 (1974).

———, ed. *The Economy of the West Indies.* Kingston: Institute of Social and Economic Research, 1960.

Demas, William G. *The Economics of Development in Small Countries with Special Reference to the Caribbean.* Montreal: McGill-Queen's University Press for the Centre for Developing-Area Studies, 1965; repr., Kingston: University of the West Indies Press, 2009.

Dookeran, Winston. "The Distribution of Income in Trinidad and Tobago, 1957–1976". *Review of Income and Wealth* 27 (June 1981).

Dumas, Reginald. *In the Service of the Public.* Kingston: Canoe Press, 1995.

Farrell, Terrence W. "Arthur Lewis and the Case for Caribbean Industrialization". *Social and Economic Studies* 29, no. 4 (December 1980).

———. 1990. *Central Banking in a Developing Economy: A Study of Trinidad and Tobago, 1964–1989.* Kingston: Institute of Social and Economic Research, 1990.

———. "Structural Adjustment and Transformation in the Caribbean: Management Strategies Based on the Lessons of Experience". In *Peace Development and Security in the Caribbean,* ed. A. Bryan, J.E. Greene and T.M. Shaw. London: Macmillan, 1990.

———. "The Structure, Organisation and Performance of Manufacturing Industry in Trinidad and Tobago". PhD diss., University of Toronto, 1979.

———. "Voops, Vaps and Vi-ki-Vi: Economic and Social Management in Trinidad and Tobago". Paper presented to the Central Statistical Office, Trinidad and Tobago. January 2007.

Farrell, Trevor. "The Multinational Corporations, the Petroleum Industry and Economic Underdevelopment in Trinidad and Tobago". PhD diss., Cornell University, 1974.

Girvan, Norman. "Caribbean Dependency Thought Revisited". *Canadian Journal of International Studies* 27, no. 3 (2006).

———. "The Development of Dependency Economics in the Caribbean and Latin America". *Social and Economic Studies* 22 no. 1 (March 1973).

Girvan, Norman, and Owen Jefferson, eds. *Readings in the Political Economy of the Caribbean.* Kingston: New World, 1971.

Government of Trinidad and Tobago. *Accounting for the Petrodollar.* Port of Spain: Government Printery, 1977.

———. *Accounting for the Petrodollar*. Port of Spain: Government Printery, 1980.

———. *Accounting for the Petrodollar*. Port of Spain: Government Printery, 1984.

———. Draft National Strategic Plan. Office of the Prime Minister, 2005.

———. *Draft Second Five-Year Plan, 1964–1968*. Port of Spain: Government Printery, 1964.

———. *FastForward: Trinidad and Tobago, Accelerating into the Digital Future*. Ministry of Public Administration and Information, 2003.

———. *Five-Year Development Programme, 1958–1962*. Port of Spain: Government Printery, 1958.

———. *The Imperatives of Adjustment: Draft Development Plan 1983–1986*. Vols. 1 and 2. August 1983.

———. *Report of the Tripartite Committee to Review the Fiscal Policy of Trinidad and Tobago*. Port of Spain: Government Printery, 1969.

———. *Restructuring for Economic Independence: Draft Medium-Term Planning Framework 1989–1995*. July 1988.

———. *Third Five-Year Plan, 1969–1973*. Port of Spain: Government Printery, 1973.

———. *Vision 2020 Operational Plan, 2007–2010*.

———. *White Paper on Public Participation in Industrial and Commercial Activities*. Port of Spain: Government Printery, 1972.

Great Britain. Colonial Office. "West Indies Royal Commission (Moyne) Report". Cmnd. 6607. HMSO 1945.

Henry, Ralph. "A Note on Income Distribution and Poverty in Trinidad and Tobago". *Central Statistical Office Research Papers* 8 (October 1975).

Hilaire, Alvin. "Economic Reaction to a Sectoral Boom: Trinidad and Tobago". PhD diss., Columbia University, 1989.

Hirschman, Albert O. *The Strategy of Economic Development*. New Haven: Yale University Press, 1958.

Julien, Ken. "The Emergence of the National Energy Sector". Nineteenth Eric Williams Memorial Lecture, Central Bank of Trinidad and Tobago, 2005.

Karl, Terry Lynn. *The Paradox of Plenty: Oil Booms and Petro-States*. Los Angeles: University of California Press, 1997.

Krugman, Paul. *Development, Geography and Economic Theory*. Cambridge, MA: MIT Press, 1997.

———. "The Myth of Asia's Miracle". *Foreign Affairs* 73, no. 6 (November–December 1994).

Landes, David. *The Wealth and Poverty of Nations*. New York: Norton, 1999.

Levitt, Kari. *Reclaiming Development*. Kingston: Ian Randle, 2005.

Lewis, Gordon K. *The Growth of the Modern West Indies*. New York: Monthly Review, 1968.

Lewis, W. Arthur. *Development Planning: The Essentials of Economic Policy*. London: Allen and Unwin, 1966.

———. "Economic Development with Unlimited Supplies of Labour". *Manchester School* (May 1954).

———. *Growth and Fluctuations, 1870–1913*. London: Allen and Unwin, 1978.

———. "The Industrialization of the British West Indies". *Caribbean Economic Review* 2 (May 1950).

———. "Jamaica's Economic Problems". Series of seven articles. *Daily Gleaner*, September 1964.

———. *Theory of Economic Growth*. London: Allen and Unwin, 1955.

Lewis, William. *The Power of Productivity*. Chicago: University of Chicago Press, 2004.

Lutz, V. *Central Planning for the Market Economy*. London: Longmans, Green, 1968.

McIntyre, Alister. "Lloyd Best: Reminiscences of the Early Days". In *Independent Thought and Caribbean Freedom: Essays in Honour of Lloyd Best*, ed. Selwyn Ryan. St Augustine, Trinidad: Sir Arthur Lewis Institute of Social and Economic Studies, 2003.

———. "Some Issues of Trade Policy in the West Indies". In *Readings in the Political Economy of the Caribbean*, ed. Norman Girvan and Owen Jefferson. Kingston: New World, 1971.

McIntyre, Alister, and B. Watson. *Studies in Foreign Investment in the Commonwealth Caribbean, No. 1: Trinidad and Tobago*. Kingston: Institute of Social and Economic Studies, 1971.

Mottley, Wendell. *Trinidad and Tobago Industrial Policy 1959–2008*. Kingston: Ian Randle, 2008.

Nettleford, Rex. *Mirror Mirror: Identity, Race and Protest in Jamaica*. Kingston: LMH Publishing, 2001.

Oxaal, Ivor. *Black Intellectuals Come to Power*. Cambridge, MA: Schenkman, 1968.

Pantin, Raoul. *Days of Wrath*. New York: iUniverse, 2007.

People's National Movement (PNM). "The People's Charter: Statement of Fundamental Principles". In *Major Party Documents*. Port of Spain: PNM Publishing, 1966.

Persad, Krishna. *The Petroleum Geology and Prospects of Trinidad and Tobago*. Port of Spain: Ministry of Energy and Energy Industries, 2008.

Porter, Michael. *The Competitive Advantage of Nations*. London: Palgrave Macmillan, 1998.

Prest, A.R. "Public Finance". In *The Economy of the West Indies*, ed. George Cumper. Kingston: Institute of Social and Economic Research, 1960.

Rampersad, Frank. *Growth and Structural Change in the Economy of Trinidad and Tobago, 1951–1961*. Kingston: Institute of Social and Economic Research, 1965.

Roberts, G.W. "Movements in Population and Labour Force". In *The Economy of the West Indies*, ed. George Cumper. Kingston: Institute of Social and Economic Research, 1960.

Rodney, Walter. *How Europe Underdeveloped Africa*. London: Bogle-L'Ouverture, 1973.

Ros, Jaime. *Development Theory and the Economics of Growth*. Ann Arbor: University of Michigan Press, 2001.

Rose-Ackerman, Susan. *Corruption and Government: Causes, Consequences and Reform*. New York: Cambridge University Press, 1999.

Ryan, Selwyn. *Eric Williams: The Myth and the Man*. Kingston: University of the West Indies Press, 2009.

———, ed. *Independent Thought and Caribbean Freedom: Essays in Honour of Lloyd Best*. St Augustine, Trinidad: Sir Arthur Lewis Institute of Social and Economic Studies, 2003.

———. *The Jhandi and the Cross: The Clash of Cultures in Post-Creole Trinidad and Tobago*. Kingston: Sir Arthur Lewis Institute of Social and Economic Studies, 1999.

———. *The Muslimeen Grab for Power*. Port of Spain: Inprint, 1991.

———. *Race and Nationalism in Trinidad and Tobago*. Toronto: University of Toronto Press, 1972.

———, ed. *Social and Occupational Stratification in Contemporary Trinidad and Tobago*. St Augustine, Trinidad: Institute of Social and Economic Research, 1991.

Ryan, Selwyn, and Lou Ann Barclay. *Sharks and Sardines: Blacks in Business in Trinidad and Tobago*. St Augustine, Trinidad: Institute of Social and Economic Research, 1992.

Ryan, Selwyn, and Taimoon Stewart, eds. *Entrepreneurship in the Caribbean*. St Augustine, Trinidad: Institute of Social and Economic Research, 1994.

Sen, Amartya. *Development as Freedom*. New York: Anchor Books, 1999.

———, ed. *Growth Economics*. Harmondsworth: Penguin, 1970.

Singh, Kelvin. *Race and Class Struggles in a Colonial State, Trinidad and Tobago 1917–1945*. Kingston: University of the West Indies Press, 1994.

Smith, M.G. *The Plural Society in the British West Indies*. Los Angeles: University of California Press, 1965.

———. *Pluralism, Politics and Ideology in the Creole Caribbean*. New York: Research Institute for the Study of Man, 1991.

Solow, Robert M. *Growth Theory: An Exposition*. Oxford: Clarendon Press, 1970.

Soverall-O'Brien, P., and A. Hilaire. "External Debt Rescheduling in Trinidad and Tobago, 1988–1992". *Central Bank Quarterly Economic Bulletin* 18, no. 1 (1993).

Stern, Robert M. *The Balance of Payments*. Chicago: Aldine, 1973.

Thomas, Clive Y. *Dependence and Transformation*. New York: Monthly Review Press, 1974.

———. *The Poor and the Powerless: Economic Policy and Change in the Caribbean*. New York: Monthly Review, 1988.

Tinbergen, Jan. *Economic Policy: Principles and Design*. Amsterdam: North Holland, 1956.

Waterston, A. *Development Planning: Lessons of Experience*. Baltimore: Johns Hopkins, 1965.

West Indian Commission. *Time for Action*. Black Rock, Barbados: West Indian Commission, 1992.

Wicker, E.R. "Colonial Development and Welfare 1929–1957". *Social and Economic Studies* 12, no. 4 (1963).

Williams, Eric E. *Economic Problems of Trinidad and Tobago*. Teachers' Educational and Cultural Association Public Affairs Pamphlet, no. 1, 1955.

———. *History of the People of Trinidad and Tobago*. Port of Spain: PNM Publishing, 1962.

———. "My Relations with the Caribbean Commission 1949–1955". Speech at Woodford Square, June 1955.

———. "The Purpose of Planning". In *The Crisis in Planning*, ed. Dudley Seers and Mike Faber. London: Chatto and Windus, 1972.

———. "Reflections on the Industrial Stabilization Bill". Series of articles in the *Nation*, April–May 1965.

Williamson, John. "Did the Washington Consensus Fail?" Speech at the Center for Strategic and International Studies, Washington, DC, November 2002.

World Bank. *The East Asian Miracle: Economic Growth and Public Policy*. New York: Oxford University Press, 1993.

———. *Poverty and Unemployment in an Oil-Based Economy.* Report No. 14382-TR. Washington, DC: World Bank, 1995.

———. *A Time to Choose: Caribbean Development in the Twenty-First Century.* Report No. 31725-LAC. Washington, DC: World Bank, 2005.

Worrell, Delisle, and Compton Bourne, eds. *Economic Adjustment Policies for Small Nations: Theory and Experience in the English-speaking Caribbean.* New York: Praeger, 1989.

Young, Allyn. "Increasing Returns and Economic Progress". *Economic Journal* 38 (December 1928).

Index